R-3972-BJS

Predicting Criminal Justice Outcomes

What Matters?

Stephen P. Klein, Patricia Ebener, Allan Abrahamse,
Nora Fitzgerald

Supported by the
Bureau of Justice Statistics,
U.S. Department of Justice

RAND

PREFACE

This report examines the extent to which the conviction rates, case disposition times, and other adjudication outcomes of defendants from 14 large urban jurisdictions across the country varied from one jurisdiction to another. All of these defendants were charged with certain types of felony burglaries and robberies. Also examined were case and defendant characteristics associated with outcome differences among these 2,263 defendants. Attempts were made, for example, to determine which types of cases were most likely to result in a plea of guilty and which would probably go to trial.

The results of these analyses were then combined to explore whether variations in outcome rates among jurisdictions are attributable to differences in case mix or, alternatively, to variations in state laws, local practices, and other factors. In short, we sought to ascertain whether the outcome of a defendant's case is driven primarily by the characteristics of that case or whether the official and unofficial policies of the jurisdiction in which that case is processed play a significant role in determining case outcomes.

We anticipate that the results of this research will be of interest to prosecutors, the defense bar, the courts, and law enforcement agencies. The report should also be pertinent to researchers who are investigating the operation of the criminal justice system as well as to policymakers and administrators who are concerned about possible disparities in this system.

The research described in this report was supported by the Bureau of Justice Statistics in the U.S. Department of Justice. This support allowed us to gather more data than are presented in this report. Specifically, at some of the 14 sites, we were also able to collect information about cases that had been dismissed by the prosecutor or filed as misdemeanors. Analyses of these additional data sets and follow-up studies with the defendants whose cases are discussed in this report are anticipated to be the subject of future research efforts.

A copy of our database has been made available to the public (see Abrahamse, Ebener, and Klein, 1990).

SUMMARY

INTRODUCTION

Does the state or county in which defendants charged with robbery or burglary have their cases heard have a bearing on the outcome of these cases, or does one criminal justice system apply to all?

Certainly it is known that large differences exist among jurisdictions in felony conviction and incarceration rates. Counties also vary in the time they usually take to process cases—i.e., from the time of arrest to the point at which a defendant is released, acquitted, or sentenced. It is not known, however, whether these variations in outcome rates and disposition times stem from divergent state laws and local practices and conditions or from differences in the case characteristics of jurisdictions. For example, cases filed for prosecution in one county could, on average, be more serious or have more evidence associated with them than those filed in another county—and these characteristics, rather than any differences in state or local adjudication policies, could give rise to varying outcome rates and disposition times.

Any investigation of the effect of jurisdiction on adjudication decisions and disposition times must therefore examine similar cases processed in different jurisdictions. If the outcomes of these cases are comparable regardless of where they are processed, it is unlikely that local policies and conditions have a unique effect. If, on the other hand, large differences among jurisdictions remain after differences in case characteristics have been held constant, support must be lent to the thesis that state laws and local practices (and the factors that affect them) influence what happens to a defendant.

Previous research on the effect of state and county on case outcomes has been hampered by a lack of requisite data on case characteristics. Existing databases simply do not contain the information that is needed to assess the extent to which cases processed in one jurisdiction are similar to those in another. Specifically, these databases do not offer *comparable* data regarding important features of a crime (e.g., victim injury), the type of evidence obtained, defendants' prior criminal records, and other factors that might influence case outcomes.

Another limitation of existing databases is that most monitor cases or charges rather than defendants and are therefore blind to the fact that some defendants may have several different charges pending against them at the same time. For example, a defendant who is out on bail on an auto theft charge might subsequently be arrested and charged with robbery—a circumstance that might increase the chances that the defendant will plead guilty to robbery, auto theft, or both. Little is known, however, about how many defendants have multiple overlapping cases, and even less is known about the effect of such overlap on case outcomes.

If only a few defendants have multiple cases or if their presence has little impact on outcomes, then the existing databases' focus on cases rather than defendants will not seriously bias conclusions. However, if many defendants have multiple overlapping cases, and if the outcomes of these cases depend in part on each other, then these relationships would need to be addressed in any comparison of outcome rates among jurisdictions.

PURPOSES

Given the foregoing issues, we set out to answer the following questions:

1. Is it feasible to gather comparable data from different large urban jurisdictions regarding the case and defendant characteristics of those charged with committing certain types of robberies and burglaries?
2. Are the adjudication outcomes in these sites related to these case and defendant characteristics?
3. Are the crime and defendant characteristics in one jurisdiction similar to those in another site?
4. Would controlling for differences among sites reduce the variation in outcome rates?
5. How often do defendants have multiple overlapping cases?
6. Is the presence of such overlapping cases related to outcomes both before and after other case and defendant characteristics have been held constant?

PROCEDURES

The sample for this study consisted of defendants who were charged with committing a felony against a stranger that involved residential burglary or armed robbery. The 1,115 burglary and 1,148 robbery defendants in the analysis sample were drawn from 14 urban sites: Montgomery County and Baltimore City, Maryland; Los Angeles, Sacramento, and San Diego, California; Dallas and Tarrant County (Fort Worth), Texas; Manhattan and Queens, New York; Kansas City and Saint Louis City, Missouri; Atlanta, Georgia; Wayne County (Detroit), Michigan; and Cook County (Chicago), Illinois. Only one of the sites invited to participate in this research declined to do so. As a group, the 14 sites represent a cross section of large metropolitan jurisdictions across the country (but certainly not the country as a whole).

At each site, we identified the population of those charged by the prosecutor with felony burglary or robbery during a 12-month period. When the prosecutor's office at a site had multiple branches, we limited our study to that branch which gave us the largest number of urban cases. We then drew from the population of burglary defendants a random sample of those whose alleged crimes involved residential burglaries against strangers. In this context, a stranger was defined as someone who was not a current or former family member, a close friend, or a crime partner of the defendant.

The prosecutor's files at a site were searched to locate the hard-copy records of the selected defendants. A RAND research team then abstracted an extensive array of data from the records that were located. These data included information about the crime (e.g., victim injury), evidence gathered (e.g., witnesses and recovery of stolen property), factors related to the arrest (e.g., whether or not it occurred at the scene of the crime), and the defendant's characteristics, including prior criminal record, racial/ethnic group, and employment status. Data were also gathered on any other charges against the defendant that overlapped in time with the adjudication of the sampled offense. Taken together, these charges and the sampled charge were designated as the defendant's *overlapping set of cases* (or OSOC).

RESULTS

We found that most of the defendants in our 14-site analysis sample were ultimately convicted and incarcerated. Of those charged with burglary, 88 percent were convicted and 74 percent were incarcerated (i.e., only 14 percent received probation). The corresponding rates for defendants charged with robbery were 84 and 78 percent. In both groups, most incarcerations involved prison rather than jail time (and therefore longer sentences).

Most defendants who were convicted pleaded guilty rather than opting to go to trial; the plea rates among convicted burglars and robbers were 89 and 81 percent, respectively. Defendants who did not plead guilty had about a 50 percent chance of being released either because their cases were subsequently dismissed or because they were acquitted at trial. However, the nonplea group did not represent a random sample of those charged; instead, they were those who stood accused of committing especially serious forms of burglary or robbery (e.g., where there was victim injury) or those against whom the evidence was weaker.

Most burglary and robbery defendants had had some prior involvement with the criminal justice system. Nearly 75 percent had a prior adult arrest, over 50 percent had a prior conviction, and more than 40 percent had a prior incarceration.

The cases against these defendants often had several features that increased the likelihood of a conviction either by plea or by trial. For example, an eyewitness other than the victim or a police officer was present in 51 percent of the burglary cases and in 37 percent of the robbery cases. The corresponding percentages of cases in which property was recovered were 60 and 48 percent. The rates at which subjects were arrested at the scene of the crime were 40 and 21 percent.

The more evidence against a defendant, the greater the conviction rate. For example, 93 percent of those charged with burglary were ultimately convicted when two or more of the following four types of evidence were present: an eyewitness, fingerprints, recovered property, or a recovered weapon. The conviction rate dropped to 75 percent when none of these types of evidence was present. The same pattern emerged for those charged with robbery.

About 23 percent of those charged with burglary or robbery were already on probation or parole at the time of their arrest or had escaped from custody on another offense. Almost all of those in this "under supervision" group were later incarcerated if they were convicted of any of the crimes in their overlapping set of cases.

As would be expected from previous research in this field (e.g., Boland et al., 1989), large differences were found among sites in the rate at which defendants pleaded guilty, were found guilty at trial, were convicted, and if convicted, were incarcerated and received a relatively short or long sentence. The 14 sites in our database also varied with respect to the time it took to adjudicate a typical defendant's case (i.e., the period from time of arrest to case disposition).

Our multivariate analyses examined how well the variation in outcome rates among sites could be explained by differences in case mix (i.e., differences in the characteristics of defendants and cases) as opposed to other factors, such as variations in local policies, practices, or conditions. For instance, did one site have a higher conviction rate than another simply because of differences in the amount and type of evidence that was available at the time of prosecution? We also examined how well various case outcomes (such as whether or not a convicted offender was sentenced to prison) could be predicted from a combination of case and offender characteristics.

This phase of our research found that some but certainly not all differences among sites could be attributed to differences in case mix. For example, a few sites had outcome rates that differed significantly from the 14-site average both before and after controlling on case mix. In other words, not all the variation among sites in outcome rates could be attributed to case mix. One example of this variation was that even after case mix had been held constant, defendants whose cases were prosecuted in one of our Texas sites were more likely to be convicted than those whose cases were adjudicated in one of our Missouri sites. Some states and sites also tended to take much longer than others to dispose of seemingly comparable cases.

Across all sites, the combination of case mix control variables allowed us to predict with 84 percent accuracy whether a defendant charged with burglary would or would not be convicted. This rate is actually less impressive than it seems in that 79 percent of the defendants would have been classified correctly simply by chance. For those charged with robbery, however, the case mix variables produced an 8-percentage-point increase in accuracy over the chance rate of 73 percent. These high chance accuracy rates resulted from high base rates—i.e., from the fact that most burglary and robbery defendants in our sample were ultimately convicted.

We also found that once this small adjustment for case mix was made, the addition of a defendant's state and site to the prediction system yielded only a 1- to 3-percentage-point increase in the accuracy with which one could predict whether a defendant would plead guilty, be convicted, or receive a relatively long or short sentence.

These findings do not mean that all state and site differences disappeared once we had controlled for case mix. Even with these controls, for example, one site had an 8-percentage-point higher-than-average conviction rate for those charged with burglary and a 15-point higher-than-average rate for those charged with robbery. The corresponding rates at another site were 5 and 9 percent below the 14-site average. In a similar manner, some sites were more likely than others to send their convicted offenders to prison. Nevertheless, the rates at most sites clustered closely around the 14-site average rate once control on case mix had been achieved. This was especially true for disposition time.

There are two possible reasons case mix controls failed to eliminate more intersite variation. First, some state and site variations could result from differences in case characteristics that we did not measure—e.g., witness credibility. Alternatively, differences in the laws, policies, and practices of the various states and sites might give rise to some variation. For example, some offenders may be more willing to plead guilty in certain sites simply because the probable alternative to entering a plea in their particular jurisdictions involves spending a long time awaiting trial in a crowded jail. In addition, the plea bargains that prosecutors are willing to accept may vary from one jurisdiction to another.

Taken together, the foregoing findings suggest that the base rates on some outcome variables are so high that one can fairly accurately predict what will happen to a defendant without knowing anything about his case other than that charges had been filed against him by the prosecutor. Once charges are filed with the court, the fate of one defendant will not vary substantially from that of another. Adding case mix control variables to the estimation process yields only a small to moderate improvement in overall classification accuracy, and adding the defendant's jurisdiction to the prediction system only slightly improves overall accuracy rates.

One important exception to these trends was that case mix variables did contribute to the ability to predict whether a defendant would or would not be found guilty at trial. State and site also contributed to classification accuracy, but to a much lesser extent.

Sites that had higher-than-average conviction rates at trial did not necessarily have lower-than-average plea or overall conviction rates. Thus, the relatively high trial conviction rates at some sites did not necessarily stem from differences among jurisdictions in the frequency with which cases went to trial. Differences in trial conviction rates among sites therefore comprised one factor that contributed to variations in overall conviction rates.

The intersite differences found in trial outcomes and case disposition times were large enough to suggest a need to examine why some sites had substantially higher rates on these outcomes than did others (even after control had been attained for case mix). This could be done by means of a more in-depth version of the case-abstracting procedures employed in this research, together with a detailed analysis of the adjudication processes of sites with markedly different outcome rates.

Our multivariate analyses also found that a defendant's racial or ethnic group bore little or no relation to conviction rates, disposition times, or other key outcome measures (that is to say, the coefficients for these variables were not significantly different from zero or large enough to have a practical effect on forecasting accuracy). These findings are consistent with those of a recent study on sentencing decisions in California (Klein, Petersilia, and Turner, 1990). Because our study was limited to burglary and robbery defendants at urban sites, however, we cannot generalize our findings to other settings or offense types (e.g., drug or morals cases).

One important feature of our research was that we tracked defendants rather than cases; in other words, we investigated what happened to a defendant in the context of all the charges pending against him. As noted above, these cases plus the one that led the defendant to be included in our analysis sample were designated as the defendant's OSOC.

We found that about one-third of the defendants in our analysis sample had at least one overlapping case in addition to the sampled offense. In other words, the adjudication of these other charges overlapped in time with the adjudication of the charge we set out to study.

Defendants with overlapping cases were much more likely than others to have high conviction and incarceration rates as well as long sentence lengths. However, these differences disappeared once control was obtained on case mix.

We also discovered that about 4 to 5 percent of the defendants in our study had been convicted of one or more of the crimes in their OSOC but had not been convicted of the charge that led to their inclusion in the study. This finding suggests that the traditional method of tracking the outcome of charges through the justice system will slightly underestimate the overall rate at which defendants are actually convicted.

CONCLUSIONS

With few exceptions, defendants with similar case characteristics and criminal records have about the same likelihood of being convicted and incarcerated regardless of where their case is adjudicated. The same holds true for the likelihood that defendants will plead guilty and for the time it usually takes to process cases from the time of arrest to final case disposition.

The jurisdiction in which a case is heard does bear a relation to whether or not a defendant is found guilty at trial—but to a much lesser extent after control has been attained for case mix. Some of the sites with higher-than-average trial conviction rates had lower-than-average plea rates. Therefore, it would appear that some tradeoffs are made in plea and trial conviction rates.

The characteristics of the cases that went to trial differed somewhat from those in which there was a plea. Specifically, the more serious the case and the more evidence against the defendant, the lower the likelihood of a plea. Thus, when defendants are more willing to take their chances at trial, the stakes are high, the evidence is weak, or both. The likelihood that a convicted offender will be sentenced to prison (or receive a relatively long term) was not related to whether that defendant pleaded guilty or was found guilty at trial.

Consideration of a defendant's full set of overlapping cases produced a small but noticeable increase in overall conviction rates; defendants with overlapping cases were much more likely to be convicted and incarcerated. But this appeared to be due to case mix—i.e., to the fact that defendants with overlapping cases also tended to have more serious prior records and case characteristics.

Taken together, the foregoing data suggest that local policies and conditions may play some role, but not a critical one, in determining what happens to a given defendant.

FUTURE RESEARCH

The research described above ended with the sentencing decision. Follow-up studies of the defendants in the analysis samples could therefore provide valuable information about equity after sentencing. For instance, do defendants with similar backgrounds and case characteristics serve comparable sentences regardless of where they were convicted? Such studies could also shed light on the factors associated with recidivism. For example, do offenders with certain case characteristics (such as having many overlapping cases) face a greater likelihood of being arrested and convicted again? And did those who were not convicted tend to disappear from the system, or were they convicted shortly thereafter of other offenses? We anticipate that future studies will explore these important issues.

ACKNOWLEDGMENTS

We appreciate the encouragement of Steven R. Schlesinger, former director of the Bureau of Justice Statistics, who supported the development of this project, and Patrick Langan and Carla Gaskins of the Bureau of Justice Statistics, who shared our desire to carry out the project and assisted the research while it was under way.

Our project advisory board members, Alfred Blumstein, Richard M. Daley, Edwin L. Miller, Stephen S. Trott, and James Q. Wilson, gave generously of their time and expertise to advise the project at critical junctures.

The chief prosecutors at the sites that participated in our study made the project possible. They allowed us to include their jurisdictions in the research and gave of their valuable time to further research in criminal justice. We especially appreciated the outstanding attendance at our conference of prosecutors participating in the study. The following individuals headed the prosecutor's offices at the time of our request for cooperation and made the research in their jurisdiction possible: Tim Curry, Criminal District Attorney, Tarrant County, Texas; Richard M. Daley, State's Attorney, Cook County, Illinois; Edwin L. Miller, District Attorney, San Diego County, California; Robert M. Morgenthau, District Attorney, New York County, New York; John D. O'Hair, Prosecuting Attorney, Wayne County, Michigan; George A. Peach, District Attorney, City of Saint Louis, Missouri; Ira Reiner, District Attorney, Los Angeles County, California; Albert A. Riederer, Prosecuting Attorney, Jackson County, Missouri; John Santucci, District Attorney, Queens County, New York; Kurt L. Schmoke, State's Attorney, City of Baltimore, Maryland; Lewis Slaton, District Attorney, Fulton County, Georgia; Andrew Sonner, State's Attorney, Montgomery County, Maryland; Henry Wade, Criminal District Attorney, Dallas County, Texas; and Steve White, District Attorney, Sacramento, California.

The project could not have been accomplished without the cooperation of many people in the prosecutors' offices that participated in the project. They provided computer-readable data, allowed access to hard-copy records, made administrative arrangements for data collection, and lent technical support to assist with our data collection activities. We particularly thank those attorneys who worked on our behalf to facilitate the study and those who patiently described their local adjudication procedures during our interviews with them.

In addition, we received excellent cooperation at many sites from court, probation, police, and county data processing personnel, who assisted by providing information that could not be obtained from the prosecutors' records.

At The RAND Corporation, Barbara Williams and Joan Petersilia, RAND's Criminal Justice Program Directors, oversaw the administration of the work that was conducted under the grant. Our colleagues Terence Dungworth and Eric Nilson assisted with the design and implementation of the project, and members of RAND's Survey Research Group, Lori Dair, Eva Feldman, Laural Hill, and Rebecca Mazel, played key roles in carrying out data collection operations of the highest quality. The people who conducted the record abstraction work in the sites were temporary RAND employees who served ably under difficult working conditions. We also appreciate Andrea Fellows' many helpful suggestions and editorial assistance.

Professor Stevens H. Clarke of the University of North Carolina at Chapel Hill and our RAND colleague, Deborah Hensler, reviewed a draft of the study, and we thank them for their many helpful suggestions for improving this report.

CONTENTS

PREFACE iii

SUMMARY v

ACKNOWLEDGMENTS xi

FIGURES xv

TABLES xvii

Section
- I. INTRODUCTION 1
  - Purposes 3
  - Design Considerations 4
- II. SITE SELECTION 6
- III. SAMPLE CHARACTERISTICS 10
  - Introduction 10
  - Sample Selection Criteria 10
  - Sampling Strata and Target Sample Size 11
  - Sample Selection Procedures 12
  - The Sampled Incident and Overlapping Cases 13
  - Effects of Criteria and Procedures on the Characteristics of the Database 17
- IV. DATA COLLECTION PROCEDURES 23
  - Preparation for Data Collection 23
  - Field Staff Recruiting 24
  - Field Staff Training 24
  - Screening Cases for Offense Type 25
  - Data Collection Instruments 26
  - Definitions Used in Data Collection 27
  - Abstracting Case Files and Coding Data Collection Instruments 28
- V. OUTCOME VARIABLE CHARACTERISTICS 29
  - Outcome Rates 29
  - Comparison of Outcome Rates Across Studies 31
  - Outcomes by Site 34
- VI. UNIVARIATE ANALYSIS RESULTS 38
  - Variables 38
  - Correlates of Case Outcomes 41
- VII. MULTIVARIATE ANALYSIS RESULTS 44
  - Relative Improvement over Chance (RIOC) 45
  - Effect of Plea/No-Plea Decision on Sentencing 51
- VIII. ANALYSIS OF OVERLAPPING CASES 54
  - Prevalence of Overlapping Cases 54
  - Relationship Between Overlapping Cases and Conviction Rates 55

	Relation of Having an Overlapping Case to Outcomes	56
	Correlates of Having an Overlapping Case	57
	Unique Effect of Overlapping Cases on Outcomes	59
IX.	PRINCIPAL FINDINGS AND CONCLUSIONS	60
	Procedures	60
	Prevalence of Case Outcomes	60
	Univariate Analyses	61
	Multivariate Analyses	61
	Analysis of Overlapping Cases	63
	Concluding Comments	64

Appendix
- A. SITE DESCRIPTIONS . . . 65
- B. DATA COLLECTION FORMS . . . 97
- C. VARIABLE NAMES . . . 144
- D. SITE CHARACTERISTICS . . . 147
- E. RELATIONSHIP OF OUTCOME VARIABLES TO CASE AND DEFENDANT CHARACTERISTICS . . . 179
- F. CALCULATION OF RELATIVE IMPROVEMENT OVER CHANCE VALUES . . . 192
- G. REGRESSION EQUATIONS . . . 195

REFERENCES . . . 199

FIGURES

3.1.	An offender's hypothetical set of overlapping cases	17
5.1.	Allocation of burglary cases to outcome categories	32
5.2.	Allocation of robbery cases to outcome categories	32
5.3.	Allocation of all RAND cases to outcome categories	33
D.1.	Site comparisons: pleaded guilty?	147
D.2.	Site comparisons: found guilty at trial?	148
D.3.	Site comparisons: convicted?	149
D.4.	Site comparisons: sent to prison?	150
D.5.	Site comparisons: relatively long sentence?	151
D.6.	Site comparisons: long disposition time?	152
D.7.	Site comparisons: had an accomplice?	153
D.8.	Site comparisons: multiple sample counts?	154
D.9.	Site comparisons: any victim a female?	155
D.10.	Site comparisons: major victim injury?	156
D.11.	Site comparisons: two or more victims?	157
D.12.	Site comparisons: nighttime arrests?	158
D.13.	Site comparisons: vulnerable victim?	159
D.14.	Site comparisons: did offender threaten use of weapon?	160
D.15.	Site comparisons: eyewitness?	161
D.16.	Site comparisons: fingerprints?	162
D.17.	Site comparisons: property recovered?	163
D.18.	Site comparisons: weapon as evidence?	164
D.19.	Site comparisons: arrested at scene?	165
D.20.	Site comparisons: arrested after 24 hours?	166
D.21.	Site comparisons: under influence of drugs at arrest?	167
D.22.	Site comparisons: exactly one overlapping case?	168
D.23.	Site comparisons: two or more overlapping cases?	169
D.24.	Site comparisons: prior adult arrest?	170
D.25.	Site comparisons: prior adult conviction?	171
D.26.	Site comparisons: prior adult incarceration?	172
D.27.	Site comparisons: prior juvenile arrest?	173
D.28.	Site comparisons: probation/parole/escape at arrest?	174
D.29.	Site comparisons: defendant black?	175
D.30.	Site comparisons: defendant white?	176
D.31.	Site comparisons: defendant unemployed?	177
D.32.	Site comparisons: defendant from out of state?	178

TABLES

2.1.	Sites eligible for selection	8
2.2.	Demographics of selected sites	9
3.1.	Sampling strata and target sample sizes	12
3.2.	Sample accounting by six strata	14
3.3.	Strata included in sample	18
3.4.	Percentage of targeted offenses filed as felonies from among those presented to the prosecutor	19
3.5.	Sample accounting for analysis sample	22
5.1.	Outcome variable rates	29
5.2.	Mean disposition times (in days) by offense type	31
5.3.	Comparison of BJS and RAND outcome rates	33
5.4.	Comparison of Boland and RAND outcome rates	34
5.5.	Comparison of Boland and RAND outcome rates in the four sites that were common to both studies	35
5.6.	Outcome rates by site: burglary	36
5.7.	Outcome rates by site: robbery	36
6.1.	Predictors of case outcomes	38
6.2.	Percentage of defendants with various characteristics	40
6.3.	Case dispositions for defendants who did and did not have a prior adult criminal record	41
6.4.	Increase (or decrease) in plea, conviction, and incarceration rates when certain case and defendant characteristics are present	42
7.1.	Relative improvement over chance percentages: burglary	46
7.2.	Relative improvement over chance percentages: robbery	46
7.3.	Percentage of cases classified correctly: burglary	48
7.4.	Percentage of cases classified correctly: robbery	48
7.5.	Deviation from the mean conviction rate before and after controlling for case characteristics	49
7.6.	Deviation from the median disposition time before and after controlling for case characteristics	50
7.7.	Disposition of convictions according to the manner in which conviction occurred	51
7.8.	Adjusted R-square values for various combinations of predictors of sentencing decisions for convicted offenders	52
7.9.	Mean imprisonment rate among convicted offenders across all sites and a site's deviation from this mean after controlling for case mix and pleas	52
8.1.	Overlapping case rate by site	55
8.2.	Relationship between overlapping cases and percentage of convictions	56
8.3.	Percentage point deviations from average outcome rate for offenders with and without overlapping cases: burglary	57
8.4.	Percentage point deviations from average outcome rate for offenders with and without overlapping cases: robbery	57
8.5.	Correlates of having an overlapping case	58
8.6.	Relative improvement over chance percentages for predicting convictions when overlapping cases enter the prediction equation after all other control variables	59

E.1.	Relationship between outcome and case characteristics incident offense: burglary	180
E.2.	Relationship between outcome and case characteristics incident offense: robbery	181
E.3.	Relationship between outcome and case characteristics evidence offense: burglary	182
E.4.	Relationship between outcome and case characteristics evidence offense: robbery	183
E.5.	Relationship between outcome and case characteristics process offense: burglary	184
E.6.	Relationship between outcome and case characteristics process offense: robbery	185
E.7.	Relationship between outcome and case characteristics overlapping offense: burglary	186
E.8.	Relationship between outcome and case characteristics overlapping offense: robbery	187
E.9.	Relationship between outcome and case characteristics prior record offense: burglary	188
E.10.	Relationship between outcome and case characteristics prior record offense: robbery	189
E.11.	Relationship between outcome and case characteristics offender offense: burglary	190
E.12.	Relationship between outcome and case characteristics offender offense: robbery	191
F.1.	Predicted versus actual conviction status among burglary defendants	193
F.2.	Chance distribution of outcomes given marginal totals	193
F.3.	Number of correct classifications with various models by outcome measure and crime type	194
G.1.	Regression coefficients for found guilty	195
G.2.	Regression coefficients for disposition time	196
G.3.	Regression coefficients for convictions	197

I. INTRODUCTION

In previous research on criminal proceedings, large differences among jurisdictions have been found on a variety of case-processing outcomes. Boland et al. (1989), for example, found that 81 percent of the felony arrests indicted in Los Angeles County in 1986 resulted in conviction, whereas only 46 percent of those in Chicago (Cook County) shared that outcome. In like manner, the median time between arrest and trial was 170 days in Los Angeles as opposed to 274 days in Washington, D.C. This variation in case outcomes could be attributable to differences in jurisdictions' laws, defendant and felony case characteristics, criminal justice resources, social and economic conditions, or local attitudes toward crime or to some combination of these and other factors influencing policies and practices.

Learning more about the relative contributions of these factors to case outcomes could have important policy implications; for example, it would be significant to find that certain legal requirements or procedures tended to increase or decrease conviction rates. The only feasible way to identify such effects, however, is to compare the outcomes of similarly situated cases within different jurisdictions. In other words, one must ascertain whether any differences in outcomes remain among jurisdictions after case characteristics have been held constant. If this proves to be the case, further research might uncover the source or sources of these variations—findings that could in turn have important implications for criminal justice policies.

Currently available case-processing databases, however, are not designed to allow for such investigations. In these databases, which were constructed by tracking cases from time of arrest (or filing with the court by the prosecutor) to final disposition (e.g., dismissal, acquittal, or jail sentence imposed), the "crime type" ascribed to a case generally corresponds to the most serious charge linked to that case at the time of arrest or initial court filing. Thus, a case in these databases would be classified as "murder" if a defendant was arrested for robbing and then murdering a store clerk.

The greater the number of categories and subcategories of crime types that are used for this purpose, the greater the likelihood that truly different crimes will be placed in separate categories and that the crimes within a category will really be akin to one another. The same holds true for alternative ways of classifying defendants. Yet the more categories that are used, the more difficult it becomes to summarize data and communicate results.

The recognition of this tradeoff between precision and simplicity, together with differences among states in the definition of various crimes, led the FBI (in its Uniform Crime Reports) and others to use a fairly small number of crime categories. Each category therefore covers a broad spectrum of crimes. Boland et al. (1989), for example, define robbery as "the unlawful taking of property that is in the immediate possession of another by force or the threat of force" and burglary as "the unlawful entry of a structure, with or without the use of force, with intent to commit a felony or theft."

Use of these broad categories makes it difficult to compare case outcomes, since jurisdictions might differ substantially in the average seriousness of their crimes within a given category. For instance, jurisdictions could vary in the relative frequency with which robberies involve the use of a gun or result in physical injury to victims—yet such variation could have a critical bearing on case disposition.

Several other potential differences among jurisdictions are not controlled in typical case-processing statistics but could nonetheless significantly affect those statistics. For example, jurisdictions could vary in their tendency to have defendants with serious prior criminal records or in the frequency with which eyewitness testimony and other evidence linking defendants to crimes are obtained.

Yet another limitation inherent in current databases lies in the fact that, by definition, case-processing statistics track cases rather than defendants through the system. This policy could produce misleading results for defendants with multiple overlapping cases. For example, an offender who is out on bail for a burglary charge might subsequently be arrested for robbery before the burglary charge is adjudicated. This situation could then influence the outcome of both the burglary and the robbery cases; for example, the prosecutor might drop the robbery charge in return for a plea of guilty to a burglary charge that carried a more stringent than normal sentence for burglary.

A typical case-tracking system would not reflect this interaction between arrests involving the same defendant and would therefore yield misleading data about them. Specifically, such a system would record one less robbery arrest resulting in a conviction and one burglary conviction carrying a more stringent sentence than normal. The significance of such a bias rests largely on the prevalence of defendants with overlapping cases—yet little is known about this prevalence or about its influence on outcomes. It is not known, for example, how many defendants actually have overlapping cases or whether such defendants are more or less likely to be convicted or to receive longer sentences than those without such cases.

Similarly, because they track only the most serious charge against a defendant, case-processing statistics fail to distinguish defendants who have multiple incidents associated with a given arrest (such as a string of liquor store robberies) from those with single incidents. Yet, it seems reasonable to expect these two case types to yield different outcomes.

In addition, case-processing statistics are generally derived from prosecutor management information systems (PROMIS)—systems that, by virtue of cost and other considerations, have a large number of cases but relatively little data on each one of them and are thus of little use in linking specific case and defendant characteristics with specific outcomes. As an example, a PROMIS database could not be used to determine if, after control has been obtained for specific features of a crime and the evidence obtained, a defendant's prior criminal record or drug use is related to his or her willingness to plead guilty.

A database that contained more than the normal amount of information about each case could address such questions, thereby providing valuable insights into the manner in which various case characteristics are related to disposition outcomes. Such information would be applicable to a variety of policy and operational decisions—e.g., in identifying a profile of those cases within a given crime type that usually go to trial rather than resulting in a plea. Given such information, more experienced prosecutors and public defenders could be assigned to cases identified as "trial prone" at an early stage of the adjudication process.

In summary, differences in outcome patterns among jurisdictions may stem from variations in case mix, in policies and laws, or in some combination of all these factors. Any investigation of the unique effect of a site's practices, policies (whether official or unofficial), and laws must therefore begin by controlling for case mix. Only then will it be possible to explore whether the same type of case is likely to yield an equivalent outcome regardless of the jurisdiction in which it is processed—or, alternatively, whether systematic differences in outcomes exist among jurisdictions that transcend differences in case mix.

Given the variety of issues that could be studied with our database, we chose to explore the source of differences in outcomes among sites because that variable illustrates the depth, breadth, and utility of these data for examining criminal justice questions. If, after controlling for case and offender characteristics, some sites were found to have more desirable outcomes than others, it would suggest that something inherent in certain sites' practices influences case outcomes. Further, if such differences emerged among prosecutorial offices within the same state, it would suggest that these differences are due to local practices and the factors that influence them rather than to laws (because the criminal code is the same throughout a state). In short, our analyses were designed to demonstrate an approach for identifying sites whose strategies (both formal and informal) might be studied and adapted by other jurisdictions.

We recognize that what happens at a site is more than a function of *official* policies and practices. In fact, actual practices and informal policies play a large role as well—and these are influenced in turn by a host of social, economic, attitudinal, and other factors. Nevertheless, finding sites that truly differ with respect to their outcomes and then studying what happens at such sites should take us one step closer to identifying effective practices that other jurisdictions can adapt to their unique situations.

PURPOSES

The research described in this report sought to ascertain whether the case outcomes of similarly situated offenders, all of whom had been arrested for robbery or burglary, varied among jurisdictions both within a given state and across states. In short, it sought to control for many of the factors that might influence case outcomes in efforts to determine the unique effect of jurisdiction on those outcomes.

One of the factors for which we controlled was the specific type of robbery or burglary committed. For example, we restricted our study to armed robberies and residential burglaries by a stranger to help ensure that the types of crimes studied in one jurisdiction were truly similar to those studied in another.

The specific outcomes studied were case processing time; whether the defendant pleaded guilty; whether the defendant was or was not convicted if he did not plead; conviction rates (whether by plea or by trial); incarceration versus probation rates; and the lengths of sentences imposed.

A second purpose of our research was to determine how well certain case characteristics predicted the outcomes outlined above. These characteristics were divided into seven categories: (1) the specific features of the crime committed, such as whether a gun or some other weapon was threatened or used; (2) evidence obtained, such as fingerprints or recovery of stolen property; (3) factors associated with the arrest, such as whether the defendant was apprehended at the scene of the crime or under the influence of drugs; (4) whether other cases were pending against the defendant; (5) the defendant's prior criminal record; (6) other defendant characteristics, such as race; and (7) the county and state in which the crime occurred.

We also examined whether use of the individual offender as our basic unit of analysis would yield a different picture of the adjudication process than would the more traditional case approach. We sought to ascertain, for example, whether offenders with multiple overlapping cases faced a higher likelihood of being incarcerated than did those who lacked such overlap. Similarly, we attempted to discover whether overlapping cases occurred frequently enough to influence policy decisions or summary descriptive statistics about case outcomes. Finally, we wished to determine if the presence of multiple pending cases against a defendant was related in any way to various case outcomes.

DESIGN CONSIDERATIONS

Four factors guided the design for this study: crime type, site characteristics, scope of the database, and unit of analysis.

We chose to assess armed robbery and residential burglary to ensure the inclusion in our analysis of personal and property crimes that were both serious and common. As will be noted in the next section of this report, our choice of robbery for this purpose restricted our study to large urban sites, since only in such jurisdictions were offenders arrested for this crime in sufficient number to provide a reliable basis for determining the outcome of such arrests.

The second critical design consideration pivoted on our need to have enough sites to reliably assess the extent of variation among jurisdictions in the outcomes of similar cases. We also wanted the final set of sites to provide adequate geographical coverage while permitting us to analyze whether outcome differences among sites stemmed from unique site characteristics or from state laws. For these reasons, we sought to include at least two sites per state in each of four regions of the country.

The third factor guiding our design was our desire to collect a large amount of information about each sampled defendant rather than a relatively small amount of data on a large number of cases. Our goal was to determine whether a wider-than-normal array of data could yield accurate predictions of outcomes, thereby providing a reasonably good control on case mix for the purposes of investigating the unique effect of site and state on these outcomes.

The fourth factor that affected our design was our decision to use the defendant rather than the case as our unit of analysis. The principal implication of this design decision was the need to study all offenses committed by the defendant that might reasonably affect the outcome of his sampled offense. All other things being equal, for example, two defendants might be treated differently if one were arrested, released on bail, and then charged with another crime.

We came to designate all the offenses that might affect the outcome of a sampled case as the defendant's *overlapping set of cases*, or OSOC. The primary implication of our decision to analyze a defendant's OSOC was the need to develop an operational definition of such cases as well as a method for finding them. This turned out to be a significant challenge in that most databases were found to be organized by case rather than by defendant—despite the fact that, as we have come to discover, a large percentage of defendants do in fact have overlapping cases.

The final design also considered tradeoffs among several factors, including (1) the fixed cost of adding another site to the study (e.g., the resources required for learning how to access and code its data and for hiring and training local staff); (2) the marginal cost of adding another defendant to a site so as to increase sample sizes and thereby bolster precision in our estimates of individual site effects; (3) the value of increasing precision within a site by having more of its cases abstracted as opposed to learning more about the variation among sites (i.e., by having more sites in the study); and (4) the sources of information that could provide data about a defendant and about the cost of accessing each source.

We initially planned to examine the outcome of cases that met our criteria for armed robbery and residential burglary and that were brought to the prosecutor by the police for filing. We wished to look at these cases in efforts to better understand the prosecutor's screening decision—i.e., to determine what factors contributed to the prosecutor's rejection of the case or to his filing of that case as a misdemeanor or as a felony. For the reasons discussed in Sec. III, however, we were unable to gather adequate data on rejected or misdemeanor cases at all sites. Thus, the current report focuses on cases that were filed as upper-court felonies.

The next three sections of this report describe the procedures that were used to develop the database. Section V presents information about the outcome variables and contrasts the outcome rates in our database with those in other databases. Sections VI and VII discuss the univariate and multivariate relationships between case characteristics and outcomes, respectively. Thus, readers who are primarily interested in these relationships may wish to skip to those sections. Section VIII describes the special analyses we conducted with respect to overlapping cases, and Sec. IX presents our conclusions.

II. SITE SELECTION

Before we selected the sites for the bulk of our research, we conducted a pilot study at two sites in Maryland—Baltimore City and Montgomery County. This pilot study investigated whether it would be feasible to gather the types of data that were needed to carry out the research. We also used it to field test the forms and procedures that were to be used for abstracting information from case files.

The records we reviewed at the pilot test sites clearly demonstrated that several types of crimes fall within the typical broad definition of a robbery or burglary. For example, both of the crimes below were called burglaries in our pilot sites even though they differ greatly in seriousness:

A divorced man returns to his former residence, lets himself in with a key, and takes the TV set while his former wife is away.

A man breaks into a home of strangers at night and takes a TV set while the family is asleep in another room.

Following a discussion of this variability in case characteristics with the project's advisory board, a decision was made to restrict our sample to *armed* robberies and *residential* burglaries committed by adult males who were strangers to their victims—crimes that are most frequently evoked when people hear the words "robbery" and "burglary."

This decision to restrict our study to two specific crimes was based primarily on two factors: (1) it would further ensure that comparisons among sites in case outcomes would be made on the basis of truly similar crimes; and (2) had we not divided a site's sampled cases among several different subcategories of robbery and burglary, we would not have had enough cases per crime per site.

Our decision to limit our research to crimes committed by strangers was driven by the fact that a prior relationship between offender and victim is likely to influence a prosecutor's decisions about a case in ways that our measures might not detect. Similarly, we excluded crimes committed by minors because of the large differences in the manner in which adult and juvenile offenders are processed by the criminal justice system.

The foregoing decisions, together with the design considerations noted in Sec. I, led us to search for sites that were likely to yield at least 120 defendants per year within each crime type, thus ensuring that we could abstract records for at least 100 offenders per crime. Our search was complicated by the fact that statistics are not readily available for most counties on the number of adult males arrested each year for the specific types of crimes we chose to study.

On the other hand, the number of armed robberies committed in a given county is usually much lower than its number of residential burglaries. Thus, all we really had to do was estimate whether a sufficiently large number of armed robbery suspects had been arrested within a county. If this was the case, that county was almost certain to have the requisite number of residential burglary suspects as well.

To obtain a rough estimate of a county's annual number of males arrested for armed robbery, we combined statistics from the 1984 Uniform Crime Report (UCR) and the *1983 County and City Data Book*. The UCR statistics indicated that 38.1 percent of all violent crimes are robberies, 49.2 percent of all robberies involve guns or knives, and 15.4 percent of every 1,000 *reported* robberies result in the arrest of an adult male. We multiplied the product of these three estimates by 1,000 to conclude that for every 1,000 violent crimes reported, there will be about 29 adult males arrested for armed robbery (1,000 × 0.381 × 0.492 × 0.154 = 29).

To be safe, we assumed a 25 percent margin of error around this estimate and concluded that for every 1,000 violent crimes, at least 22 adult males will be arrested for armed robbery. We then used data from the *County and City Data Book,* which contains the number of violent crimes for each county, to identify those jurisdictions in which we were almost certain to find at least 120 such cases per year. This process permitted us to draw up a list of 45 possible jurisdictions, presented in Table 2.1.

We selected sites from this list according to three criteria. First, we sought regional diversity—i.e., at least one site in each of the four major census regions. Second, in order to compare within-state and between-state variation in outcomes, we wanted about two sites per state. Third we wanted at least one site in New York City, widely regarded as the "robbery capital of the world."

The foregoing considerations led us to select the counties listed in Table 2.2. As this table shows, the sites selected exhibit considerable demographic diversity with respect to income, minority presence, and lower-income population. In addition, five states contain more than one site. Consequently, the 14 sites selected, although in no sense a random sample, exhibit significant variability along a number of important dimensions and, in particular, represent a number of the large population centers of the United States. Only one of the sites that we invited to participate in this research declined to do so.

Table 2.1

SITES ELIGIBLE FOR SELECTION

Region and County	State	Estimated Minimum Number of Armed Robbery Defendants	1980 Population
NORTHEAST			
Kings	NY	1,093	2,239,836
Queens	NY	923	1,891,325
New York	NY	697	1,428,285
Bronx	NY	576	1,168,972
Philadelphia	PA	388	1,688,210
Essex	NJ	366	851,116
Suffolk	MA	335	650,142
Allegheny	PA	185	1,450,085
Richmond	NY	172	352,121
Hartford	CT	120	807,766
SOUTH			
Dade	FL	659	1,625,781
Baltimore City	MD	391	786,775
Dallas	TX	321	1,556,390
Washington	DC	319	638,333
Harris	TX	315	2,409,547
Fulton	GA	239	589,904
Broward	FL	227	1,018,200
Hillsborough	FL	184	646,960
Orleans	LA	179	557,515
Shelby	TN	168	777,113
Palm Beach	FL	153	576,863
Tarrant	TX	143	860,880
Prince Georges	MD	143	665,071
Baltimore	MD	137	655,615
Orange	FL	130	471,016
Duval	FL	129	571,003
NORTH CENTRAL			
Cook	IL	711	5,253,655
Wayne	MI	633	2,337,891
Cuyahoga	OH	328	1,498,400
Saint Louis City	MO	228	453,085
Jackson	MO	155	629,266
Franklin	OH	136	869,132
Marion	IN	120	765,233
WEST			
Los Angeles	CA	2,187	7,477,503
San Francisco	CA	268	678,974
San Diego	CA	257	1,861,846
Alameda	CA	257	1,105,379
Maricopa	AZ	217	1,509,052
Orange	CA	198	1,932,709
King	WA	168	1,269,749
San Bernardino	CA	162	895,016
Multnomah	OR	160	562,640
Santa Clara	CA	156	1,295,071
Sacramento	CA	140	783,381
Clark	NV	127	463,087

Table 2.2

DEMOGRAPHICS OF SELECTED SITES

Region	Jurisdiction	State	Per Capita Income	Percent Black	Percent Hispanic	Percent Poor
Northeast	Queens	NY	12,012	18.8	13.9	9.1
	New York	NY	16,368	21.8	23.5	18.7
South	Fulton	GA	12,357	51.5	1.3	17.5
	Montgomery	MD	16,966	8.8	4.0	3.0
	Baltimore City	MD	9,842	54.8	1.0	18.9
	Tarrant	TX	11,219	11.7	7.9	6.9
	Dallas	TX	13,530	18.4	9.9	7.9
North Central	Cook	IL	12,570	25.6	9.5	10.8
	Wayne	MI	11,486	35.5	1.9	11.8
	Jackson (Kansas City)	MO	10,514	19.9	2.6	7.9
	Saint Louis City	MO	10,336	45.5	1.2	16.6
West	Sacramento	CA	10,849	7.5	9.4	8.9
	San Diego	CA	10,951	5.6	14.7	8.4
	Los Angeles	CA	12,544	12.6	27.6	10.5

III. SAMPLE CHARACTERISTICS

INTRODUCTION

Although our research design as well as our criteria for inclusion in the sample remained the same across sites,[1] the characteristics of our final sample and our sampling procedures varied across sites owing to differences in the way sites organized and stored their data.

As noted earlier, the unit of analysis for our research was the individual offender rather than the offense. However, the computerized information systems at our sites were typically case based. Moreover, each system had its own definition of a case that conformed with the information-tracking needs and the legal and administrative structure of that jurisdiction. For example, sites differed in the manner in which they defined offenses and cases as well as in the population of offenders over whom they exercised jurisdiction. In addition, we found varying record retention practices among the jurisdictions with which we worked. Such differences affected our decisions about which cases could be included and about the period of time from which we were to draw our cases at each site. We describe below our multistaged sampling and data coding process, which was designed to accommodate this variation and hence to produce a comparable offender-level database across all jurisdictions.

SAMPLE SELECTION CRITERIA

Nature of Offense

To control for the effect of case type diversity on case outcomes, we targeted offenders who had been arrested for two offense types: burglary and robbery, the most prevalent serious property and personal crimes in most urban communities. To further control for variation among case characteristics within these offense types, we limited our selection process to residential burglary and armed robbery involving criminal incidents perpetrated against strangers—i.e., against individuals with whom the offender had no known personal relationship.[2] A stranger was defined in this context as someone who was not a current or former family member, a domestic partner or roommate, or a crime partner. Neighbors, co-workers, and acquaintances were therefore considered strangers.

To be included in our sample, an armed robbery or residential burglary charge had to be among the initial charges in a case presented to the prosecutor for a filing decision (i.e., among the charges the prosecutor would formally file against the defendant with the court, thereby officially initiating the adjudication process). The sampled charge might have been the only offense charged or one of several charges brought at the same time. The charges actually filed by the prosecutor in most cases included the armed robbery or residential burglary, but this target offense may have been dropped or reduced as the case proceeded through the adjudication process. Offenders with more than one case involving armed robbery or a residential burglary were more likely to be included in our sample.

---

[1] The sample design was finalized only after the three pilot sites had been completed. The criteria for selection of cases in the pilot sites differed considerably from those used in the other 11 sites. See App. A for a description of sample selection procedures at each site.

[2] These two additional restrictions were put into effect after the completion of fieldwork in Montgomery County, Baltimore, and San Diego County.

Offender Characteristics

We targeted only certain offenders in efforts to limit some of the variation in outcome arising from offender characteristics. Specifically, we excluded female offenders and limited the sample to males facing adjudication in adult court. With very few exceptions, all created by waiver of jurisdiction from juvenile court, our sample consisted of adult males.

Urban Caseloads

As noted previously, sufficient numbers of armed robbery and residential burglary cases could be obtained only through the use of large urban jurisdictions. In fact, many of our jurisdictions, such as Baltimore, Manhattan, Queens, and Saint Louis, were entirely urban. Others, however, extended beyond the central city to outlying suburban and rural areas, encompassing several branch offices of the prosecutor and hence several different police departments, cities, and/or branches of the court—all with separate databases. In such jurisdictions, we limited our scope to the *largest* urban sampling frame. In Los Angeles County, for example, which subsumes more than 25 relatively large cities (and many smaller ones) with over a dozen prosecutorial branch offices, we chose the downtown Los Angeles office and examined cases brought to that office by the Los Angeles Police Department.

Our decision to limit sampling to cases filed in the largest branch of a prosecutor's jurisdiction meant that our sample generally reflects a caseload generated by the largest metropolitan police department in each urban jurisdiction. Hence, the cases in our sample arise largely from offenses that are committed in the central city and then adjudicated in urban courts. Data presented throughout this report thus reflect this portion of a jurisdiction's caseload rather than its entire caseload.

Window Period

The final criterion for case selection centered on the period of time during which cases were presented to the prosecutor for screening. Our estimates of caseload size, described in Sec. II, suggested that 12 months' worth of filings would be needed to ensure that sufficient armed robbery and residential burglary cases were found to meet our target sample sizes (described below). In this context, we wished to select relatively recent cases so that our results would reflect as closely as possible the current situation at a given site. At the same time, however, we wanted our cases to have been largely disposed by the time data collection began. In addition, we had to find sampling frames with which to work, and local data retention practices restricted the time frames from which we could choose. At the onset of the study, we selected from among 1985 caseloads. Data collection at later sites used a 12-month window that included 1986 cases.

SAMPLING STRATA AND TARGET SAMPLE SIZE

At each site, we attempted to draw a stratified random sample of cases with a fixed target sample size for each stratum, or a quota sample. Our design called for sampling to be derived from all cases in the universe of cases presented to the prosecutor. The branching process beginning at this point includes cases rejected by the prosecutor, cases filed as misdemeanors or referred to misdemeanor jurisdictions, and cases filed as felonies. However, the offenses presented to the prosecutor, not those subsequently filed, were the charges sampled. Our focus on armed robbery and residential burglary meant that in almost every jurisdiction, very few cases proceeded past the point of screening with these charges as misdemeanors. For the analyses discussed in subsequent sections of this report, we use only those cases filed as felonies. Table 3.1 summarizes the strata and target sample sizes.

SAMPLE SELECTION PROCEDURES

In an ideal research setting, cases would be sampled directly from the universe of cases of interest. Such a sample would thus consist of a list of unique individuals—none of whom would appear more than once—who had been charged with one of the target offenses during the window period. On this list, we would find all the information we needed to stratify the sample according to our design. No jurisdiction, however, had such a framework. Thus, we began instead by identifying the available record systems and by learning the characteristics of the cases that these systems contained. Then, after investigating a number of possibilities—sometimes including handwritten intake logs, computerized records, and court and other agency databases—we identified a source list known as the *sample frame*.

We began the multiple stages of sampling in each site by drawing a sample from the frame or frames available to us, each of which consisted of an exhaustive list, usually machine readable, of all offenders charged with certain offenses during a certain period of time. This list usually differed from our targeted universe in a number of ways. For example, it generally contained more than one record for some offenders; included females, juveniles, or cases that occurred outside the sample window; encompassed persons charged with nontarget offenses (e.g., strong-arm robbery or nonresidential burglary); subsumed cases for only a portion of the 12-month window period; and, in some jurisdictions, excluded lower-court and rejected cases, thus requiring that we either work with more than one frame or eliminate these strata from the sample.

From the frame, we drew a random sample of cases called an *extract*. The number of cases in this extract exceeded that of the ultimate sample to allow for the misfit mentioned above. Each case in the extract was assigned a random number and was then ordered in terms of this number. Extracted cases were subsequently processed in this order until the required number of cases was coded. This usually left several extracted cases that we never considered—a set called the *oversample*.

We called a case *lost* when we encountered an extracted record but could find no further field information—i.e., if the case file could not be located. The balance—that is, the extracted cases minus the lost cases and the oversample—was designated the *field sample*. For the

Table 3.1

SAMPLING STRATA AND TARGET SAMPLE SIZES

Offense Brought by Police	Prosecutor's Initial Decision			
	Reject	File in Lower Court	File in Upper Court	Total
Residential burglary	15	25	60	100
Armed robbery	15	25	60	100
Total	30	50	120	200

purpose of making inferences about the target population, we have assumed that the field sample constitutes a random sample of cases from the original sample frame.

Certain cases were eliminated from the field sample—for example, duplicates (i.e., cases in which the offender's name appeared more than once); cases that were not in the sampling universe (e.g., cases in which the offender was a female or a juvenile, or in which the offense occurred outside the target-window period); and frame errors (i.e., data processing mistakes in the preparation of the original frame or of the extract). Cases remaining after these had been eliminated were collectively designated the *screening sample*. Cases that did not satisfy the target offense definitions were then eliminated as well—e.g., burglaries of commercial buildings rather than residences; strong-arm rather than armed robberies; and robberies or burglaries of family members rather than strangers.

The sample that remained after all these cases had been eliminated constituted our final *coded sample*. Given the size of the final coded sample, we could then estimate the number of target cases in the *universe* by assuming that the coded sample bore the same relation to the field sample as the universe bore to the frame. That is, we assumed that:

$$\text{Universe} = (\text{Frame})(\text{Coded Sample/Field Sample})$$

Table 3.2 shows the number of defendants for each offense type in each site as we proceeded through the stages of selecting the extract, locating records for the field sample, eliminating ineligible cases, and screening the resulting sample for targeted offenses. This information is broken down by sampling stratum—reject, lower-court misdemeanor, and upper-court felony—within each offense type. The *analysis sample* consisted of the coded cases with sufficiently complete data to permit analysis.

THE SAMPLED INCIDENT AND OVERLAPPING CASES

The case that resulted in the offender's selection is called the *sampled incident*. At any given point in time, however, an offender may have committed several offenses, may be the subject of several prosecutions, or both. Such differing offenses may result in different prosecutions, or offenses might be combined and prosecuted simultaneously. Moreover, different prosecutions may proceed independently but may nonetheless be "related." For example, an offender could be arrested for an incident that occurred while he was awaiting trial for another offense, and this could affect the decision to prosecute as well as other decisions made in the course of the prosecution.

"Related" incidents involving a single offender are what we define as an *overlapping set of cases*, or OSOC. Such incidents may be related in at least two ways:

(1) Two different offenses can be adjudicated together; or
(2) Two different adjudications can overlap.

An *adjudication window (or processing period)* begins (or opens) on the day of a screening decision (intake date) for a case and ends (or closes) on the day the case is finally disposed. Two windows (or periods) are said to *overlap* if at least one day is common to both.

With respect to a sampled incident, an *overlapping case* is either (1) a criminal incident that differs from the sampled incident but is adjudicated together with the sampled incident, or (2) a criminal incident that was not adjudicated with the sampled incident but whose window overlapped with the sampled incident's window. The following examples illustrate the distinction between a sampled case and an overlapping case:

Table 3.2

SAMPLE ACCOUNTING BY SIX STRATA

Site	Offense Type and Status[a]	Estimated Universe	Extract			Screened Sample	Coded Sample
			Over-sample	Lost	Field Sample		
Montgomery	B Rej	12	0	5	15	9	9
	B Low	32	0	10	25	23	23
	B Up	68	0	1	79	67	67
	R Rej	13	0	3	12	10	10
	R Low	16	0	7	12	10	10
	R Up	66	0	0	74	66	66
Baltimore	B Rej	16	0	4	15	13	13
	B Low	19	0	0	54	19	19
	B Up	69	13	0	58	56	56
	R Rej	17	0	3	16	14	14
	R Low	15	0	0	54	15	15
	R Up	72	13	0	60	59	59
San Diego	B Rej	216	128	34	25	23	16
	B Low	0	0	0	0	0	0
	B Up	839	0	36	235	229	127
	R Rej	71	71	12	23	22	14
	R Low	0	0	0	0	0	0
	R Up	319	0	79	218	215	120
Sacramento	B Rej	65	0	40	36	33	17
	B Low	0	0	0	0	0	0
	B Up	351	0	37	151	143	71
	R Rej	38	0	31	34	32	20
	R Low	0	0	0	0	0	0
	R Up	201	0	32	156	151	83
Los Angeles	B Rej	259	75	9	41	40	16
	B Low	0	0	0	0	0	0
	B Up	539	150	11	139	135	90
	R Rej	599	65	11	49	48	17
	R Low	0	0	0	0	0	0
	R Up	685	1	17	282	278	89
Fort Worth	B Rej	29	0	1	24	23	16
	B Low	0	0	0	0	0	0
	B Up	399	0	5	105	97	83
	R Rej	24	0	0	32	31	21
	R Low	0	0	0	0	0	0
	R Up	293	0	4	140	124	83
Dallas	B Rej	66	15	2	18	18	15
	B Low	0	0	0	0	0	0
	B Up	847	2	17	101	89	85
	R Rej	222	34	5	21	18	15
	R Low	0	0	0	0	0	0
	R Up	431	38	40	112	87	85
Manhattan	B Rej	1	0	0	4	4	1
	B Low	262	0	26	74	73	35
	B Up	438	0	73	92	91	70
	R Rej	25	0	3	22	22	9
	R Low	1,687	0	22	78	78	31
	R Up	2,315	0	66	149	148	66

Table 3.2—continued

Site	Offense Type and Status[a]	Estimated Universe	Extract Over-sample	Lost	Field Sample	Screened Sample	Coded Sample
Queens	B Rej	0	0	0	0	0	0
	B Low	78	0	42	58	53	31
	B Up	341	9	64	92	85	72
	R Rej	0	0	0	0	0	0
	R Low	166	0	51	64	55	30
	R Up	526	0	100	125	118	71
Detroit	B Rej	0	0	0	0	0	0
	B Low	0	0	0	0	0	0
	B Up	357	54	5	121	115	101
	R Rej	0	0	0	0	0	0
	R Low	0	0	0	0	0	0
	R Up	518	49	5	126	115	109
Chicago	B Rej	0	0	0	0	0	0
	B Low	0	0	0	0	0	0
	B Up	1,092	0	26	149	109	104
	R Rej	0	0	0	0	0	0
	R Low	0	0	0	0	0	0
	R Up	1,289	18	45	117	106	102
Kansas City	B Rej	0	0	0	0	0	0
	B Low	0	0	0	0	0	0
	B Up	248	58	9	113	111	105
	R Rej	0	0	0	0	0	0
	R Low	0	0	0	0	0	0
	R Up	181	51	15	114	110	105
Saint Louis	B Rej	0	0	0	0	0	0
	B Low	101	25	8	52	52	26
	B Up	232	36	18	186	174	77
	R Rej	0	0	0	0	0	0
	R Low	13	0	7	17	16	9
	R Up	184	4	28	118	108	94
Atlanta	B Rej	20	7	0	23	22	15
	B Low	0	0	0	0	0	0
	B Up	325	95	0	145	139	83
	R Rej	24	11	0	18	18	15
	R Low	0	0	0	0	0	0
	R Up	149	39	1	100	98	90
Totals	B Rej	684	225	95	201	185	118
	B Low	492	25	86	263	220	134
	B Up	6,145	417	302	1,766	1,640	1,191
	R Rej	1,033	181	68	227	215	135
	R Low	1,897	0	87	225	174	95
	R Up	7,229	213	432	1,891	1,783	1,222

[a] B = burglary, R = robbery, Rej = rejected, Low = lower court, Up = upper court. The analysis sample for this report was restricted to upper-court cases.

A defendant robs one store. Five people are in the store, each of whom is robbed. No other charges overlap this one in time. This is counted as one case with no overlapping cases.

A defendant robs two stores on the *same* night. No other charges overlap this one in time, and both robberies are prosecuted at the same time. This is counted as one case with no overlapping cases.

A defendant robs two stores on the *same* night. He also steals a car that night. If the auto theft is prosecuted along with the robberies (e.g., because the car was used in the robberies), then the auto theft is classified as an "extra" case but not as an overlapping case. However, if the auto theft is not joined with the robberies but is adjudicated separately, it is counted as an overlapping case.

A defendant robs two stores, each one on a *different* night. The first incident is the one sampled. The two incidents are prosecuted together (e.g., two counts of robbery). No other charges are filed against the defendant. This is counted as two separate cases (the sampled case plus one overlapping case).

Because most jurisdictions maintain files that are case rather than offender based, and because the definition of a case varies across jurisdictions in terms of the number of incidents it may include, the process of identifying defendants and their OSOC involved two stages. First, a random sample of armed robbery and residential burglary cases was selected. Then a unique set of individuals was chosen from this sample. If an individual had two or more cases, the chronologically earlier case was designated the sampled incident.

The window of the sampled incident was defined as the span of time from the intake date to final adjudication within the trial court of general jurisdiction, with appeals excluded. All other cases with a similarly defined window that overlapped the sampled incident window were then identified and included in the database.

Consequently, although each record in our database involves only one offender, a given record may have data on more than one incident and more than one adjudication. For example, there may be *multiple incidents*, or more than one incident adjudicated at the same time. As an example, two different robberies constitute two different criminal incidents, but if both occurred on the same day and were allegedly performed by the same person, that person might be convicted for both offenses in a single trial and then be given a single sentence. For certain statistical analyses, this type of overlapping case is designated an "extra" case.

The database may also contain *related adjudications*, or different adjudications of the same offender for different incidents that may nonetheless be related. For example, an ongoing adjudication may cause a prosecutor to think differently about a new case at the screening decision. Or, as described by one prosecutor, a plea about to be entered on one case may be thrown out upon addition of another case against the offender.

Figure 3.1 shows how cases overlapping in their period of adjudication are considered together in our database. Practices across sites varied considerably with regard to how they joined incidents into cases, but our database has taken this variation into account by assembling data for all "cases" at the level of the criminal "incident." Our disposition and sentencing information is linked across cases so that we can determine the net sentence imposed for the OSOC.

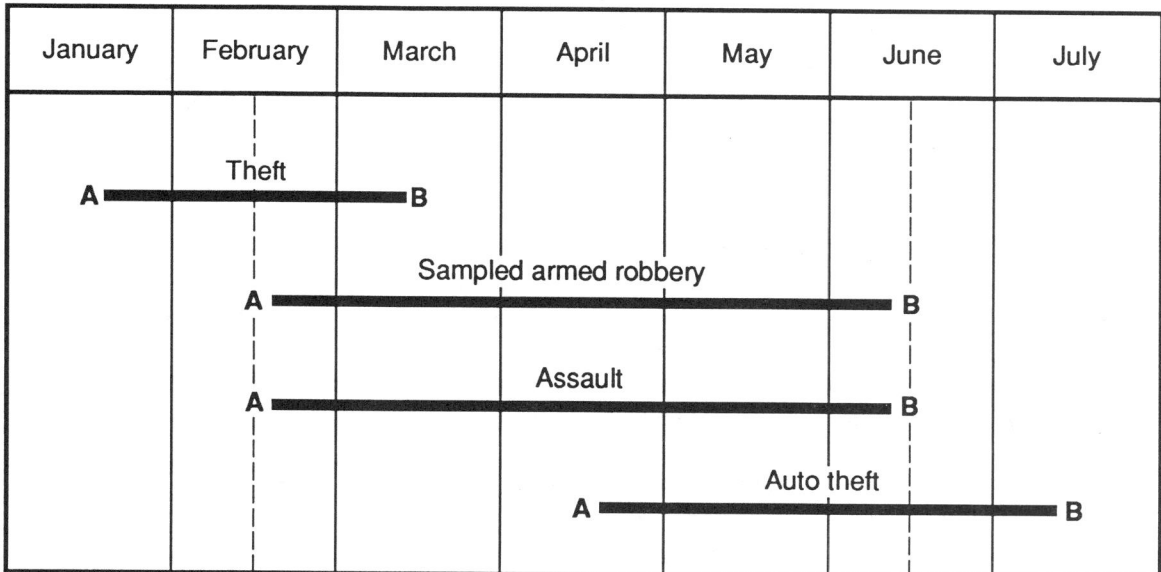

A = Date case presented to the prosecutor
B = Date case closed (rejected, dismissed, not guilty, sentenced)

Fig. 3.1—An offender's hypothetical set of overlapping cases

EFFECTS OF CRITERIA AND PROCEDURES ON THE CHARACTERISTICS OF THE DATABASE

Intake Sample

Although the process by which felony arrests are adjudicated differs in its details from one jurisdiction to another, one general procedure is usually followed in all jurisdictions. Specifically, when an arrest is made, the police may release the arrestee and take no further action. Alternatively, the police may seek a filing from the prosecutor—which is the norm around the country—or file the case directly with the court for a preliminary hearing. The latter practice occurs in Maryland and in Georgia. At an early point, the case must be referred to the prosecutor, who then decides whether it merits prosecution as a felony. The decision made at this point—to reject the case or to proceed with prosecution and, if so, what charge to make—is called the *prosecutorial screening decision*. With it, the adjudication process for an arrest formally begins.

For accepted cases, the prosecutor files charges with the court—charges that may or may not be the same as the arrest charges and that may also differ from the disposition charges. Some prosecutors have jurisdiction over misdemeanor filings as well as felony filings, but others have jurisdiction only over felony filings; the latter policy exists in California, Texas, Michigan, Illinois, and Kansas City, Missouri. Our intention was to sample from among all cases presented to the prosecutor for an initial screening decision.

Depending on the policy of each jurisdiction, the universe of cases presented to the prosecutor varied. In some jurisdictions, the police did relatively little screening; in others, screening was extensive (Petersilia, Abrahamse, and Wilson, 1987). Similarly, in some sites the police had the discretion to decide whether a case should be referred to the county prosecutor or to a misdemeanor court handled by a separate prosecutor, such as the city attorney or the police. In such jurisdictions, the police did a portion of the case screening that was ordinarily done by prosecutors.

Excluded Sample Strata

In some sites, it proved impractical or impossible to sample any rejected cases—usually because the prosecutor had not retained a record of rejections or because such records had been purged from the information system after a short period of time. Similarly, in some sites we did not sample any lower-court cases because such cases had been referred to a separate prosecutor for adjudication. When we were unable to draw a rejection sample, a lower-court sample, or both, we increased the upper-court sample size so that the total number of cases would remain approximately 100 within each offense class. Table 3.3 shows sites with all three strata, sites with only felony and misdemeanor filings, sites with only felonies and rejects, and sites with only felony cases included in the sample. The specific reasons for failing to sample a stratum are outlined in the site-specific descriptions in App. A.

As mentioned above, few state laws allow armed robbery and residential burglary to be classified as misdemeanors; hence few cases of this nature were missed as a result of failure to include misdemeanors in each jurisdiction. In some instances, however, cases initially presented by the police as armed robbery or residential burglary were not likely to be provable as charged. This would sometimes result in a lesser misdemeanor filing, and hence such cases were likely to be omitted by our sampling procedure.

Our data also suggest that few cases of armed robbery and residential burglary with no relationship between the victim and offender are rejected in the jurisdictions we studied.

Table 3.3

STRATA INCLUDED IN SAMPLE

Site	Felony Filings	Misdemeanor Filings	Rejects
Montgomery	x	x	x
Baltimore City	x	x	x
San Diego	x		x
Sacramento	x		x
Los Angeles	x		x
Dallas	x		x
Tarrant (Fort Worth)	x		x
New York	x	x	x
Queens	x	x	
Wayne (Detroit)	x		
Cook (Chicago)	x		
Jackson (Kansas City)	x		
Saint Louis City	x	x	
Atlanta	x		x
Total	14	5	9

Although we have data on rejections from only a few sites, the vast majority of cases that met our sampling criteria in most such sites were filed rather than rejected. Table 3.4 shows the proportion of armed robberies and residential burglaries filed as felonies among the jurisdictions for which we were able to determine whether rejected cases met our definitions of burglary and robbery.

In most jurisdictions, 80 to 90 percent of the armed robbery and residential burglary cases presented to the prosecutor were filed as felonies. This rate is substantially higher than that typically found among all felonies (Boland et al., 1989), suggesting that more serious offenses, such as our target offenses of residential burglaries and armed robberies committed by strangers, are prosecuted at a much higher rate than are felonies in general.

Los Angeles had a significantly lower filing rate for robbery than did the other sites for which we had data about rejected cases. The prosecutor at this site suggested that this low rate might be attributable to the fact that many of its robbery victims in this area were Skid Row residents—individuals who are very difficult to locate and whose cooperation as witnesses is difficult to obtain. In Dallas, the prosecutor's office presents all cases to the grand jury rather than rejecting cases without filing—but in cases it does not want prosecuted, it recommends that the grand jury fail to indict. This occurs at a somewhat later stage than the normal screening process. Fort Worth follows the same process, but it has a higher rate of felony filings for armed robbery than does Dallas.

It is somewhat surprising that we did not observe more variation in filing rates among jurisdictions given the wide variation in their screening procedures.

Unlocated Cases

Overall, we were able to locate the hard-copy files for 80 percent of the felony cases we attempted to field. The remaining 20 percent were misplaced, not returned from the prosecuting attorney, or sealed. The presence of unlocated cases is not surprising in light of the limited facilities for retention of files and in view of the file destruction and sealing policies in effect in certain jurisdictions. In each jurisdiction, we had concerns that the cases we could not locate in the file room may not have been representative of all the extracted cases. Sealed cases, for example, were typically resolved in favor of the defendant.

Table 3.4

PERCENTAGE OF TARGETED OFFENSES FILED
AS FELONIES FROM AMONG THOSE
PRESENTED TO THE PROSECUTOR

Site[a]	Armed Robbery	Residential Burglary
Fort Worth	93	92
Dallas	66	93
Atlanta	86	94
Sacramento	84	84
Los Angeles	53	67

[a]In this and other tables, site does not include the entirety of the prosecutor's jurisdiction because we did not gather data on cases adjudicated in suburban and rural branch offices.

We had approximately the same rate of unlocated cases among the burglary defendants and robbery defendants. We had a lower rate of unlocated cases—16 percent—among the felony filings than among the lower-court cases (26 percent) or the rejects (28 percent). In seven sites, over 90 percent of the felony cases were located, but in the two New York sites the rate was between 30 and 40 percent. Only the New York sites had procedures providing for the automatic sealing of cases resolved in favor of the defendant.

We do not believe that unlocated cases were still pending because the computerized records indicated that these cases had been disposed. In the absence of hard-copy records, however, we could not determine whether a case met our target criteria for offense characteristics.

One jurisdiction advised us that its prosecutors sometimes retained as "trophies" the files of especially difficult cases whose outcomes were successful. We were therefore able to retrieve some cases that might otherwise have been lost. At other times, files were provided by the records division, and therefore we could not determine the reason for missing cases.

In most jurisdictions, especially for the felony filings, we believe that the unlocated cases were so rare as to have little effect on the characteristics of the final coded sample. In Manhattan and Queens, however, the unlocated cases were probably resolved in favor of the defendants. Omission of a substantial portion of cases resolved in favor of the defendant therefore yielded an unusually high conviction rate in these two New York sites.

Varying Defendant Tracking Systems

Variations in record systems affected our ability to link an individual across cases overlapping in their adjudication with the sampled incident's window period. In sites whose records facilitated the linking of defendants to multiple cases, for example, we were likely to have found more overlapping cases than in jurisdictions lacking such built-in mechanisms. However, some sites had no defendant identifier—in which case we used a name search to identify additional cases. We also conducted a search of the hard-copy case records for other case ID numbers; we then requested these cases and checked the records to determine whether they belonged to the same defendant. This check was difficult to make in jurisdictions with branch offices, where an overlapping case might have been pending in an office other than that in which we were working. We encountered this problem in Los Angeles, a site that does not have a unique identifier for each defendant entered into the prosecutor management information system (PROMIS). We systematically checked cases of the same name filed in other offices for a subset of the sample and found that few were true matches with the sampled defendant. It is possible, however, that the number of overlapping cases we identified is somewhat lower than the actual number owing to identification problems encountered at a few sites.

Varying Case Definitions

Rules of joinder varied among the sites in our study. Some had fairly liberal rules for the joining of multiple criminal incidents into a single case; others required that each criminal incident be filed as a separate case. This variation could affect the number of overlapping cases we found. We applied a coding procedure that captured each criminal incident whether it was filed with others or separately. Thus, the rate of overlapping cases can be compared across jurisdictions despite the intersite variation in joinder rules.

Different Window Periods

The fact that we coded cases in some sites from 1985 and others from 1986 might produce differences across sites if changes had been made in the penal code of statewide policies between these two periods. We minimized this possibility by coding both sites in a state at the same time, with the exception of California. For that state, Los Angeles data were coded for 1986, while San Diego and Sacramento data were coded for 1985. However, we know of no substantive change in criminal law during this period that would produce differences between Los Angeles and the other two California sites.

Urban Caseload

Since we were not able to cover the entire jurisdictions of certain sites, the nature of our sample must be qualified. For the most part, ours is a study of the central, most intensely urbanized part of each jurisdiction selected. This means that the results obtained with our sample cannot be generalized to the jurisdiction as a whole. A description of that part of each site which was actually covered in our study is given in App. A.

As noted in Table 3.3, data were available on misdemeanors at five sites and on rejects at nine. Moreover, there were far more unlocated cases among the rejects and misdemeanors than among the upper-court filed cases. These and related factors led us to focus our current report only on cases filed in the upper court. Table 3.5 shows the number of defendants with such cases by site and crime type as well as those who had sufficiently complete data to be included in the analyses discussed in the remainder of this report.

With the exception of Montgomery County, relatively few cases had to be excluded from our analysis sample because of missing or incomplete data. This is a testimony to the perseverance of our data collection team. The relatively small percentage of cases with complete data from Montgomery County was due not to missing data but rather to the fact that we decided, after data collection was completed at this site, to focus exclusively on crimes involving residential burglaries and armed robberies that had been committed by strangers.

Table 3.5

SAMPLE ACCOUNTING FOR ANALYSIS SAMPLE

Site	Offense	Estimated Universe	Extract Over-sample	Extract Lost	Field Sample	Screen Sample	Coded Sample	Analysis Sample
Mont-	Burglary	68	0	1	79	67	67	22
gomery	Robbery	66	0	0	74	66	66	25
Baltimore	Burglary	69	13	0	58	56	56	54
	Robbery	72	13	0	60	59	59	55
San Diego	Burglary	839	0	36	235	229	127	119
	Robbery	319	0	79	218	215	120	116
Sacra-	Burglary	351	0	37	151	143	71	71
mento	Robbery	201	0	32	156	151	83	83
Los	Burglary	539	150	11	139	135	90	89
Angeles	Robbery	685	1	17	282	278	89	86
Fort	Burglary	399	0	5	105	97	83	81
Worth	Robbery	293	0	4	140	124	83	78
Dallas	Burglary	847	2	17	101	89	85	85
	Robbery	431	38	40	112	87	85	85
Manhattan	Burglary	438	0	73	92	91	70	65
	Robbery	2,315	0	66	149	148	66	61
Queens	Burglary	341	9	64	92	85	72	70
	Robbery	526	0	100	125	118	71	64
Detroit	Burglary	357	54	5	121	115	101	93
	Robbery	518	49	5	126	115	109	106
Chicago	Burglary	1,092	0	26	149	109	104	102
	Robbery	1,289	18	45	117	106	102	101
Kansas	Burglary	248	58	9	113	111	105	105
City	Robbery	181	51	15	114	110	105	104
Saint Louis	Burglary	232	36	18	186	174	77	76
	Robbery	184	4	28	118	108	94	94
Atlanta	Burglary	325	95	0	145	139	83	83
	Robbery	149	39	1	100	98	90	90
Totals	Burglary	6,145	417	302	1,766	1,640	1,191	1,115
	Robbery	7,229	213	432	1,891	1,783	1,222	1,148

IV. DATA COLLECTION PROCEDURES

PREPARATION FOR DATA COLLECTION

At each site we began our data collection process by visiting the prosecutor's office with the goal of learning about local procedures, identifying a sampling frame, exploring the sources of information contained in case files, and making arrangements for the fieldwork that would follow. The data collection manager and site coordinator always made these trips together, usually devoting six or seven days to such tasks. An important aspect of this trip lay in evaluating data sources to determine which contained the most useful information and which would be the easiest to work with. These efforts required close coordination with site staff, who would explain local procedures, help us interpret information in case files and automated systems, and direct us to sources that could provide a sampling frame. At a number of sites, we also met with court personnel as well as with county data processing departments that maintained on-line systems for the prosecutor's office.

Local criminal justice data systems offer a rich and valuable source of data for research studies. However, cross-site studies must be conducted in the knowledge that each jurisdiction and state has its own unique systems for managing criminal justice data, with variation occurring in state laws, court jurisdictions, criminal procedures, and prosecutor and police operations. The information retained in records, both automated and paper, therefore reflects each jurisdiction's individual definitions and procedures. Incorporating this variation into our data collection procedures required careful adherence to study design definitions. For example, while all jurisdictions file felony cases in court, jurisdictions differ with regard to the specific court in which such cases are filed and with respect to the number of charges or offenders that can be included in a case. Hence, if a study examined only those charges filed in a court of general jurisdiction, felony cases initially filed and resolved at the lower-court level would be omitted. Similarly, if researchers defined cases according to local definitions, commonality across jurisdictions would be lacking as some jurisdictions include multiple offenders in one case, multiple charges, or multiple criminal incidents while others limit a case to only one offender, charge, or incident.

Because our study relied on local records for its data, with 14 different jurisdictions in eight states, we remained acutely sensitive to the substantial differences in procedures and record-keeping practices that we found among sites. During our initial site visits, for example, we had to learn about case-processing procedures and documentation so that we could reliably abstract information from local files and then fit that information into our overall data collection protocol. As an example, each site had its own means of identifying and documenting rejected cases. Thus, we had to learn how to identify these cases in the local records and to determine if in fact they had been retained. In addition, we learned how each site defined a case and developed procedures for each that would enable us to capture comparable information across sites. Our data collection instruments, selection of coders, training procedures, and intensive supervision were all designed to ensure the collection of a database that was standardized across sites.

FIELD STAFF RECRUITING

In each site, we aimed to recruit a team of four field coders and one supervisor to work in the prosecutors' offices. This was the maximum number of coders we wanted for one supervisor; the actual number used depended primarily on the space available and on the quality of the pool of candidates. If little space was available, we worked with fewer staff and extended the length of the field period. Where possible, we recruited five coders to allow for attrition during training and fieldwork. The local supervisory position was the most difficult to recruit because we wanted highly qualified individuals, and such persons are often unavailable for temporary work.

Whenever possible, we recruited from the staffs of local survey research organizations, which provided a pool of reliable, experienced fieldworkers, some with prior experience in coding from agency records. At other sites, we recruited from the social science departments of local colleges and universities and from temporary employment agencies. In the latter case, we arranged with one or more agencies in advance to interview a number of candidates. The actual hiring decision was the responsibility of the RAND data collection coordinators. Because the abstracting and coding work was complex and required careful attention to detail as well as a thorough understanding of case-processing information, the hiring decision was highly pertinent to the success of data collection in each site. Hence it was not unusual for as many as 15 candidates to be interviewed before the small coding staff required to complete the work was ultimately assembled.

FIELD STAFF TRAINING

Training for this study was extensive. One full week was spent on training before record abstraction for the sampled cases began. Such training included an overview of the project's purpose, instruction on the general principles of coding, detailed specifications for screening the fielded sample, and instructions on how to use the source materials and which source provided the information for the items on our coding forms. General definitions were provided as well as specific rules for each site. In addition, work rules and schedules were covered along with procedures for setting aside problem cases for review by the supervisor and data collection coordinator.

The training process combined classroom lectures on definitions and specifications with practice in using the source materials contained in defendant files and in coding the data collection forms. In advance of training, the data collection coordinator prepared several practice files using actual case materials. These files were assembled in efforts to familiarize coders with all the source materials and examples of cases disposed at different points in the process. Special attention was given to preparing material that helped coders learn how to use our multiple data collection forms for recording information about multiple incidents in a case and about supplemental cases being processed in the same period as the sampled incident.

Training at each site was conducted by the RAND site coordinator and an assistant. This provided two trainers for a maximum of six field staff. The field supervisor and the coders were trained at the same time. The site coordinator spent the entire training week and the first week of fieldwork at the site. During the first week, the trainers and the field supervisor checked each coder's cases in their entirety. In about half the sites, the site coordinator then made a second trip to the site during the four- to five-week field period. When not at the site, the site coordinator conducted daily telephone conversations with the supervisor to discuss problems and resolve coding difficulties.

At some sites, coders were trained to use an automated information system that served as an information source about overlapping cases. At other sites, special instruction was given on the use of hard-copy card files or other logs or lists in which related case information was retained. At almost all sites, coders were held responsible for pulling and returning case files to the records department and thus received special training on site procedures for file use.

The main responsibility of the supervisor was to check at least 10 percent of the work of the coders and to resolve problems thus encountered. Coders therefore received feedback continuously throughout the field period, and retraining was conducted as necessary. Most coders performed extremely well after the intense training that they had received. In almost all sites, however, it was necessary to replace one coder. High productivity among all the coders was sometimes difficult to attain because one or two coders would almost invariably be much slower than others in handling the source materials in the files. Hence, we sometimes reallocated tasks so that the slowest coder could handle case screening or a similar task.

SCREENING CASES FOR OFFENSE TYPE

In the screening process, individual case files were first pulled from the prosecutor's central records using the local identifier contained in the sampling frame, and they were then placed on the information sheet used in the field. When individual files were not found, steps were taken to locate them elsewhere in the prosecutor's office. Files were usually pulled by RAND staff members, but in some sites local staff handled this activity for us. A related step involved checking that the file did in fact belong to the sampled defendant. Toward this goal, a series of identifiers was checked against information derived from the sampling frame. If any discrepancies were found, the case was set aside for review.

Next, the coder searched for file records containing information about the sampled charge—i.e., whether it was a burglary or robbery. In some sites, sampling could be performed from a frame that already identified residential burglary and/or armed robbery, thereby eliminating part of the screening task. In many sites, however, we had to locate the specified source document and determine whether our sampled robbery or burglary defendant was eligible for inclusion in our field sample. During training, coders were told which document to use for this purpose. In some sites, for instance, the police report was used; in others, the complaint or some other document was used. The definitions that follow were used at all sites for sample selection.

Armed Robbery. For a crime to be considered armed robbery, a weapon must have been present at the scene and its presence known to the victim or victims. Not included were weapons discovered later by the police (e.g., those in the defendant's pocket, car, or home) unless these weapons were involved in the incidents. Coders also did not include as armed robbery a victim's unsubstantiated report of a weapon. Weapons included guns, knives, and deadly blunt objects.

Residential Burglary. Sites defined as residences included private residences, apartments, permanent mobile homes, farm houses (only buildings designated for living), vacation residences or short-term rentals, guest houses, servants' quarters, residential garages (if attached, or no mention made), institutional living facilities (dormitories or nursing/retirement homes), and hotel or motel rooms, whether short- or long-term occupancy.

Sites considered nonresidences included nonresidential buildings or areas within a residential building or on residential property (barns, hotel laundry rooms, or hotel lobbies); outside buildings on residential property (detached garages, playhouses, or sheds); uninhabited dwelling places (vacant apartments or abandoned buildings); commercial buildings (stores, warehouses, offices, or restaurants); vehicles; and nonresidential institutions (schools, hospitals, or churches).

Victim/Offender Relationship. Once the offense type had been determined, coders screened cases to ascertain the relationship of the victim to the offender. Additional documentation, usually contained in police reports, was often needed for this purpose.

Coders screened out any case in which the victim of armed robbery or residential burglary was a current or former family member, a crime partner or an accomplice, or a domestic partner or roommate.

If there were multiple victims, one of whom met one of the above criteria, the case was screened out. Cases were not screened out, however, on the basis of a codefendant's relationship. If the victim was related to a codefendant but not to the sampled defendant, the case was allowed in.

Coders also screened in cases where the victim was a neighbor, co-worker, acquaintance, or friend—in other words, cases in which the victim knew but was not related to and did not live with the defendant.

DATA COLLECTION INSTRUMENTS

Information Sheet

We printed summary data on each sampled case at a given site on an information sheet generated from information contained in our sampling frame. Field coders added additional identifiers and tracked the status of fieldwork on the case using this form. Because it contained names and other personal identifiers, data on this sheet were maintained in a separate computer file. The information sheet was used to identify a defendant, to locate his case or cases, to confirm information found in case files, and to record the status of the case. It is therefore not part of the public-use file for this study.

Defendant Main Form (DMF)

The Defendant Main Form (DMF) was the primary instrument for recording information about each defendant (see App. B). This form had the following five sections:

- A— Identification of related incidents. This section was used as a worksheet with which to identify related cases—i.e., with which to pinpoint any cases that were pending against the defendant during the time the sampled case was being processed.
- B— Criminal incident description (for sampled incident). This section collected detailed information about the armed robbery or residential burglary incident on the basis of reports prepared by police, prosecutor, and probation officers.
- C— Adjudication process (for sampled incident). This section was designed to follow a case through the criminal justice system, from the time it was filed or rejected by the prosecutor to final disposition (e.g., acquittal, or conviction and sentencing). Sources of data for this section included prosecutor and court records.
- D— Defendant's personal background. This short section contains demographic data about the defendant as found in probation, police, and prosecutors' reports.

E— Criminal history record. In this section we coded a defendant's juvenile and adult criminal history using local, state, and federal rap sheets.

Supplemental Case Form (SCF)

A Supplemental Case Form was coded for every related case identified in Section A of the DMF. This form contained two sections that were nearly identical to those in the DMF: criminal incident description and adjudication process.

Supplemental Incident Form (SIF)

When a defendant is charged with a number of different incidents, charges are sometimes combined into one case so that they can be processed together. When this happened, we coded each incident separately in an SIF, which contains only one section for the criminal incident description.

Record Folder

All the forms for a defendant were kept together in a manila folder, which was also used for sample accounting purposes. A copy of these forms appears in App. B.

DEFINITIONS USED IN DATA COLLECTION

Incident. As a general rule, offenses that occurred at the same place and time were treated as one incident, whereas offenses committed at different times were considered separate incidents. For example, if a defendant robbed three people at the same time, the offenses were treated as a single incident; but if the defendant robbed these individuals on separate days, each was treated as a separate incident.

The number of incidents bore no relation to the number of arrests or filing charges. A single incident could result in arrest on a number of arrest charges or counts; conversely, one arrest could involve one incident or multiple incidents.

Case. A number of incidents or charges were sometimes combined into one case, with practice varying across sites. We captured information about each incident included in a case. Cases against multiple defendants who committed a crime together might be combined under one case number, with a one-digit suffix to identify defendants within a case. We gathered information only about our sampled defendants.

Sample Incident/Sampled Case. A case was eligible for inclusion in our analysis sample if it included filed charges of either armed robbery or residential burglary. Some cases included both but were selected only on the basis of the "sampled charge."

The incident involving the sampled charge was coded in the DMF. Other incidents that had different case numbers were coded in SCFs. Information about incidents that were combined with a DMF or SCF case (as described above) was coded in an SIF.

ABSTRACTING CASE FILES AND CODING DATA COLLECTION INSTRUMENTS

The contents of individual case files were used for coding the DMF and the supplemental forms.[1]

Instructions were prepared for each site telling coders which documents to use for each section of the forms. In this process, special attention was paid to the task of identifying each sampled defendant's clutch cases; additional worksheets were often used for this purpose. In some sites, this task was handled by the field supervisor or by one or two specially trained coders, who identified the related cases using additional source materials. The additional cases were then located and placed with the case containing the sampled incident for coding by the regular coders.

The coders first completed the DMF and, in this process, identified the number of SCFs and SIFs that would be completed for the sampled defendant. Effort was made to link these multiple documents to the sampled case and to ensure that sentencing information was coded correctly to eliminate double counting of concurrent sentences across cases. Defendant background and criminal history information was contained only in the DMF and was coded only once for each sampled defendant.

---

[1] In one pilot site—Baltimore—the court's individual case files were used to code information about cases filed as felonies and misdemeanors. It was determined that while court files contained excellent information about the processing of the case, they contained much less detail about the characteristics of the cases than did the prosecutors' records. In all other sites, prosecutors' records were used, often supplemented with data from countywide, on-line information systems used by prosecutors, courts, jail, and police.

V. OUTCOME VARIABLE CHARACTERISTICS

The six major outcome variables studied in our research were:

- Did the defendant plead guilty (i.e., waive trial)?
- If the defendant did not plead guilty, was he nonetheless found guilty at trial (rather than being acquitted at trial or having his case dismissed prior to trial)?
- Was the defendant convicted (whether or not he pleaded guilty)?
- If the defendant was convicted, was he sentenced to jail or prison?
- If the defendant was incarcerated, was his sentence short or long in relation to others in his state who were incarcerated for the same offense?
- How many days elapsed between the date the case was filed and its ultimate disposition (acquittal or sentencing date)—i.e., how long did it take to adjudicate the case?

OUTCOME RATES

Table 5.1 shows the rate across all sites at which various outcomes occurred in our samples of burglary and robbery cases. As can be seen, 78 percent of the burglary defendants and 68 percent of the robbery defendants pleaded guilty. Of the defendants who did not plead guilty, just under half were found guilty. Some defendants who were not found guilty had their

Table 5.1

OUTCOME VARIABLE RATES

Outcome Variable	Definition of Cases at Risk	Number of Cases at Risk		Percentage of Cases with This Outcome	
		Burglary	Robbery	Burglary	Robbery
Pleaded guilty	All completed cases with a disposition	1,115	1,148	77.9	68.2
Found guilty at trial	Cases where there was no plea	246	365	45.5	49.9
Convicted	All completed cases with a disposition	1,115	1,148	88.0	84.1
Convicted of sampled offense	All cases convicted of any offense	981	965	95.3	94.6
Incarcerated	All cases convicted	981	965	84.0	92.5
Had a long sentence	All cases sentenced to incarceration[a]	804	869	50.0	50.0
Above median time to disposition	All completed cases for which disposition time was available	1,109	1,151	50.0	50.0

[a]Excludes 20 burglary and 24 robbery cases in which the sentence length could not be computed because of missing data. A "long" sentence was one that was greater than the median sentence for the crime in the sample of defendants from the same state who were incarcerated.

cases dismissed before going to trial, whereas others were acquitted at trial. In short, about half the defendants who did not plead guilty had their cases disposed in their favor. It should be noted, however, that most burglary and robbery defendants did plead guilty.

The combination of pleas and finding of guilt at trial led to overall conviction rates of 88 and 84 percent for burglary and robbery, respectively. The fourth row in Table 5.1 shows that of those convicted, about 95 percent were convicted of the sampled offense. The remaining 5 percent of the convictions were therefore attributable to other cases whose adjudication overlapped that of the sampled offense. Thus, if we had not considered the outcome of the overlapping cases, we would have slightly underestimated the true overall conviction rate.

The row for incarcerations in Table 5.1 shows that 84 percent of the 981 convicted burglars and 92.5 percent of the 965 convicted robbers were incarcerated. In short, an adult male defendant in our study who was convicted of a burglary and especially of a robbery was very likely to be incarcerated.

The last two rows of Table 5.1 show that 50 percent of the defendants in both burglary and robbery cases received long sentences. These rates stem from the manner in which these variables were constructed.

In this study, a *long sentence* was defined as one that was greater than the median sentence for the defendant's state—a value computed on the basis of the defendants in our sample. We used this definition because of the large differences among states in sentencing laws and because the true meaning of a given sentence (in terms of the time the offender would actually serve) was also likely to vary among states. A four-year sentence in one state, for example, might normally result in an offender actually serving less than two years, whereas in another state the actual time served might be closer to three years. Moreover, some states give a range for a sentence—e.g., two to five years—rather than a specific number. In such cases, we used the minimum number as the designated sentence length.

Case disposition time was defined in our study as the number of days between the first arrest date in a defendant's set of overlapping cases and the date at which the last case in this set was adjudicated (i.e., the date the defendant was sentenced or acquitted). These data were for 1,115 burglary defendants and 1,148 robbery defendants. The mean disposition times in these two groups were 167 and 195 days, respectively. A defendant was considered to have had a "long" disposition time if the number of days it took to adjudicate his set of overlapping cases exceeded the median for his offense group.

We also examined how long it took to adjudicate a defendant's sampled offense. Restricting the data to these cases reduced the overall mean time to 145 and 173 days for burglary and robbery, respectively; in other words, it cut about three weeks off each average. Regardless of whether the time to disposition was based on all cases or just the sampled case, however, defendants with overlapping cases waited much longer to have the charges against them adjudicated than did other defendants. Table 5.2 illustrates this trend.

Figure 5.1 shows that of the 1,115 completed burglary cases, 74 percent resulted in incarceration. Across all sites, in other words, a defendant charged with burglarizing a stranger's home had about three chances in four of being incarcerated.

Figure 5.2 shows the corresponding information for persons charged with robbery. Interestingly, these data indicate that a defendant charged with armed robbery of a stranger had about the same probability of being incarcerated as a defendant charged with a burglary (78 percent versus 74 percent). However, burglary and robbery cases differ in the route they take to this outcome. Specifically, burglary defendants are more likely to plead than are robbery defendants, but robbery defendants are more likely to be found guilty at trial than are burglary defendants.

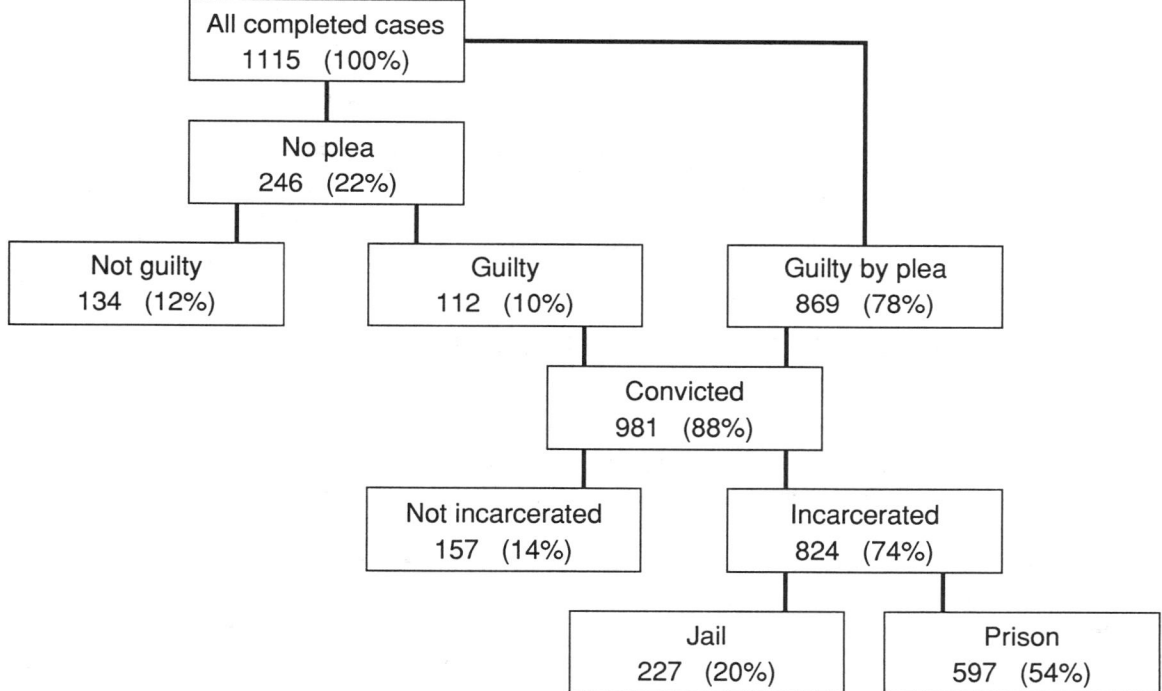

Fig. 5.1—Allocation of burglary cases to outcome categories

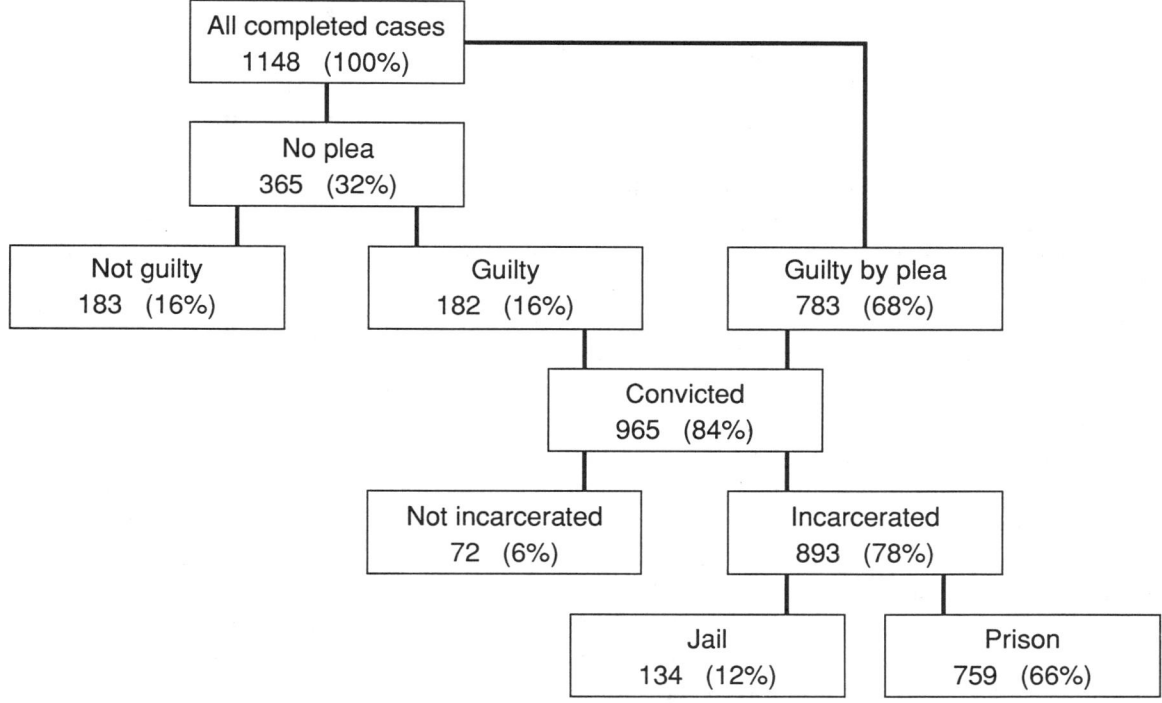

Fig. 5.2—Allocation of robbery cases to outcome categories

Table 5.2

MEAN DISPOSITION TIMES (IN DAYS) BY OFFENSE TYPE

Type of Defendant	Sampled Offense		All Cases	
	Burglary	Robbery	Burglary	Robbery
No overlapping cases	136	162	136	162
With overlapping cases	164	194	234	259
Total sample	145	173	167	195

COMPARISON OF OUTCOME RATES ACROSS STUDIES

The results presented above often differ from those reported by others. The Bureau of Justice Statistics (BJS, 1988), for example, investigated the outcomes of felony arrests prosecuted in 1984 using offender-based transaction system (OBTS) data from 11 states. Eight of the 14 sites in our research were located in four of these BJS states (California, Georgia, Missouri, and New York).

Table 5.3 contrasts the BJS results with those of our research. As these data indicate, RAND outcome rates tended to be slightly higher than those reported by BJS. One possible source of these differences is that BJS looked at the outcome of all felony arrests, including those that were prosecuted as a misdemeanor, whereas the RAND database was restricted to cases prosecuted as felonies (although the case outcome may have involved the defendant pleading or being found guilty of a misdemeanor).

This divergence in outcome rates might also be attributable to our use of large urban sites or to differences in these studies' definition of what constituted a burglary and a robbery (see Secs. I and IV). The latter consideration may help explain why the differences between the BJS and RAND studies were more pronounced for robbery than for burglary cases (i.e., we restricted our analyses to *armed* robbery).

Figure 5.3 presents results for the combination of burglary and robbery cases in our study. These data also differ from those based on 1986 PROMIS and court data as reported by Boland et al. (1989).

Boland's database consisted of all felony arrests in 10 large urban areas as well as the subset of these arrests that resulted in a felony indictment (i.e., reached felony court). These two levels of case processing bracket those in the RAND database discussed in this report. This occurred because we focused on all cases filed as felonies. Our database thus excluded felony arrests that led to misdemeanor filings but included cases that did not necessarily result in felony indictments, such as those in which the defendant pleaded guilty to a misdemeanor and those in which the court ruled that there was insufficient evidence to bind the defendant over to felony court.

Table 5.4 presents outcome rates on various measures in the Boland and RAND databases. To provide a more appropriate basis for making comparisons between these rates, the percentages in the Boland "felony arrest" column are based solely on the cases that went to court (which comprised 73 percent of all felony arrests in the Boland study; 22 percent were rejected at screening and 5 percent were diverted or referred).

Table 5.4 shows that the Boland and RAND studies had similar plea rates, but different conviction and incarceration rates. Disposition times were also quite different. We investigated possible sources of these differences by examining the conviction and incarceration rates

Table 5.3

COMPARISON OF BJS AND RAND OUTCOME RATES

Outcome Variable	Burglary			Robbery		
	BJS	RAND	Diff.	BJS	RAND	Diff.
Percentage of filed cases that resulted in conviction	81	79	2	70	75	5
Percentage of filed cases that resulted in incarceration	59	65	6	53	69	16
Percentage of convictions that resulted in incarceration	74	83	9	77	92	15

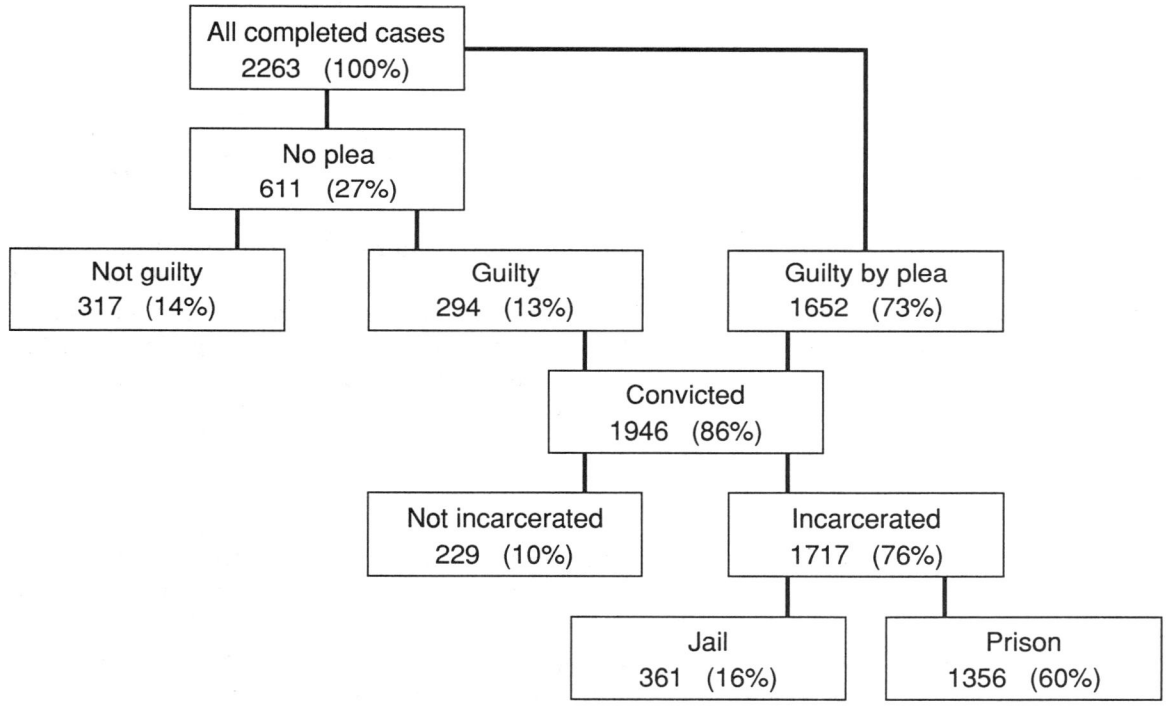

Fig. 5.3—Allocation of all RAND cases to outcome categories

Table 5.4

COMPARISON OF BOLAND AND RAND OUTCOME RATES
(ALL SITES IN BOTH STUDIES)[a]

	Boland		RAND
Outcome Variable	Felony Arrests	Felony Indictments	Felony Filings
Disposed by guilty plea	71	72	73
Percentage convicted	74	80	86
Percentage incarcerated	41	47	76
Percentage of convictions that led to an incarceration	56	59	88
Mean time from arrest to disposition	177	207	159

[a]Figures 1 and 2 in Boland et al. (1989) were the source of the percentages in columns 1 and 2 after the base for column 1 was restricted to those arrests that went to court. Mean disposition times were derived from Tables 8 and 9.

of those defendants who had been arrested for robbery and burglary in the four sites that were common to both studies: Los Angeles and San Diego, California; Manhattan, New York; and Saint Louis, Missouri.

Table 5.5 shows that when we control on site, there is fairly close agreement in outcome rates and disposition times between the RAND sample of felony filings and Boland's sample of felony indictments. The differences that remain most likely stem from the previously noted differences between these two samples with respect to level of case processing, differences in the definition of what constitutes burglary and robbery, RAND's use of cases processed in the central branch of jurisdictions with multiple offices, and chance.

OUTCOMES BY SITE

Since most of the differences in outcome rates between the Boland and RAND studies were eliminated when we controlled for site, it may be inferred that the differences between the overall rates of these studies stemmed primarily from the particular set of sites used in each. This conclusion is consistent with the finding of relatively large differences in outcome rates among sites both within each study and between the RAND and BJS investigations.

Table 5.6 shows the rate on four key outcome variables by site as well as the average of the rates across the 14 sites. It is evident from this table that some sites had much higher rates and case disposition times than did others. In San Diego, for example, 70 percent of defendants charged with burglary pleaded guilty, and it usually took about three months (97 days) to process their cases. The corresponding values for Baltimore were 87 percent and 128 days. Table 5.7 shows the rates on these variables by site for defendants whose sampled cases involved armed robbery.

The data in Tables 5.6 and 5.7 should be interpreted with caution for two reasons. First, there were usually only about 80 completed cases at risk per site, and some outcomes had even

Table 5.5

COMPARISON OF BOLAND AND RAND OUTCOME RATES IN THE
FOUR SITES THAT WERE COMMON TO BOTH STUDIES[a]

	Boland		RAND
Outcome Variable	Felony Arrests	Felony Indictments	Felony Filings
Disposed by guilty plea			
Burglary	74	88	79
Robbery	59	76	74
Percentage convicted			
Burglary	77	93	90
Robbery	66	87	86
Percentage incarcerated			
Burglary	59	79	82
Robbery	54	77	80
Percentage of convictions that led to an incarceration			
Burglary	78	85	91
Robbery	85	89	93
Mean number of days from arrest to disposition			
Burglary	131	141	123
Robbery	117	177	152

[a]The source of plea and conviction rates in columns 1 and 2 was appendix Tables 2 and 3 in Boland et al. (1989). In both of these tables, dismissals include diversions and referrals for other prosecution. The sources for incarceration rates for these two columns were appendix Tables 6 and 7, respectively. The disposition times came from Tables 8 and 9. Sites were weighted equally to compute the tabled rates. All rates are based on cases in which sentencing outcome was known.

fewer at risk per site. Thus, some of the observed deviations from the overall average rate may simply represent chance fluctuations.

The second reason caution should be exercised in interpreting the observed differences in outcome rates among sites is that such differences may stem from intersite variation in case characteristics rather than from differences in local or state policies and practices. For instance, one site may have had more cases whose characteristics were likely to lead to a plea than did another site. Section VII of this report examines the extent to which the observed differences in outcome rates among sites (and states) remain after case characteristics have been held constant. In addition, the plea and conviction rates at the New York sites cannot be compared to those at other sites because of the biases associated with the sample selection at these sites, as discussed in Sec. III and App. A.

The mean rate among the 14 sites on a given outcome variable is presented at the bottom of each table. This mean corresponded closely with the mean rate across all defendants. For example, when site is used as the unit of analysis, the mean number of days to disposition was 146 for burglary defendants and 175 for robbery defendants. When the individual defendant was used as the unit of analysis, the corresponding means were 145 and 173. The same pattern

Table 5.6

OUTCOME RATES BY SITE: BURGLARY

Site	Pleaded Guilty	Convicted	Incarcerated	Mean Days to Disposition[a]
Montgomery	78	95	82	160
Baltimore	87	89	82	128
San Diego	70	94	90	97
Sacramento	85	87	86	123
Los Angeles	76	79	78	120
Fort Worth	70	90	51	153
Dallas	89	94	85	95
Manhattan	88	100	92	166
Queens	86	96	87	226
Detriot	75	89	71	116
Chicago	56	72	58	246
Saint Louis	82	85	66	107
Kansas City	79	83	61	192
Atlanta	85	90	61	118
Mean rate	79	85	75	146

[a]Results are presented for the sampled offense. On average, the mean rate increased by about 20 days if the disposition time was based on the full set of overlapping cases.

Table 5.7

OUTCOME RATES BY SITE: ROBBERY

Site	Pleaded Guilty	Convicted	Incarcerated	Mean Days to Disposition[a]
Montgomery	64	84	72	173
Baltimore	64	73	67	181
San Diego	60	91	86	132
Sacramento	60	83	74	126
Los Angeles	77	81	80	150
Fort Worth	83	94	86	243
Dallas	87	93	87	122
Manhattan	89	98	89	173
Queens	83	98	92	245
Detroit	42	79	74	139
Chicago	53	77	72	243
Saint Louis	68	75	65	153
Kansas City	64	79	71	226
Atlanta	79	88	77	139
Mean rate	70	85	78	175

[a]Results are presented for the sampled offense. On average, the mean rate increased by about 20 days if the disposition time was based on the full set of overlapping cases.

occurred with the other outcome variables and with the case mix variables discussed in Sec. VI. Thus, it did not appear necessary to weight the data to adjust for some sites having more defendants than others. All the remaining analyses in this report use the individual defendant as the unit of analysis.

VI. UNIVARIATE ANALYSIS RESULTS

This section summarizes our analyses of the frequency with which various case and defendant characteristics occurred in our database and the extent to which the outcomes discussed in Sec. V are correlated with these characteristics. The variables outlined below are those we used to control for possible differences in case characteristics among sites. Readers who are interested primarily in the policy implications of our research may therefore wish to review the "variables" portion of this section and then skip to Sec. VII.

VARIABLES

Table 6.1 lists the variables that were used as controls for case characteristics. Appendix C provides variable names in the database and location in the survey instrument.

Table 6.1

PREDICTORS OF CASE OUTCOMES

INCIDENT CHARACTERISTICS
- Did the defendant have an accomplice?
- Were there multiple counts?
- Were there any female victims?
- Did any victim receive major injuries?
- Was there more than one victim?
- Did the incident happen at night?
- Was any victim vulnerable (handicapped, elderly, or juvenile)?
- Did the defendant use or threaten to use a weapon?

EVIDENCE
- Were the defendant's fingerprints linked to the crime?
- Was stolen property recovered?
- Did the police obtain the weapon(s) used?
- Was there at least one witness who was not a police officer or a victim?

APPREHENSION
- Was the defendant arrested at the scene of the crime?
- Was the defendant arrested more than 24 hours after the crime?
- Was the defendant under the influence of drugs or alcohol at the time of arrest?

OVERLAPPING CASES
- Did the defendant have one or more overlapping cases?

PRIOR RECORD
- Did the defendant have a prior juvenile (nontraffic) arrest?
- Did the defendant have a prior adult criminal arrest?
- Did the defendant have a prior adult criminal conviction?
- Did the defendant have a prior adult criminal incarceration?
- Was the defendant on probation, parole, or escape status when arrested?

DEFENDANT CHARACTERISTICS
- Was the defendant white?
- Was the defendant black?
- Was the defendant Hispanic?
- Was the defendant unemployed at time of arrest?

Variables were selected for inclusion in the analysis on the basis of two criteria: (1) they were conceptually or empirically associated with the case outcomes of interest; and (2) data on them were available across all 14 sites. For example, we examined the evidence that was available to the prosecution because a stronger case presumably could be brought against a defendant if more factors linked him to the crime. Similarly, being arrested at the scene would weigh against the defendant as well. We looked at the offender's racial/ethnic group in light of the extensive research that has been conducted on this topic (e.g., Klein, Petersilia, and Turner, 1990). Some variables, such as the defendant's income, were not included in the analyses because relevant data were not readily available for all or most defendants. Variables that were included in the analysis did not have serious missing-data problems; nor was their basic meaning affected by any changes made in the case-abstracting form during the course of the project.

One important exception to the foregoing considerations was that prior-record data were more likely to be available for convicted than for nonconvicted defendants. Specifically, 16 percent of the completed cases did not have prior-record data. Within this "missing data" group, 82 percent of the burglars but only 72 percent of the robbers were convicted of a sampled and/or overlapping case. By contrast, the conviction rates among those for whom prior-record data were available were 89 and 86 percent, respectively. The missing data rates for convicted and not-convicted cases were approximately 15 percent and 26 percent, respectively. We had no way of knowing whether the missing data signified that a given defendant did not have a prior record or whether such a record simply never found its way into the defendant's permanent folder in the prosecutor's office.

For the analyses presented in this report, a defendant who did not have prior-record information in his folder was considered to have no prior record. We chose this approach for two reasons. First, we wanted to examine case outcomes from the prosecutor's perspective. Thus, if there was no prior-record information in the defendant's file, the prosecutor had to assume that the defendant did not have such a record. Second, among the 84 percent of the cases for whom prior-record data were available, the defendants who had prior convictions and incarcerations were more likely to be convicted again than were those with a clean record. Thus, the course we chose for handling missing data was consistent with the observed relationships in the preponderance of our database.[1]

Table 6.2 shows the percentage of defendants with various case and individual characteristics. For instance, 48 percent of those charged with burglary had an accomplice. In addition, there was an eyewitness (other than the victim or a police officer) in 51 percent of the burglary cases and 37 percent of the robbery cases. In the case of burglary, this might have been a neighbor or friend. This finding suggests that the residential burglary and armed robbery cases that actually result in a charge are those in which there is a fairly solid case against the defendant.

Table 6.2 also shows that 57 percent of the burglary defendants and 53 percent of the robbery defendants were known to have had at least one prior adult conviction (and most of those with a prior adult conviction had had a prior adult incarceration as well). The prior adult arrest rates for burglars and robbers were 74 (rounded) and 70 percent, respectively. More than one out of five of the defendants was on probation or parole (or had escaped) at the

---

[1]The plan for the present study envisioned the gathering of complete prior-record data as part of a subsequent follow-up study of the completed cases in our analysis sample. Any bias that may have been introduced by the missing prior-record data into the prediction models discussed in the next section of this report could therefore be identified and corrected after collection of the follow-up data.

Table 6.2

PERCENTAGE OF DEFENDANTS WITH VARIOUS CHARACTERISTICS

Defendant/Case Characteristic	Burglary	Robbery
Had an accomplice	48	65
Multiple sample charges	6	12
Any victim a female	20	40
Major victim injury	2	11
Two or more victims	10	40
Nighttime arrest	48	69
Vulnerable victim	7	12
Offender threatened use of a weapon	5	69
Eyewitness	51	37
Fingerprints	13	5
Property recovered	60	48
Weapon as evidence	7	35
Arrested at scene	40	21
Arrested after 24 hours	41	49
Under influence of drugs at arrest	10	12
Had at least one overlapping case	31	35
Prior juvenile arrest (no incarceration)	6	7
Prior juvenile incarceration	8	9
Prior adult arrest (no conviction)	16	17
Prior adult conviction (no incarceration)	14	13
Prior adult incarceration	43	40
Probation/parole/escape at arrest	24	22
Black	56	71
White	28	17
Hispanic	15	11
Unemployed	40	42
From out of state	5	5

time they were arrested for the crime that led to their inclusion in our database. These findings are generally consistent with those of other studies that have found that persons charged with crimes are likely to have had prior criminal records.

The data on prior juvenile record probably greatly underestimate the actual percentage of defendants with juvenile offenses. This bias occurred because information on juvenile arrests and convictions was often excluded from the prosecutors' records and hence from the coding procedure as well.

The remainder of this section discusses how the variables in Table 6.1 were individually related to the outcomes discussed previously. Section VII discusses how well the six clusters of variables in this table, as well as state and site, predict case outcomes. Appendix D provides information about the similarities and differences among the 14 sites with respect to case mix variables.

CORRELATES OF CASE OUTCOMES

Table 6.3 shows the relationship between case disposition and whether the defendant did or did not have a prior adult criminal record (i.e., an arrest, conviction, or incarceration). These data show that defendants with prior criminal records were slightly more likely to be convicted than were those who did not have prior records. Once convicted, offenders with prior records were much more likely to go to prison than were those lacking such records.

Table 6.4 shows the relationship between three key adjudication outcomes and various case and defendant characteristics. For instance, the rate at which burglary defendants pleaded guilty was 12 percentage points higher in cases where stolen property was recovered than in cases in which such property was not recovered. There was an 11-point swing for robbery. Similarly, the conviction rate was 10 percentage points higher among defendants charged with robbery who had their fingerprints linked to the crime than it was among robbery cases lacking this type of evidence.

Defendants who had one or more overlapping cases were much more likely to plead guilty and be convicted and incarcerated than were other offenders. As will be discussed in Sec. VIII, however, these defendants also tended to have other characteristics generally associated with elevated outcome rates.

Appendix E contains data that show the direction and strength of the relationship between the variables in Table 6.1 and each adjudication outcome. An inspection of these data suggests that the variables most closely associated with the outcomes studied were number of counts, victim injury, types of evidence available, presence of one or more overlapping cases, and prior record. A few variables were highly related to one outcome but not to another. For example, being under the influence when arrested was related to being found guilty at trial but not to whether the defendant entered a plea.

Table 6.3

CASE DISPOSITIONS FOR DEFENDANTS WHO DID AND DID NOT HAVE A PRIOR ADULT CRIMINAL RECORD[a]

	Burglary		Robbery	
Disposition	No Prior Record (N = 296)	With Prior Record (N = 819)	No Prior Record (N = 342)	With Prior Record (N = 806)
In favor of defendant	15%	11%	20%	14%
Convicted by:				
Plea	76	79	66	69
Trial	9	10	14	17
Total	100%	100%	100%	100%
Sentence if convicted:				
Probation	29%	12%	13%	5%
Jail	29	21	17	13
Prison	42	67	70	82
Total	100%	100%	100%	100%

[a]Prior record consisted of documentation in the prosecutor's file for the case that the defendant had at least one adult arrest and/or conviction.

Table 6.4

INCREASE (OR DECREASE) IN PLEA, CONVICTION, AND INCARCERATION RATES
WHEN CERTAIN CASE AND DEFENDANT CHARACTERISTICS ARE PRESENT

Case or Defendant Characteristic	Pleaded Guilty		Convicted		Incarcerated[a]	
	Burglary	Robbery	Burglary	Robbery	Burglary	Robbery
Had an accomplice	3	1	1	1	−3	−1
Multiple counts	−2	3	11	9	12	7
Female victim	−3	11	−2	8	0	3
Victim injured	−4	−9	7	−1	11	6
Two or more victims	−1	6	−2	5	2	5
Nighttime crime	3	6	0	6	1	−2
Vulnerable victim	−4	−1	−9	2	−4	4
Weapon threatened	−8	11	−6	7	10	5
Eyewitness	5	10	6	10	7	3
Fingerprints	2	11	5	10	8	4
Recovered property	12	11	10	10	7	0
Recovered weapon	1	7	6	6	11	1
Arrested at scene	9	14	10	8	10	3
On drugs at arrest	3	7	10	4	3	0
Had one or more overlapping cases	19	23	14	17	24	23
On probation/parole at time of arrest	1	−1	4	4	16	10
Unemployed	8	9	4	7	9	4

[a]The "incarceration rate" is the percentage of defendants who were sentenced to jail or prison from among those who were convicted.

The tables in App. E reveal some unanticipated relationships. For example, the variables "arrested at the scene" and "delayed" (i.e., arrested more than 24 hours after the crime) are both positively correlated with a defendant's willingness to plead guilty (and therefore those arrested not at the scene but within a day of its commission are less willing to plead guilty). We suspect that this curvilinear relationship with time stems from two quite different mechanisms. Specifically, those arrested at the scene are more likely to be caught red-handed and therefore to face a very strong case against them. By contrast, those apprehended much later are tied to the crime through good police work, "sting" operations, and the like. Those in the middle time slot may be apprehended as a result of instructions to "round up the usual suspects."

Only about 11 percent of those charged with burglary or robbery were known to be under the influence of drugs at the time of their arrest. However, we suspect that sites varied in the effectivenss with which they documented this characteristic. Thus, the actual percentage may well be much higher. Moreover, we had information about drug use only at the time of arrest as distinct from when the crime was committed. It is also important to note that the case mix variables discussed in this section are not independent of each other. For example, defendants with overlapping cases are also more likely to have prior criminal records. Thus, the predictive power of a given combination of case characteristics is far less than that obtained from a simple addition of their individual abilities to forecast a given outcome.

Comparison of the data in Table 6.2 with those in App. E provides several interesting insights about case characteristics and their relationship to adjudication outcomes. For instance, stolen property was recovered in 48 percent of the cases in which a defendant was charged with robbery. One explanation for this remarkably high recovery rate is that prosecutors may be more willing to file cases when stolen property is recovered (see Table E.4). Such a tendency is certainly consistent with the fact that the overall plea rate is six percentage points higher than average when property is recovered and five points below average when it is not recovered. Put another way, the recovery of stolen property corresponds to an 11-point swing in the likelihood of a plea and is therefore something that prosecutors are likely to heed in their filing decisions.

It is evident from the foregoing discussion that differences among jurisdictions' outcome rates could stem from differences in case mix. In other words, the characteristics of cases and defendants in one jurisdiction could differ substantially from those in another in ways that are related to case outcomes. Thus, if one is to determine the unique effect of state and county on outcomes, one must control for important differences among sites in the characteristics of their cases and defendants. The effects of these controls are discussed in Sec. VII.

VII. MULTIVARIATE ANALYSIS RESULTS

The primary goal of our research was to assess the extent to which state and local policies and practices were related to case outcomes. We recognized that observed differences in outcomes among states and sites might stem from a variety of factors, including their mixes of case characteristics. As noted in the previous section, for example, a defendant is somewhat less likely to plead guilty if his victim sustained major injury. Thus, one site may have a lower plea rate than another not because of intersite differences in adjudication policies but rather because that site merely has more cases involving injuries.

To investigate this matter, we used the defendant as the unit of analysis with the intent of examining how well the combination of all the factors discussed in the previous section correctly classified a defendant's status with respect to each outcome. We then examined whether inclusion of a defendant's state and site in the prediction system increased classification accuracy. If adding state and site to the system does not improve accuracy, it can be inferred that state and site policies and practices probably do not have a significant bearing on case outcomes—suggesting in turn that a given defendant will face roughly the same outcome regardless of the jurisdiction in which he is charged.

It is, of course, possible that state or site policies may not enhance classification accuracy but may nonetheless have an indirect effect on outcomes. This could occur if such policies led to stronger (or weaker) cases against defendants—e.g., if they influenced the extent to which witnesses and evidence are obtained.

If the inclusion of state and site in the prediction system were found to produce a significant increase in accuracy, support would be lent to the hypothesis that state and local policies (and the factors that drive them) influence outcomes. An alternative explanation is that the variables we used to adjust for differences in case characteristics among sites were not sufficient to capture all the differences that actually affect outcomes. In other words, any state and site differences that remained after we adjusted for case characteristics could well have disappeared if the prediction system had contained more variables (or if the current variables had been combined in a different way). For example, we did not measure witness credibility—yet one site may in fact have a higher conviction rate than another because its police/prosecutor screening process retains only those cases with highly credible witnesses or similarly strong evidence.

In summary, a finding that state and site contribute uniquely to predictive accuracy would open the door to the possibility that local policies and practices influence outcomes. Thus, if one site were found to have a significantly higher conviction rate than another even after controlling for available case characteristics, an examination of the practices at these sites would be warranted. If, however, site did not significantly enhance predictive accuracy, such an investigation would be far less likely to reveal any policy differences that affect outcomes.

With the foregoing considerations in mind, we examined how well various case outcomes could be predicted when the variables discussed in the previous section were combined into a single prediction system. We then examined the *size* of the increase in classification accuracy when this system was modified to include the defendant's state and site.

Our goal in this research was not to find the best combination of variables to predict a given outcome but rather to investigate whether the use of a simple and common adjustment procedure—ordinary least-squares multiple regression—would eradicate the differences among sites in the outcome rates discussed in the previous section. This approach also enabled us to assess the extent to which the addition of a given cluster of variables enhanced the classification accuracy obtained solely with the use of the other variables already in the regression equation. We sought to ascertain, for example, how much accuracy increased when the defendant's demographic characteristics were added to a prediction system that already included his other case and prior-record variables.

Variables were placed into the regression equations in the sequence presented in Table 6.1. Thus, we entered all the incident characteristics, measured predictive accuracy, added the evidence variables, measured the increase in accuracy, and continued in this manner until all the variables listed in Table 6.1 had been considered.[1] We then added a defendant's state and site to the system to determine the extent to which unique state and site characteristics were related to case outcomes.

There are two ways to measure the degree to which case mix and other variables contribute to the accuracy with which one can predict a given outcome. One method focuses on the relative improvement over chance, and the other examines the actual degree of that improvement. The results obtained with both approaches are discussed below.

RELATIVE IMPROVEMENT OVER CHANCE (RIOC)

The "relative improvement over chance," or RIOC, method looks at how much of the difference between chance and perfect accuracy can be explained by a given prediction system (Loeber and Dishion, 1983). Computation of the RIOC value is illustrated by the following example in the sample of 1,115 completed burglary cases—a group containing 981 defendants who were convicted and 134 who were not. A prediction system based on chance would classify 879 of these defendants into their correct outcome categories. If 939 of the defendants had their outcome categories classified correctly by a prediction system, this would represent a 25 percent improvement over chance.

The data used to calculate this RIOC value are shown below; the specific procedures used to compute RIOC values presented in this report are discussed in more detail in App. F.

```
1,115 = perfect prediction
  879 = chance correct predictions
  236 = difference between chance and perfect = 1,115 − 879
  939 = number of correct predictions
   60 = difference between chance and correct predictions = 939 − 879
   25 = (100)(60/236) = RIOC value
```

The results of the RIOC analyses are presented in Tables 7.1 and 7.2. These tables show the effect on overall classification accuracy of adding each group of variables to the prediction system. For example, it is evident from the first column of Table 7.1 that the incident characteristics, even when used together, did not improve accuracy over the chance rate. Evidence

---

[1]The predictive equation used in the computation of relative improvement over chance was specified as a linear combination of the predictor variables and was estimated using ordinary least squares. We did not draw any inferences from the estimated coefficients because we were interested only in using the estimated equation as a predictor. Moreover, since the outcomes were, on the average, bounded away from both 0 and 1, it was not necessary to use a more complicated specification and estimation procedure such as logit.

Table 7.1

RELATIVE IMPROVEMENT OVER CHANCE PERCENTAGES: BURGLARY[a]

Equation Variables	Pleaded Guilty	Found Guilty	Convicted	Incarcerated	To Prison	Sentence Length	Case Time
Incident	0	7	6	5	0	5	10
Evidence	10	13	17	9	17	19	14
Arrest	11	23	23	9	21	19	14
Overlapping	17	30	24	15	28	28	25
Priors	17	36	26	33	33	37	27
Offender	21	36	26	35	36	37	28
State	28	44	34	39	45	37	36
Site	29	51	35	46	48	37	37

[a]The prediction equation for a row contains the variables in that row plus the variables in the row(s) above it; e.g., the prediction equation for the "arrest" variable includes incident and evidence variables. Case time refers to number of days between arrest and case disposition.

Table 7.2

RELATIVE IMPROVEMENT OVER CHANCE PERCENTAGES: ROBBERY[a]

Equation Variables	Pleaded Guilty	Found Guilty	Convicted	Incarcerated	To Prison	Sentence Length	Case Time
Incident	14	4	11	15	15	25	12
Evidence	18	21	20	17	16	28	13
Arrest	18	21	20	17	22	33	15
Overlapping	24	27	22	23	27	42	23
Priors	25	28	28	23	27	44	23
Offender	29	28	28	26	29	44	26
State	36	42	35	26	34	44	35
Site	36	44	39	26	36	44	40

[a]The prediction equation for a row contains the variables in that row plus the variables in the row(s) above it; e.g., the prediction equation for the "arrest" variable includes incident and evidence variables. Case time refers to number of days between arrest and case disposition.

factors, on the other hand, did improve classification accuracy by 10 percent over chance. The inclusion of all the other control variables led to an accuracy rate that was 21 percent better than that which would be obtained by chance.

The 11-percentage-point increment from 10 to 21 percent in RIOC values for "pleaded guilty" reflects the unique contribution of arrest, overlapping case, prior-record, and offender characteristics to overall predictive accuracy after incident and evidence variables are already in the prediction system. This combined set of factors alone would have an RIOC value exceeding 11 percent because they shared some predictive power with the incident and evidence factors already in the system (that is to say, case mix variables were often correlated with each other). This caveat also applies to the interpretation of differences between any two adjacent sets of factors, such as the six-percentage-point increase that was observed in RIOC values when the presence versus absence of overlapping cases in a defendant's file was included in the prediction system.

Adding state and site to the prediction produced a seven-percentage-point gain in the RIOC value. As will be discussed later in this section, however, this RIOC-value increase translates into only a three-point gain in the model's ability to predict whether a given burglary defendant will or will not plead guilty.

The fact that offender characteristics slightly improved accuracy even after other factors were in the prediction system suggests that these factors (or variables correlated with them) may influence the decision to plead. Looking back to Table 6.4, we see that this was most likely attributed to the fact that unemployed defendants were more likely to plead than were employed defendants.

As with the other case characteristics examined, however, offender characteristics do not stand alone; instead they are correlated with other aspects of an offense. For example, unemployed defendants may be more likely than employed defendants to commit the types of offenses that tend to result in a plea. Thus, the observed correlation between offender characteristics and outcome variables may stem from the association of these characteristics with certain crime and prior-record variables rather than from offender characteristics per se. As a consequence of this situation, a given factor may correlate with an outcome variable in one direction when used alone but in the opposite direction when joined with other variables in a prediction system. Moreover, the specific combination of variables in the prediction system can affect their algebraic sign. Thus, readers should exercise caution in interpreting the nature of the contribution to prediction that actually stems from a given variable.

Taken together, Tables 7.1 and 7.2 show that offender characteristics played little or no role in the prediction of most outcome variables once other factors were in the prediction system.

Actual Improvement over Chance

Tables 7.3 and 7.4 show the actual (as distinct from relative) levels of classification accuracy achieved (see App. F). These data indicate that case characteristics alone predicted a given outcome with only a moderate degree of accuracy. For instance, 84 percent of the burglary defendants had their conviction status estimated correctly by use of the case mix variables, but this is only 5 percentage points better than the percentage of correct classifications that would be obtained by chance.

Adding state to a prediction system that already included case characteristics had little or no effect on most outcomes but did produce a small increase in the accuracy with which convictions at trial were predicted. This finding suggests that state laws and practices may have some impact on whether a defendant will or will not be found guilty if he does not plead guilty.

The last column in Tables 7.3 and 7.4 shows the percentage of defendants with each outcome (see Table 5.1 for details). For example, 78 percent of the burglary defendants pleaded guilty. Thus, an estimation system would be correct 78 percent of the time if it simply said that every burglary defendant pleaded guilty. Moreover, such a system would make only one type of error: it would predict that an offender pleaded when in fact he did not do so. Thus, if the base rate for an outcome is very high or very low, not much utility will result from the use of a sophisticated prediction system. By contrast, when the base rate is close to 50 percent (as it is with sentence length and disposition time), the regression models yielded a substantial increase in classification accuracy.

Table 7.3

PERCENTAGE OF CASES CLASSIFIED CORRECTLY: BURGLARY

Outcome Variable	Chance	With All Controls	All Controls + State	All Controls + State and Site	Base Rate
Pleaded guilty	66	74	76	77	78
Found guilty	50	72	76	80	46
Convicted	79	84	86	86	88
Incarcerated	73	83	84	86	84
Long term	50	70	70	70	50
Long disposition	50	65	69	70	50

Table 7.4

PERCENTAGE OF CASES CLASSIFIED CORRECTLY: ROBBERY

Outcome Variable	Chance	With All Controls	All Controls + State	All Controls + State and Site	Base Rate
Pleaded guilty	57	70	73	73	68
Found guilty	50	68	75	76	50
Convicted	73	81	83	84	84
Incarcerated	86	90	90	90	93
Long term	50	72	73	73	50
Long disposition	50	64	68	71	50

Differences Among Sites

Table 7.5 shows the deviation from the overall mean conviction rate before and after adjustment for case characteristics. The expected value for a site was obtained by applying the prediction equation for a given outcome to the defendants at that site. For instance, if the application of this equation resulted in a prediction that 85 percent of the defendants at this site would plead guilty, the expected value for this site would be 85 percent. Before controlling for case mix, the conviction rate for the burglary defendants in our sample from Montgomery was 10 percentage points higher than the mean rate of 85 percent across all 14 sites. After controlling for case mix, this differential shrank to three percentage points higher than average. Thus, for this site, the case characteristics eliminated almost all the observed deviation from the 14-site mean rate.

An inspection of Table 7.5 indicates that after control for case mix had been achieved, the New York and Texas sites had consistently higher conviction rates than would be expected. By contrast, the Missouri sites tended to have lower-than-expected conviction rates. The New York rates are biased upward for the reasons discussed in Sec. III (i.e., because of state law, we generally did not have access to the records of defendants who were not convicted at these sites). Even setting aside the New York data, however, some apparent differences among states and sites remained—differences that could not be explained simply by the available case mix variables.

Although the differences depicted in Table 7.5 are suggestive of state effects, they certainly do not offer conclusive evidence of such effects. As noted in Tables 7.3 and 7.4, unique state and site effects translate into an increase of only a few percentage points in the accuracy

Table 7.5

DEVIATION FROM THE MEAN CONVICTION RATE BEFORE AND AFTER
CONTROLLING FOR CASE CHARACTERISTICS

Site	Burglary		Robbery	
	Before	After	Before	After
Montgomery	10	3	−1	6
Baltimore	4	0	−12	−5
San Diego	9	2	6	9
Sacramento	2	−5	−2	−13
Los Angeles	−6	−9	−4	−6
Fort Worth	5	3	9	5
Dallas	9	8	8	10
Manhattan	15	7	13	12
Queens	11	8	13	15
Detroit	4	4	6	−2
Chicago	−13	−13	−8	−7
Saint Louis	0	−1	−10	−9
Kansas City	−2	−5	−6	−9
Atlanta	5	5	3	5
Mean rate	85		84	

of forecasting whether a defendant will have a given case outcome. In addition, the trends in San Diego were the opposite of those in the other two California sites.

More important, it should be noted that the case mix control process is far from perfect. The intersite differences that remained after controlling for case characteristics could well have stemmed from unmeasured case or defendant variables that are correlated with site rather than from the manner in which cases were processed once charges were actually filed. For example, the prosecutors at the two Texas sites may have been relatively less willing to file charges when they did not have especially credible witnesses. Similarly, prosecutors in sites with below-average conviction rates may have been somewhat more willing to take a chance on a case in which they had the same number of witnesses as some other site, even if the witnesses were less credible. Alternatively, site could play a role. For instance, Texas juries may be slightly more willing to convict.

Site by itself had little bearing on the prediction of outcomes once the other variables were already in the model. Specifically, less than a one-percentage-point increase in forecasting accuracy generally resulted when site was added to a system that already included case mix variables and state. This finding suggests that most of the differences among sites that remained after controlling for case mix were related to state rather than local practices.

The only exceptions to this trend were cases in which (1) a burglar was found guilty at trial (i.e., among those who did not plead), (2) a defendant was incarcerated for burglary, and (3) a robbery defendant had a relatively long disposition time. Tables 7.3 and 7.4 show, however, that the unique effect of site on overall accuracy was quite small (two to four percentage points) even for these variables.

Taken together, the foregoing findings indicate that intersite differences in policies and practices generally had little effect on what happened to a particular defendant. For example, Table 7.3 shows that after controlling for case characteristics, only one site—Chicago—had a conviction rate for burglars that deviated more than 10 percentage points from the mean across all sites. Moreover, the Chicago rate would have been even closer to the mean if the New York data had been excluded from the analysis for the reasons discussed above.[2]

Table 7.6 shows the real power of the case mix control procedure. Before the controls were used, 77 percent of the burglary defendants at the Kansas City site had a longer-than-median disposition time (i.e., 27 percent *more* than expected). By contrast, only 27 percent of the Dallas burglars had a longer-than-median time (i.e., 23 percent *less* than expected). Thus, there was a 50-percentage-point swing between these two sites in disposition times. After control had been attained for differences in case mix, however, this difference shrank to nine percentage points. In other words, little difference was found in the length of time sites took to dispose of a particular type of case once control had been attained for differences in the characteristics of cases these sites processed. Nonetheless, the small differences that remained appeared to be fairly systematic, as indicated by the fact that the inclusion of site and state in the estimation equation increased predictive accuracy.

Appendix G contains the regression equations that were used to control for case mix in the estimation of conviction rates, trial outcomes, and disposition times.

Table 7.6

DEVIATION FROM THE MEDIAN DISPOSITION TIME BEFORE AND AFTER CONTROLLING FOR CASE CHARACTERISTICS[a]

Site	Burglary		Robbery	
	Before	After	Before	After
Montgomery	8	10	12	11
Baltimore	6	0	10	2
San Diego	−17	−3	−21	−4
Sacramento	−8	−2	−14	−5
Los Angeles	−6	−3	−16	0
Fort Worth	6	0	17	5
Dallas	−23	−5	−24	−6
Manhattan	12	0	12	0
Queens	33	9	21	7
Detroit	−17	−3	−22	3
Chicago	16	11	19	5
Saint Louis	−9	−6	1	−4
Kansas City	27	4	30	6
Atlanta	−6	−2	−15	−4

[a]If site was not related to disposition time, 50 percent of a site's defendants would be expected to have a longer-than-median disposition time. The values in this table show the deviation from 50 percent—the higher the value, the greater the percentage of cases with longer-than-expected disposition times.

---

[2]There were not enough defendants going to trial at most sites to provide a reliable basis for making cross-site comparisons in trial conviction rates.

EFFECT OF PLEA/NO-PLEA DECISION ON SENTENCING

Some defendants go to trial while others confess (i.e., "plead guilty"). Pleas are much less costly for prosecutors to process than are trials. Given their limited resources, prosecutors are therefore generally willing to drop or reduce charges if defendants are willing to plead guilty rather than exercise their constitutional right to a full trial. Defendants, for their part, are willing to enter a plea of guilty because it presumably means that they will receive a lesser sentence than would have been the case had they gone to trial and been found guilty of all the offenses with which they were initially charged (as well as enhancements, such as use of a gun in commission of a felony). Judges also recognize the utility of the plea-bargaining process in the knowledge that without it they would be inundated with trials. Public defenders' offices face similar pressures to make the bargaining process work.

The assumption underlying plea bargaining is that defendants who are guilty receive less severe sentences if they confess than if they take their chances at trial. Such a pattern has been observed in other studies (e.g., Clarke and Turner-Kurtz, 1983). The analyses discussed below examined whether the route to a conviction (plea versus trial) was associated with a defendant's chances of going to prison or receiving a relatively long or short sentence for his state.

Of the 981 burglary defendants who were convicted, 869 pleaded guilty. The other 112 were found guilty at trial. The corresponding counts for the 965 convicted robbery defendants were 783 and 182. Table 7.7 shows that the route a defendant took to conviction was not systematically related to that defendant's likelihood of going to prison or receiving a relatively long term. For instance, 62 percent of the burglary defendants who pleaded guilty were sentenced to prison, whereas 54 percent of those who did not plead (but were nevertheless convicted) went to prison. The opposite pattern occurred among robbery defendants who were convicted.

We also constructed three regression equations on the sample of convicted offenders. These equations were constructed for each combination of crime type and outcome variable discussed above. The first equation contained all the case mix variables, the second contained these same variables plus whether or not the defendant pleaded guilty, and the third contained the same variables plus state and site. The adjusted R-square values for these equations are presented in Table 7.8.

The data in Table 7.8 again show that whether a defendant was convicted as a result of a plea or a trial had no real effect on the likelihood that the defendant would go to prison or receive a relatively long sentence. These data do show, however, that the addition of a

Table 7.7

DISPOSITION OF CONVICTIONS ACCORDING TO THE MANNER IN WHICH CONVICTION OCCURRED

Case Outcome	Burglary		Robbery	
	Plea	Trial	Plea	Trial
Percentage going to prison	62	54	78	81
Percentage receiving a relatively long term	50	49	49	54

Table 7.8

ADJUSTED R-SQUARE VALUES FOR VARIOUS COMBINATIONS
OF PREDICTORS OF SENTENCING DECISIONS
FOR CONVICTED OFFENDERS

Variables in Model	Prison		Long Term	
	Burglary	Robbery	Burglary	Robbery
Case mix	.165	.125	.190	.247
Case mix + plea	.166	.127	.190	.254
Case mix + plea + site	.251	.174	.210	.264

defendant's site to the model did improve the ability to predict whether or not that defendant would be sent to prison. In other words, even after control for case mix had been attained, the jurisdiction in which a defendant was convicted was related to his chances of going to prison.

Table 7.9 shows these differences. For instance, of the 981 burglary defendants who were convicted, 61 percent were sentenced to prison. After controlling for case mix (and for whether the defendant pleaded guilty), the imprisonment rate among burglary defendants in Dallas was 29 percentage points higher than the average rate, while in Sacramento it was 23 points below this average. In short, a defendant convicted in Dallas was much more likely to go to prison than was one convicted in Sacramento. No systematic state effects appeared to be in operation.

Why did defendants who pleaded guilty have no apparent advantage over those who were found guilty at trial? One possible explanation is that some offenders who might be charged with felony burglary or robbery are probably not in our analysis sample because they pleaded

Table 7.9

MEAN IMPRISONMENT RATE AMONG CONVICTED OFFENDERS
ACROSS ALL SITES AND A SITE'S DEVIATION FROM THIS MEAN
AFTER CONTROLLING FOR CASE MIX AND PLEAS

Site	Burglary	Robbery
Montgomery	9%	−12%
Baltimore	21	13
San Diego	−16	−7
Sacramento	−23	−15
Los Angeles	3	5
Fort Worth	−9	2
Dallas	29	13
Manhattan	−1	3
Queens	10	1
Detroit	−7	5
Chicago	4	5
Saint Louis	0	−6
Kansas City	1	4
Atlanta	−2	1
Average rate	61%	79%

guilty to a lesser offense shortly after their arrest and thus were never charged with burglary or robbery—that is to say, they quickly agreed to plead guilty to an offense that carried a lesser sentence. Another explanation is that the court (juries) may have convicted defendants for some but not all the crimes with which they were charged. Our database did not allow us to trace the source of the similarity between the outcomes of those who pleaded guilty and the outcomes of those who did not. This issue should, however, be explored in future studies.

VIII. ANALYSIS OF OVERLAPPING CASES

An important feature of our research is that, unlike many previous studies of the adjudication process, we examined the extent to which a given case outcome was related to whether a defendant had one or more other cases pending in the same court system. These other cases plus the sampled offense were collectively designated the defendant's *overlapping set of cases*, or OSOC. Thus, the "unit of analysis" in our study was the defendant rather than the case. This approach, although not unique to our study (see Clarke and Turner-Kurtz, 1983), is rarely taken in the compilation of large-scale criminal justice databases (e.g., PROMIS or those used for the FBI's Uniform Crime Reports).

We took this approach after several prosecutors advised us that the outcome on a sampled offense could be influenced by that of other cases in the defendant's OSOC. For instance, a defendant might be more or less likely to plead, or the nature of the bargain offered and accepted might change, as a function of whether that defendant had one or more other cases pending in the system.

Because gathering data on the OSOC promised to be a complex task, we wanted to find out whether overlapping cases truly made a difference in an analysis of case outcomes. We therefore sought to answer the following questions:

- What percentage of the defendants had one or more overlapping cases?
- To what extent did sites differ with respect to whether a defendant had one or more overlapping cases?
- What percentage of offenders were convicted for a case in the OSOC but not for the sampled offense?
- What case and defendant characteristics were associated with having an overlapping case?
- To what degree did having an overlapping case add to a defendant's likelihood of being convicted?
- After controlling for other case and offender characteristics, did defendants with overlapping cases have different outcomes (e.g., longer sentences) than defendants who did not?

The remainder of this section discusses the answers to these questions.

PREVALENCE OF OVERLAPPING CASES

Across all 14 sites, about 33 percent of the defendants in our study had at least one overlapping case; in other words, about one of three offenders had another case in the court system whose adjudication overlapped in time with the adjudication of the sampled offense. However, this rate underestimates how many offenders actually have overlapping cases in that it does not include crimes committed by the defendants while they were on the street awaiting adjudication of their case but for which they were not arrested or charged.

There are several ways in which defendants might have overlapping cases. For one, they might be arrested and charged for an offense while out on bail for another offense. They might also be arrested and charged for a different offense while in custody for the sampled offense—

for example, if there were a prior warrant for a defendant's arrest on another offense or if a warrant were issued after his arrest for another crime (such as when the police linked him to additional offenses on the basis of his or a codefendant's interrogation). In any event, it is evident that a large percentage of defendants have multiple cases that are processed concurrently. Some of these cases are joined and some are not.

Table 8.1, which shows the frequency with which offenders had an overlapping case at each site, indicates that the prevalence of overlapping cases varied across sites. For example, 64 percent of the robbery defendants in Fort Worth had at least one overlapping case, whereas only 19 percent of the robbery defendants in San Diego had an overlapping case. The sites that had a relatively high proportion of robbers with overlapping cases also tended to have a relatively high proportion of burglars with such cases. The correlation between these rates across the 14 sites was .45 and would have been much higher were it not for the unusually high rate for robbery defendants in Fort Worth.

One possible source of this intersite variation in overlapping case rates may lie in differences in these sites' average disposition times. In other words, if a case takes a relatively long time to adjudicate, then there is more opportunity for another case to overlap it. An investigation of this hypothesis, however, revealed that only a small portion of this variation could be traced to differences in average disposition times. The R-square between case disposition time and the percentage of defendants at a site with an overlapping case was .06 for burglary and .24 for robbery.

RELATIONSHIP BETWEEN OVERLAPPING CASES AND CONVICTION RATES

One important question addressed by our research was whether conviction rates were affected by consideration of an offender's OSOC. Table 8.2 shows that only 4.1 percent of the burglary defendants and 4.5 percent of the robbery defendants were convicted of an

Table 8.1

OVERLAPPING CASE RATE BY SITE

Site	Burglary	Robbery
Montgomery	33	23
Baltimore	40	37
San Diego	25	19
Sacramento	34	34
Los Angeles	24	30
Fort Worth	37	64
Dallas	27	32
Manhattan	43	38
Queens	35	28
Detroit	29	43
Chicago	21	28
Saint Louis	29	32
Kansas City	40	35
Atlanta	33	34
Median rate	33	34

Table 8.2

RELATIONSHIP BETWEEN OVERLAPPING CASES
AND PERCENTAGE OF CONVICTIONS

Offender's Status	Burglary	Robbery
No overlapping cases and not convicted of sampled offense	11.3	14.4
No overlapping cases and convicted of sampled offense	57.3	51.0
With an overlapping case and convicted of the sampled offense and an overlapping offense	2.1	2.3
With an overlapping case, but convicted only of sampled offense	24.5	26.3
With an overlapping case, but convicted only of an overlapping offense	**4.1**	**4.5**
With an overlapping case, but not convicted of any offense	0.7	1.6
Total	100.0	100.0

overlapping case without being convicted of the sampled offense as well. Thus, including the outcomes of overlapping cases in the computation of overall conviction rates produces a small but noticeable increase in these rates.

Only 7 percent of the 748 defendants with overlapping cases were convicted of both the sampled offense and the overlapping case. This finding suggests that the overlapping cases may have been used primarily as bargaining chips in the plea negotiation process rather than as truly separate adjudications.

RELATION OF HAVING AN OVERLAPPING CASE TO OUTCOMES

Tables 8.3 and 8.4 show that offenders with overlapping cases were much more likely to have more serious case outcomes than were offenders who did not have overlapping cases. For example, 54 percent of the 1,115 burglary defendants went to prison. However, 75 percent of the 350 burglary defendants with overlapping cases went to prison, compared with only 44 percent of those without overlapping cases. Thus, the presence of an overlapping case corresponded to a 31-percentage-point swing in the likelihood that an offender would go to prison. Similar findings were obtained for other outcomes and for defendants whose sampled cases involved robbery.

Table 8.3

PERCENTAGE POINT DEVIATIONS FROM AVERAGE OUTCOME RATE FOR OFFENDERS WITH AND WITHOUT OVERLAPPING CASES: BURGLARY[a]

Outcome	Average Rate	Deviation from Average Rate for Offenders		Difference in Rates
		With an Overlapping Case	Without an Overlapping Case	
Pleaded guilty	78	13	−6	19
Found guilty	46	30	−5	35
Convicted	88	10	−4	14
Incarcerated	74	16	−8	24
Sent to prison	54	21	−10	31
Long sentence	50	17	−11	28
Long disposition	50	20	−9	29

[a]All percentages are based on the total sample of defendants within an offense type except for "found guilty" (which was based on those who did not plead) and "long sentence" (which was based on those who were convicted).

Table 8.4

PERCENTAGE POINT DEVIATIONS FROM AVERAGE OUTCOME RATE FOR OFFENDERS WITH AND WITHOUT OVERLAPPING CASES: ROBBERY[a]

Outcome	Average Rate	Deviation from Average Rate for Offenders		Difference in Rates
		With an Overlapping Case	Without an Overlapping Case	
Pleaded guilty	68	15	−8	23
Found guilty	50	24	−5	29
Convicted	84	11	−6	17
Incarcerated	75	15	−8	23
Sent to prison	66	21	−11	32
Long sentence	50	21	−15	36
Long disposition	50	15	−8	23

[a]All percentages are based on the total sample of defendants within an offense type except for "found guilty" (which was based on those who did not plead) and "long sentence" (which was based on those who were convicted).

CORRELATES OF HAVING AN OVERLAPPING CASE

Table 8.5 shows the correlates of having an overlapping case. Each plus and minus sign in this table represents one standard error of difference between the fraction of overlapping cases in the sample and the fraction of overlapping cases in the subsample with or without the indicated factor present. For example, the three plus signs in the top-right entry means that for robbers, the fraction of defendants with an overlapping case among those who pleaded guilty was about three standard errors more than the average rate at which all robbery defendants had overlapping cases. In short, if a robbery defendant pleaded guilty, he was more likely to have an overlapping case than were robbery defendants in general. The reverse was true for those who did not plead—that is to say, such defendants were less likely to have overlapping cases (see App. E for a discussion of standard errors).

A review of the factors in Table 8.5 indicates that defendants with overlapping cases generally had more serious case characteristics than did other defendants. The case mix characteristics that were most closely related to having an overlapping case were generally the same for burglars and robbers—i.e., multiple counts on the sampled offense, nighttime arrest,

Table 8.5

CORRELATES OF HAVING AN OVERLAPPING CASE

Factor Present?	Burglary		Robbery	
	No	Yes	No	Yes
Outcome Variables				
Pleaded guilty	− − − − −	++	− − − − −	+++
Found guilty at trial	− −	+	− −	++
Convicted	− − − − − − −	+	− − − − − −	++
Sent to prison	− − − −	+++	− − − − −	++
Relatively long sentence	− − − −	++++	− − − − −	++++++
Long disposition time	− − − − −	+++++	− − − −	++++
Case Mix Variables				
Had an accomplice	−	+	−	+
Multiple sample counts	*	++++	*	++
Any victim a female	*	+	− − − −	+++++
Major victim injury	*	*	*	*
Two or more victims	*	*	− −	+++
Nighttime arrest	− −	+++	− −	+
Vulnerable victim	*	*	*	+++
Offender threatened to use a weapon	*	++	− − −	++
Eyewitness	− −	++	− − −	++++
Fingerprints	−	+++	*	++
Property recovered	− − −	++	−	+
Weapon as evidence	*	++	*	*
Arrested at scene	−	++	*	+
Arrested after 24 hours	− − − − −	++++++	− − − − − −	++++++
Under influence of drugs at arrest	*	+	*	*
Prior adult arrest	*	++	*	*
Prior adult conviction	*	*	*	+
Prior adult incarceration	*	+	*	+
Prior juvenile arrest	*	+	*	*
Prior juvenile incarceration	*	*	*	+
Probation/parole/escape at arrest	*	+	*	*
Defendant black	*	*	−	+
Defendant white	*	*	*	*
Defendant Hispanic	*	*	*	− −
Defendant unemployed	*	*	*	*
Defendant from out of state	*	− −	*	− −

NOTE: Each plus and minus sign indicates one standard error, and an asterisk indicates less than one standard error.

weapon threatened, eyewitness, fingerprints, and arrested after 24 hours. Having an overlapping case was related to the recovery of property among burglary defendants and to victim vulnerability among robbery defendants. Offender race and employment status were not related to having an overlapping case.

The relative improvement over chance (RIOC) values for predicting (on the basis of the case mix variables) whether or not a defendant had an overlapping case were 43 percent for burglary defendants and 42 percent for robbery defendants. Adding site and state to the prediction equation had no appreciable effect on predictive accuracy. Taken together, these data indicate that having or not having an overlapping case can be predicted with a reasonably high degree of accuracy and, further, that site and state have virtually no unique effect on whether or not a defendant has an overlapping case once these other variables are included in the prediction system.

UNIQUE EFFECT OF OVERLAPPING CASES ON OUTCOMES

It is evident from the discussion above that offenders with overlapping cases tend to have different crime and individual characteristics than do those without overlapping cases. Thus, the disparity in case outcomes between these two groups may stem from these differences rather than from whether a defendant does or does not have an overlapping case per se. We investigated this matter by examining whether the accuracy in predicting a given case outcome increased when the variable of having or not having an overlapping case was added to an estimation model that already included all the other case characteristics discussed in Sec. VI.

The results of this analysis, summarized in Table 8.6, show that there was no increase in the accuracy of predicting a given case outcome that was uniquely associated with having an overlapping case once the other case mix variables were already in the prediction system. This finding and the other analyses above strongly suggest that the reason offenders with overlapping cases are much more likely to have more serious case outcomes is that they are more likely to commit crimes (and have the case characteristics) that are associated with these outcomes.

Table 8.6

RELATIVE IMPROVEMENT OVER CHANCE PERCENTAGES
FOR PREDICTING CONVICTIONS WHEN OVERLAPPING
CASES ENTER THE PREDICTION EQUATION
AFTER ALL OTHER CONTROL VARIABLES[a]

Equation Variable	Burglary	Robbery
Incident	6	11
Evidence	17	20
Arrest	23	20
Priors	25	24
Offender	25	24
Overlapping	25	24
State	34	35
Site	35	39

[a]The prediction equation for a row contains the variables in that row plus the variables in the row(s) above it.

IX. PRINCIPAL FINDINGS AND CONCLUSIONS

Our 14-site study of 1,115 defendants charged with residential burglary and 1,148 defendants charged with armed robbery provided information about the characteristics of these defendants and about the factors that were related to the disposition of their cases. The principal findings of this research are delineated in the paragraphs that follow.

PROCEDURES

Criminal justice data systems offer a rich and valuable source of data for research studies. However, cross-site studies are difficult to conduct because each jurisdiction and state has its own unique systems for the management of criminal justice processing, with variation occurring in laws, court jurisdiction, criminal procedures, and prosecutor and police operations. For example, jurisdictions differ with regard to the court in which they file felony cases and with respect to the number of charges and/or offenders that may be included in a case.

The information retained in records, both automated and paper, also reflects individual jurisdictions' definitions and procedures. Incorporation of this variation into cross-site data collection procedures therefore requires careful adherence to study design definitions. These definitions must also be crafted to incorporate the wide variation found in multiple sites.

Despite these concerns, we found that it was feasible to develop the necessary definitions and decision rules as well as to train coders to implement them reliably. We also found that with some effort it was possible to locate the requisite data on each case. The two notable exceptions were as follows: (1) we were not able to obtain adequate data on rejected cases at most sites (but at the sites where such data were available, we found that about 80 percent of the cases that met our screening criteria were filed as felonies); and (2) because of state laws, data on acquitted defendants in the two New York sites were often missing. As a result of the latter situation, overall conviction rates are slightly inflated (and the accuracy with which conviction outcomes could be predicted was slightly lowered).

PREVALENCE OF CASE OUTCOMES

Our initial analyses revealed that most defendants charged with burglary or robbery were convicted and incarcerated, although not always for these crimes. Among those charged with burglary, 88 percent were convicted and 74 percent were incarcerated. The corresponding rates for defendants charged with robbery were 84 and 78 percent.

In both groups of defendants, over three-fourths of the incarcerations involved prison rather than jail. Taken together, these findings debunk the common belief that defendants found guilty of serious burglaries or robberies are usually set free.

Most of the defendants in our sample who were convicted decided to plead guilty rather than go to trial. Of the 981 burglary defendants who were convicted, 89 percent pleaded guilty. Of the 965 robbery defendants who were convicted, 81 percent pleaded guilty.

UNIVARIATE ANALYSES

The defendants who did not plead guilty had about a 50 percent chance of being released as a result of having their case dismissed before trial or because they were acquitted at trial. However, the defendants in the nonplea group were not a random sample of those charged. Instead, they were those accused of committing especially serious forms of burglary or robbery (e.g., crimes involving victim injury) or where the evidence against them was weaker. In robbery cases, for example, a defendant was much more likely to enter a plea if he was arrested at the scene of the crime and if the evidence against him included an eyewitness, fingerprints linking him to the offense, recovered property of the victim(s), and the weapon used. These factors were also correlated with the trial outcomes of defendants who chose not to enter a plea.

Our univariate analyses further revealed that both burglary and robbery defendants usually had prior involvement with the criminal justice system. Nearly 75 percent had a prior adult arrest, over 50 percent had a prior conviction, and more than 40 percent had a prior incarceration.

The presence of a given type of evidence was often associated with a greater likelihood that a defendant would plead guilty or otherwise be convicted. For example, the rate at which defendants charged with robbery pleaded guilty was 11 percentage points higher when property was recovered than when it was not. Similarly, among the robbery defendants who went to trial rather than pleading guilty, there was a 20-percentage-point swing in conviction rates between cases in which fingerprints linked the defendant to the crime and cases in which such evidence was lacking. In short, the better the police work and the less adept the offender, the higher the conviction rate.

About 23 percent of those charged with burglary or robbery were, at the time of their arrest, already on probation or parole or had escaped from custody on another offense. Moreover, almost all of those in this "under supervision" group were later incarcerated if they were convicted of any of the crimes in their overlapping set of cases.

As expected by previous research in this field (e.g., Boland et al., 1989), we found relatively large differences among sites in the rate at which defendants pleaded guilty, were found guilty at trial, were convicted, and, if convicted, were incarcerated and received a relatively short or long sentence. The 14 urban sites in our database also varied considerably with respect to the time it took to adjudicate a typical defendant's case (i.e., the time from arrest to disposition).

MULTIVARIATE ANALYSES

We examined whether the variation in outcome rates among sites was related to differences in the characteristics of sites' cases, policies, and practices or to some combination of these and other factors. We also examined how well various case outcomes could be predicted from a combination of case and offender characteristics.

This phase of our research found that some but certainly not all differences among sites could be attributed to differences in case characteristics. For example, a few sites had outcome rates that differed significantly from the 14-site average both before and after controlling on case mix. In other words, not all the variation among sites in outcome rates could be attributed to case characteristics.

Across all sites, the combination of all case characteristics could predict with 84 percent accuracy whether a defendant charged with burglary would or would not be convicted. This rate is actually less impressive than it seems in that 79 percent of the defendants would have been classified correctly simply by chance. These high chance accuracy rates occurred because most defendants were convicted.

A comparison of the correct classification rates with and without case mix controls indicates that controls added only five percentage points to the overall accuracy rate. For those charged with robbery, the case mix variables produced an eight-percentage-point increase in accuracy over the chance rate of 73 percent. Thus, the controls produced some improvement in the accuracy with which defendants could be classified into their actual outcome categories.

We also found that once this small adjustment was made for case mix, adding a defendant's state and site to the prediction system yielded only a one- to three-percentage-point increase in the accuracy with which we could classify whether a defendant would or would not plead guilty, be convicted, or receive a relatively long or short term.

These findings do not mean that all state and site differences disappeared on these outcomes once we had controlled for case mix. Even with these controls, for example, one site had an eight-percentage-point higher-than-average conviction rate for those charged with burglary and a 10-point higher-than-average rate for those charged with robbery. The corresponding rates at another site were five and nine percentage points below the 14-site average. Nevertheless, the rates at most sites clustered closely around the average once there was control on case mix.

The fact that case mix controls did not eliminate more intersite differences can be explained in two ways. First, this variation could be due to intersite differences in case characteristics that we failed to measure. For example, prosecutors at some sites may have been somewhat more willing than those at other sites to file cases when the witnesses were not as credible as they would have liked them to be.

Differences in the laws, policies, and practices of the various states and sites constitute the other explanation for the variation in outcome rates that remained after controlling for case mix. For example, offenders may be somewhat more willing to plead in some sites than in others because the likely alternative to a plea in their jurisdiction involves spending a long time awaiting trial in an especially crowded jail as opposed to being on the street. The bargains prosecutors are willing to accept in some jurisdictions may also differ from those accepted in others.

Taken together, the foregoing findings suggest that the base rates on some outcome variables are so high that one can make a reasonably accurate prediction of what will happen to a defendant without knowing anything about his case other than the fact that the prosecutor filed charges against him. Once charges are filed, what happens to one defendant will generally be the same as what happens to another. Moreover, adding case mix control variables to the estimation process will yield only a small to moderate improvement in overall classification accuracy. This situation underscores the importance of the charging decision.

One important exception to the foregoing trends was that case mix variables did make a relatively large contribution to the prediction of whether a defendant was or was not found guilty at trial. Nevertheless, state and site still had a relatively large unique effect on predictive accuracy.

The variation among sites in conviction rates at trial that remained after controlling for case mix could, of course, be due to unmeasured differences among sites in their case types. In addition, because the sample size for the trial outcome analyses was much smaller than that of the other outcomes studied (27 percent of the total sample within each offense group), there was more opportunity for chance to operate. Thus, site may actually have had less of a systematic effect than it appeared to have.

We also noted that the sites that had higher-than-average conviction rates at trial did not necessarily have higher-than-average plea or overall conviction rates. In other words, there was only some offsetting of relatively low plea rates by relatively higher overall conviction rates at trial. Thus, trial conviction rates clearly constituted one factor contributing to intersite variations in overall conviction rates.

The difference among sites in trial outcomes and case disposition times was large enough to suggest that it may be fruitful to examine why some sites had substantially higher rates on these outcomes than did others (even after control had been attained for case mix). This could be done with a more in-depth version of the case-abstracting procedures employed in this research coupled with a detailed analysis of the adjudication process in sites with markedly different outcome rates.

It must also be noted that for all outcomes, a defendant's status could not be predicted with 100 percent accuracy even when all the variables—including state and site—were put into the estimation equations. Therefore, other factors that are related to outcomes are not closely related to the variables we studied.

Finally, an important by-product of our multivariate analyses lay in the fact that they gave us the opportunity to examine whether the inclusion of a defendant's racial or ethnic group in the regression equations contributed to the accuracy with which various case outcomes could be estimated. This analysis found that such characteristics bore little or no relationship to convictions, disposition times, or other key outcome measures (i.e., their coefficients were not significantly different from zero or large enough to make a practical impact on forecasting accuracy). These results, which are consistent with those in a recent study of sentencing decisions in California (Klein, Petersilia, and Turner, 1990), further support the conclusion that there is generally one justice system for all.

ANALYSIS OF OVERLAPPING CASES

One important feature of our research was that we tracked defendants rather than simply cases. In other words, we investigated what happened to a defendant in the context of all of the charges pending against him. These cases plus the one that led to the inclusion of the defendant in our analysis sample were designated as the *defendant's overlapping set of cases*, or OSOC.

We found that about one-third of the defendants in our analysis sample had at least two cases in their OSOC. In other words, the adjudication of other charges overlapped in time with the adjudication of the charge we set out to study.

We further found that defendants with overlapping cases were much more likely than others to have high conviction and incarceration rates as well as relatively long sentences. However, these large differences in outcome rates were tied closely to differences in case mix. For example, defendants with multiple overlapping cases also tended to have more severe prior records and types of case characteristics (such as victim injury) that often led to more severe outcomes. Once there was control on these characteristics, no difference was found between the outcomes of defendants who had overlapping cases and the outcomes of those who did not.

We also discovered that about 4 to 5 percent of the defendants in our study were convicted of one or more of the crimes in their OSOC but were not convicted of the charge that led to their inclusion in the study. For example, a defendant may have agreed to plead guilty to some other lesser charge in his OSOC in return for the prosecutor dropping the charge or charges that got him into our database.

The finding that 4 to 5 percent of our cases were convicted of an overlapping offense but not the sampled offense suggests that the traditional method of tracking the outcome of charges through the justice system will slightly underestimate the overall rate at which defendants are actually convicted.

CONCLUDING COMMENTS

The project described in this report was conducted in part to determine the feasibility and utility of developing an in-depth, multisite database on adjudication outcomes. We found that it was certainly feasible (albeit costly and difficult) to gather the requisite data in a way that would make them appropriate for cross-site analyses. This effort also enabled us to construct a database that provided several interesting insights into the characteristics of robbery and burglary cases that are filed for prosecution.

We have not analyzed all the data that were gathered in this project. Thus, we anticipate that this report will be only the first of a series of studies that will be conducted with this database. To that end, we have made our data available to other researchers.

Moreover, given the wealth of data gathered on the defendants studied, even more can be learned by using these data in analyses of what happened to defendants after their cases were adjudicated. For example, how much time was actually served by those sentenced to prison, and was the length of term served (as distinct from imposed) related to case or defendant characteristics? And did those who were not convicted tend to disappear from the system, or were they convicted of other offenses shortly thereafter? We anticipate that future studies will address these important issues.

Appendix A

SITE DESCRIPTIONS

This appendix contains information about procedures used in each site to select the sample and identify overlapping cases for sampled defendants.

MONTGOMERY COUNTY: SITE 1

I. THE SAMPLE UNIVERSE

A. Sample Universe Background: Case Filing Procedure

Police agencies in Montgomery County bring their misdemeanor and felony arrests to the district (lower) court before prosecutor review.

Most misdemeanors are disposed in the lower court, whereas felonies and more serious misdemeanors are taken to the circuit court following the state attorney's review and grand jury indictment. The state attorney's review determines whether the case is to be presented to the grand jury with felony (or misdemeanor) charges, returned to the district court for disposition there, or dropped for prosecution at this stage (prosecutor's "nolle prosequi").

B. Sample Strata

The sample universe includes:

- Upper-court cases (robbery and burglary arrests that the prosecutor decided to present to the grand jury).

- Lower-court cases (robbery and burglary arrests that the prosecutor referred to the lower court for prosecution).

- Rejected cases (robbery and burglary arrests that the prosecutor decided to reject for prosecution altogether).

C. Sample Universe Charges

The site-specific definitions of burglary and robbery are:

- Burglary: "Breaking and entering with intent to commit a felony"
"Breaking and entering"
"Burglary"
"Forcible entry"
"Nighttime housebreak"
"Daytime housebreak"
"Housebreak"
"Entering a dwelling"
"Unlawful entry"
"Storehouse breaking"

- Robbery:
  - "Robbery with a deadly weapon"
  - "Armed robbery"
  - "Accessory to robbery with a deadly weapon"
  - "Accessory to armed robbery"
  - "Robbery"
  - "Robbery/common law"
  - "Conspiracy to rob"
  - "Accessory to robbery"

II. BUILDING THE SAMPLE FRAME

The sample frame was constructed from information provided by a printout of the district court's docket of cases set for preliminary hearing, which included the defendant's name and charges for all felonies and serious misdemeanors filed in the district court. On this printout, the state attorney's office recorded the outcome of its review to decide the charges and the level at which to file the case.

A. Defining Cases for the Sample Frame

Arrests in Montgomery County are generally brought by the police to the district (lower) court and filed as cases individually by criminal incident. There can be multiple charges in a single case, but normally they would all be associated with one incident. Cases were thus sampled on the assumption that each would provide information about an individual incident.

B. Selecting Cases for the Sample Frame

A defendant's case was selected for inclusion in the sample frame if it met the following conditions:

- One of the charges for which the defendant was arrested was robbery or burglary as defined above.

- The defendant's case was reviewed for charging decision by the state's attorney between the dates of January 1, 1985, and December 31, 1985.

III. IDENTIFICATION OF A SAMPLED DEFENDANT'S OVERLAPPING CASES

A. Source for Identifying Overlapping Cases

Additional cases against the defendant pending at the same time as the sampled case were identified using Montgomery County's automated criminal justice tracking system containing case-processing information for all cases filed in the district court.

B. Process of Identifying Overlapping Cases

To identify additional cases for the defendant, the county's computer was queried using the system's defendant identification number, which links defendants in the system in multiple cases under the same name or other names. Additionally, the computer's name index was queried to find cases where the defendant's name was the same as or similar to the defendant's name in the sampled case but not linked by county ID number. In such cases, birthdate and race were used to confirm that the different names belonged to the same person.

C. Problems with Identifying Overlapping Cases

Lower-court and reject cases were underrepresented in the set of overlapping cases owing to the county's policy of purging those kinds of cases from its computer six months after disposition.

BALTIMORE CITY: SITE 2

I. THE SAMPLE UNIVERSE

A. Sample Universe Background: Case Filing Procedure

The Baltimore police bring their misdemeanor and felony arrests to the district (lower) court to file complaints without prosecutor review in advance of filing.

B. Sample Strata

The sample universe includes:

- Upper-court cases (those that the prosecutor decided to take to preliminary hearing).

- Lower-court cases (those that the prosecutor decided to prosecute as misdemeanors).

- Rejected cases (those with which the prosecutor decided not to proceed, immediately following initial filing in the lower court).

C. Sample Universe Charges

The site-specific definitions of burglary and robbery are:

- Burglary: "Breaking and entering with intent to commit a felony"
  "Breaking and entering"
  "Burglary"
  "Forcible entry"
  "Nighttime housebreak"
  "Daytime housebreak"
  "Housebreak"
  "Entering a dwelling"
  "Unlawful entry"
  "Storehouse breaking"

- Robbery: "Robbery with a deadly weapon"
  "Armed robbery"
  "Accessory to robbery with a deadly weapon"
  "Accessory to armed robbery"
  "Robbery"
  "Robbery/common law"
  "Conspiracy to rob"
  "Accessory to robbery"

II. BUILDING THE SAMPLE FRAME

The sample frame was constructed from a listing of all cases brought by the police to the court for filing. The listing was obtained from the Judicial Information System (JIS) used to track all cases.

A. Defining Cases for the Sample Frame

Arrests in Baltimore City are generally brought by the police to the district (lower) court and filed as cases individually by criminal incident. There can be multiple charges in a single case, but normally they would all be associated with one incident. Cases were thus sampled on the assumption that each would provide information about an individual incident. In Baltimore, it became evident during data collection that some cases filed initially in district court had resulted in multiple felony indictments in circuit court. To the extent that this occurred, it had the effect of reducing the number of chances an offender had of being selected in the initial sample.

B. Selecting Cases for the Sample Frame

A defendant's case was selected for inclusion in the sample frame if it met the following conditions:

- One of the charges brought by the police was robbery or burglary as defined above.

- The defendant's case was filed in the lower court on or between the dates of January 1, 1985, and December 31, 1985.

III. IDENTIFICATION OF OVERLAPPING CASES

A. Source for Identifying Overlapping Cases

Additional cases against the defendant pending at the same time as the sampled case were identified through the circuit (upper) court's automated case-tracking system. The system includes all cases bound over to the circuit court from the district (lower) court.

B. Process of Identifying Overlapping Cases

The circuit (upper) court and district court computers were queried separately to identify additional cases for the defendant using the police department ID number, which links multiple cases for the same defendant.

The district court computer was queried using the defendant's name to locate additional district court cases.

C. Problems with Identifying Overlapping Cases

The set of overlapping cases includes only cases that were filed in court. Information about cases rejected for prosecution is not contained in the circuit or district court's computers, and no hard-copy log of reject cases was available.

SAN DIEGO COUNTY: SITE 3

I. THE SAMPLE UNIVERSE

A. Sample Universe Background: Case Filing Procedure

The San Diego County prosecutor's office is located in downtown San Diego with branch offices in three other locations in cities outside San Diego. The prosecutor handles all felony cases for the county and misdemeanors for unincorporated areas. Misdemeanors brought by the San Diego police and law enforcement agencies in other cities are prosecuted by the city attorney.

All felony (and certain misdemeanor) cases are reviewed by the prosecutor prior to the defendant's first appearance in the lower court. The reviewing attorney decides to go forward with felony charges, refer the case to the city attorney for prosecution with misdemeanor charges, or reject for prosecution altogether.

B. Sample Strata

The sample universe includes:

- Upper-court cases (robbery and burglary arrests that the prosecutor decided to file with felony charges).

- Rejected cases (robbery and burglary arrests that the prosecutor decided to reject for prosecution altogether).

The sample universe excludes:

- Lower-court cases (robbery and burglary arrests filed with misdemeanor charges only).

C. Sample Universe Charges

The site-specific definitions of burglary and robbery are:

- Burglary: Penal code 459 ("Burglary")

  This definition does not conform to the project definition of residential burglary.

- Robbery: Penal Code 211 ("Robbery")

  This definition does not conform to the project definition of armed robbery.

II. BUILDING THE SAMPLE FRAME

The sample frame was generated from the prosecutor's automated case-tracking system (JURIS). The system contains information on all arrests brought by the police for prosecutor review, including those rejected for prosecution.

A. Defining Cases for the Sample Frame

For the purpose of sampling, each case contained in the system was treated as a single sampling unit, although it was possible that multiple criminal incidents were represented by one case.

B. Selecting Cases for the Sample Frame

A defendant's case was selected for inclusion in the sample frame if it met the following conditions:

- One of the charges for which the defendant was arrested was robbery or burglary as defined above.

- The defendant was arrested and booked between the dates of January 1, 1985, and December 31, 1985.

III. IDENTIFICATION OF OVERLAPPING CASES

A. Source for Identifying Overlapping Cases

Additional cases against the defendant pending at the same time as the sampled case were identified through the prosecutor's automated case-tracking system (JURIS).

B. Process of Identifying the Overlapping Cases

JURIS was queried for additional cases using the system's defendant identification number. This identification number links defendants who are in the system in multiple cases under the same or assumed names.

C. Problems with Identifying Overlapping Cases

No other means of identifying additional defendant cases was used.

SACRAMENTO COUNTY: SITE 4

I. THE SAMPLE UNIVERSE

  A. Sample Universe Background: Case Filing Procedure

  The Sacramento County prosecutor handles both felony and misdemeanor cases.

  The prosecutor's office has attorneys assigned to the police and sheriff's offices, who review all arrests and decide whether and how to charge each case.

  B. Sample Strata

  The sample universe includes:

  - Upper-court cases (robbery and burglary arrests that the prosecutor decided to file with felony charges).

  - Rejected cases (robbery and burglary arrests that the prosecutor decided to reject for prosecution altogether).

  The sample universe excludes:

  - Lower-court cases (robbery and burglary cases that the prosecutor decided to file with misdemeanor charges).

    The case files for misdemeanor cases are destroyed 30 days after disposition in this site. Therefore, although the cases could be identified for inclusion in the sample universe, it was not possible to code them because the case files were unavailable.

  C. Sample Universe Charges

  The site-specific definitions of burglary and robbery are:

  - Burglary: Penal Code 459 ("Burglary")

    This definition does not conform to the project definition of residential burglary.

  - Robbery: Penal Code 211 ("Robbery")

    This definition does not conform to the project definition of armed robbery.

II. BUILDING THE SAMPLE FRAME

The sample frame was constructed from information provided by the municipal jail's booking log of arrested persons in conjunction with a log that records the prosecutor's charging decision for each arrest.

  A. Defining Cases for the Sample Frame

  For the purpose of sampling, each arrest was treated as a single sampling unit, although it was possible that multiple criminal incidents were represented by one arrest.

  B. Selecting Cases for the Sample Frame

  A defendant's case was selected for inclusion in the sample frame if it met the following conditions:

- One of the charges for which the defendant was arrested was robbery or burglary as defined above.

- The defendant was arrested and booked between the dates of January 1, 1985, and December 31, 1985.

III. IDENTIFICATION OF OVERLAPPING CASES

A. Source for Identifying Overlapping Cases

Cases were identified for inclusion in the set of overlapping cases through use of PROMIS, the Sacramento County prosecutor's office system for tracking case-filing information for all arrests (including those rejected for prosecution) in the jurisdiction.

B. Process of Identifying Overlapping Cases

To identify additional cases for the defendant, PROMIS was queried using the defendant's state criminal identification number. This identifier links up cases in the system belonging to a single defendant even when there are differing names and/or birthdates recorded for him among his cases. The method was considered sufficient for identifying additional cases. There may be defendants in Sacramento's PROMIS system under multiple identification numbers, but this was not considered likely in this jurisdiction.

LOS ANGELES COUNTY: SITE 5

I. THE SAMPLE UNIVERSE

A. Sample Universe Background: Case Filing Procedure

The Los Angeles police screen arrests before presenting them to the prosecutor. The screening decision is to (1) release the arrestee, (2) present the case to the city attorney for prosecution on misdemeanor charges, or (3) present the case to the district attorney for felony prosecution.

The central branch of the Los Angeles prosecutor's office handles only felony prosecutions referred by the central division of the Los Angeles Police Department. The attorneys screen cases brought by the police to decide whether to file felony charges, refer the case to the city attorney for misdemeanor prosecution, or reject the case for prosecution.

B. Sample Strata

The sample universe includes:

- Upper-court cases (those that the prosecutor decided to charge with felony charges).

- Rejected cases (those that the prosecutor did not want to file).

The sample universe excludes:

- Lower-court cases.

    These cases could not be identified because they are handled by a separate prosecutor.

C. Sample Universe Charges

The site-specific definitions of burglary and robbery are:

- Burglary: Penal code 459 ("Burglary"—excluding auto)

    This definition does not conform to the project definition of a residential burglary.

- Robbery: Penal Code   211   ("Robbery")
    211a ("Robbery of operator of motor vehicle")
    213.5 ("Robbery in an inhabited dwelling")
    209.b ("Kidnapping/robbery")
    214 ("Train robbery")

    This definition does not conform to the project definition of armed robbery.

II. BUILDING THE SAMPLE FRAME

The sample frame was generated from the prosecutor's automated case tracking system (PROMIS).

A. Defining Cases for the Sample Frame

If the defendant is charged for multiple criminal incidents at the time of filing, each is charged in a separate case. Therefore, cases could be sampled on the basis of incident rather than arrest or filing.

B. Selecting Cases for the Sample Frame

A defendant's case was selected for inclusion in the sample frame if it met the following conditions:

- One of the charges brought by the police was robbery or burglary as defined above.

- The defendant's case was brought to the prosecutor's office on or between the dates of January 1, 1986, and December 31, 1986.

- The arrest was brought to the Los Angeles County district attorney's central branch for prosecution.

III. IDENTIFICATION OF OVERLAPPING CASES

A. Source for Identifying Overlapping Cases

Additional cases against the defendant pending at the same time as the sampled case were identified through the PROMIS case-tracking system.

B. Process of Identifying Overlapping Cases

PROMIS was queried for additional cases using the defendant's name as shown on the sampled case. This query produced cases for defendants in the system with the names that were the same as or similar to the sampled defendant's. Cases were reviewed for potential inclusion in the OSOC if the defendant's date of birth was within five years of the sampled defendant's, and the case was filed in the central (downtown) branch of the prosecutor's office. Once the case file was pulled, it was determined whether the defendant in the case was the same as the sampled defendant.

C. Problems with Identifying Overlapping Cases

The Los Angeles County prosecutor's office PROMIS system does not contain a reliable defendant identification number that can be used for identifying all cases against a defendant in the system. This would not be as great a problem in a jurisdiction with a smaller caseload, but in Los Angeles County the number of similar defendant names contained in PROMIS is great. The defendant's date of birth contained in PROMIS for various cases is likely to differ, perhaps by more than five years, and cannot be used to identify additional defendant cases.

The set of overlapping cases contains only additional cases filed against a defendant in the central branch of the Los Angeles County criminal courts. There are 11 additional branches of the Los Angeles County criminal courts.

TARRANT COUNTY: SITE 6

I. THE SAMPLE UNIVERSE

A. Sample Universe Background: Case Filing Procedure

The Tarrant County district attorney handles both felony and misdemeanor arrests brought by the Fort Worth police and 42 other law enforcement agencies in the county.

The prosecutor presents all felony arrests to the grand jury for indictment. The prosecutor recommends that they find "no true bill" on the cases his office does not wish to prosecute, screening out a substantial number of the cases brought for felony prosecution. The remaining are "true billed" and bound over for prosecution in the upper court or in the lower court on misdemeanor charges.

B. Sample Strata

The sample universe includes:

- Upper-court cases (those for which the grand jury found a "true bill of indictment").

- Rejected cases (those for which the grand jury found "no bill of indictment").

The sample universe excludes:

- Lower-court cases.

    These cannot be identified in this jurisdiction. A "lower-court case" is defined by the project as a felony arrest that the prosecutor decided to charge as a misdemeanor at the time of initial screening. These are filed with an information rather than indictment, and no complete listing of misdemeanor filings could be obtained.

C. Sample Universe Charges

The site-specific definitions of burglary and robbery are:

- Burglary: "Burglary Habitation" (burglary of a residence)

    This definition conforms to the project definition of residential burglary.

- Robbery: "Aggravated Robbery with a Deadly Weapon" (weapon used in the commission of a robbery)

    "Aggravated Robbery with Serious Bodily Injury" (robbery that in some cases involves the use of a weapon)

    This definition does not conform to the project definition of armed robbery.

II. BUILDING THE SAMPLE FRAME

The sample frame for Tarrant County was constructed from a county data processing report on cases (i.e., charges) filed with the grand jury by the prosecutor by category of offense for the entire year of 1985.

A. Defining Cases for the Sample Frame

Typically, the prosecutor presents one charge for indictment in a case for a single criminal incident. It is not unusual, however, for multiple burglaries to be brought by the police for one individual at one time. The prosecutor applies a rule of filing at most three burglaries at one time against a defendant. The police investigative file for the additional burglaries is kept in the prosecutor's file with the information about the cases that were filed. Burglaries were sampled, however, by indictment. Therefore, a burglary case represents a single burglary presented by the police and charged by the prosecutor. Identification of the additional burglary incidents was made during field coding.

Robbery, on the other hand, can be charged with multiple counts/indictments if there is more than one victim in the case. For that reason, a robbery case was defined by the complete set of robbery charges (i.e., cases) presented to the grand jury on a single day. In some instances, these multiple charges actually represented multiple robberies. The charges were later separated into multiple cases during data abstraction, when the file was available to determine how many separate incidents were included in a single case.

B. Selecting Cases for the Sample Frame

A defendant's case was selected for inclusion in the sample frame if it met the following conditions:

- One of the charges brought by the police was robbery or residential burglary as defined above.

- The defendant's case was brought to the district attorney's office on or between the dates of January 1, 1985, and December 31, 1985.

III. IDENTIFICATION OF OVERLAPPING CASES

A. Source for Identifying Overlapping Cases:

Additional cases against the defendant pending at the same time as the sampled case were identified through the county's automated management information system used by the prosecutor for tracking criminal cases. The system tracks all criminal (felony and misdemeanor) cases presented to the office for prosecution.

B. Process of Identifying Overlapping Cases

The computer's records were queried using the name index, which searched for cases where the defendant's name was the same as or similar to the defendant's name in the sampled case. In a jurisdiction as small as Tarrant County, little difficulty was encountered in identifying the defendant's additional cases, since for the most part the database of criminal cases was small and the county was able to maintain records for each defendant under a single name.

DALLAS: SITE 7

I. THE SAMPLE UNIVERSE

A. Sample Universe Background: Case Filing Procedure

The Dallas County district attorney handles both felony and misdemeanor arrests brought by the Dallas police and by several smaller neighboring suburban communities.

The prosecutor presents all felony arrests to the grand jury for indictment. The prosecutor recommends that they find "no true bill" on the cases his office does not wish to prosecute, screening out a substantial number of the cases brought for felony prosecution. The remaining are "true billed" and bound over for prosecution in the upper court or in the lower court on misdemeanor charges.

B. Sample Strata

The sample universe includes:

- Upper-court cases (those for which the grand jury found a "true bill of indictment").

- Rejected cases (those for which the grand jury found "no bill of indictment").

The sample universe excludes:

- Lower-court cases.

  These cannot be identified in this jurisdiction. A "lower-court case" is defined by the project as a felony arrest that the prosecutor decided to charge as a misdemeanor at the time of initial screening. These are filed with an information rather than indictment and no complete listing.

C. Sample Universe Charges

The site-specific definitions of burglary and robbery are:

- Burglary: "Burglary Habitation" (burglary of a residence)

  This definition conforms to the project definition of residential burglary.

- Robbery: "Aggravated Robbery with a Deadly Weapon" (weapon used in the commission of a robbery)

  This definition conforms to the project definition of armed robbery.

II. BUILDING THE SAMPLE FRAME

The sample frame was generated from the Dallas County justice system's automated case-tracking system.

A. Defining Cases for the Sample Frame

Typically, the prosecutor presents one charge for indictment in a case for a single criminal incident. Burglary is always filed with one count, for instance. Robbery, however, may be charged with multiple counts if there is more than one victim.

Burglary cases in the sample frame were defined by a single charge. A robbery case was defined by the complete set of robbery charges presented to the grand jury on a single day. In some instances, these multiple charges actually represented multiple robberies. The charges were later separated into multiple cases during data abstraction, when the file was available to determine how many separate incidents were included in a single case.

B. Selecting Cases for the Sample Frame

A defendant's case was selected for inclusion in the sample frame if it met the following conditions:

- One of the charges brought by the police was armed robbery or residential burglary as defined above.

- The defendant's case was brought to the district attorney's office on or between the dates of January 1, 1985, and December 31, 1985.

III. IDENTIFICATION OF OVERLAPPING CASES

A. Source for Identifying Overlapping Cases

Additional cases against the defendant pending at the same time as the sampled case were identified through the prosecutor's automated management information system.

The Dallas County district attorney's office uses an automated case-tracking system maintained by the county. The system tracks all criminal (felony and misdemeanor) cases presented to the office for prosecution.

B. Process of Identifying Overlapping Cases

The computer's records were queried using the name index, which searched for cases where the defendant's name was the same as or similar to the defendant's name in the sampled case. The name index also linked cases where the defendant used a name differing from that used in the sampled case.

In order to determine whether the case with the same or similar defendant name actually belonged to the sampled defendant, date of birth and race were taken into consideration. If the date of birth and race both differed from the sampled defendant's date of birth and race, the defendants were assumed to be different people. If the date of birth was the same and the race different, the case was selected as potentially belonging to the sampled defendant. If race was the same and date of birth was within five to ten years, the case was selected as potentially belonging to the sampled defendant. Once the case file was pulled, it was possible to determine if the defendants in both cases were the same person.

NEW YORK COUNTY (MANHATTAN): SITE 8

I. THE SAMPLE UNIVERSE

A. Sample Universe Background: Case Filing Procedure

The Manhattan district attorney prosecutes both felonies and misdemeanors.

Arrests made by the New York City police for crimes committed within New York County (Manhattan) are brought to the Manhattan district attorney's office for review and charging decision. If the case warrants felony charges, the prosecutor will take it to the upper court through grand jury indictment—or the charges may be reduced or allowed to stay at the misdemeanor level and prosecuted in the lower court. The prosecutor may also decide to reject all charges in the case for prosecution.

B. Sample Strata

The sample universe includes:

- Upper-court cases (those that the prosecutor decided to take to the grand jury).

- Lower-court cases (those that the prosecutor decided to prosecute with reduced charges in the lower court).

- Rejected cases (those for which all charges were dropped for prosecution).

  Rejected cases were identified and included in the sample. The numbers of robbery and burglary cases rejected by the prosecutor were small, however. After all cases in the sample frame were screened to remove any that were not stranger-to-stranger residential burglaries and armed robberies, only 10 reject cases eligible for coding remained.

C. Sample Universe Charges

The site-specific definitions of burglary and robbery are:

- Burglary: Penal Code 140.30 ("Burglary First Degree"). A person knowingly enters or remains unlawfully in a dwelling with intent to commit a crime therein, and . . . he or another participant in the crime: (1) is armed with explosives or a deadly weapon; (2) causes physical injury to someone not a participant in the crime; (3) uses or threatens to use a dangerous instrument; or (4) displays what appears to be a deadly weapon.

  Penal Code 140.25 ("Burglary Second Degree"). A person knowingly enters or remains unlawfully in a building with intent to commit a crime therein, and . . . he or another participant in the crime: (1) is armed with explosives or a deadly weapon; (2) causes physical injury to someone not a participant in the crime; (3) uses or threatens to use a dangerous instrument; or (4) displays what appears to be a deadly weapon. Or a person knowingly enters or remains unlawfully in a building with intent to commit a crime therein, and the building is a dwelling.

  This definition does not conform to the project definition of residential burglary.

- Robbery: Penal Code 160.15 ("Robbery First Degree"). A person forcibly steals property and he or another participant in the crime: (1) causes serious physical injury to someone not a participant in the crime; (2) is armed with a deadly weapon; or (3) uses or threatens the immediate use of a dangerous instrument.

Penal Code 160.10 ("Robbery Second Degree"). A person forcibly steals property and: (1) is aided by another person actually present; or (2) in the course of the commission of the crime he or another participant: (a) causes physical injury to someone not a participant in the crime; or (b) displays what appears to be a deadly weapon.

This definition does not conform to the project definition of armed robbery.

II. BUILDING THE SAMPLE FRAME

The sample frame was generated from the prosecutor's automated case-tracking system (AGIS).

A. Defining Cases for the Sample Frame

The prosecutor's case-tracking system requires that each case represent one criminal incident for a defendant. In a small number of cases, the collected charges in the case represented more than one incident. These multiple incidents could not be identified until the case was selected for coding and the prosecutor's file reviewed.

The sample frame was based on the cases as defined by the automated system, which in most cases were single criminal incidents.

B. Selecting Cases for the Sample Frame

A defendant's case was selected for inclusion in the sample frame if it met the following conditions:

- One of the charges brought by the police was robbery or burglary as defined above.

- The defendant's case was brought to the circuit attorney's office on or between the dates of January 1, 1986, and December 31, 1986.

III. IDENTIFICATION OF OVERLAPPING CASES

A. Source for Identifying Overlapping Cases

Additional cases against the defendant pending at the same time as the sampled case were identified through the AGIS case-tracking system.

B. Process of Identifying Overlapping Cases

AGIS was queried for additional cases using the defendant's system identifier. This identification number links multiple cases under the same or different names.

C. Problems with Identifying Overlapping Cases

Additional cases not linked by the system's defendant identification number were not included in the set of overlapping cases.

QUEENS COUNTY: SITE 9

I. THE SAMPLE UNIVERSE

A. Sample Universe Background: Case Filing Procedure

The Queens County district attorney prosecutes both felonies and misdemeanors.

Arrests made by the New York City police for crimes committed within Queens County are brought to the Queens district attorney's office for review and charging decision. If the case warrants felony charges, the prosecutor will take it to the upper court through grand jury indictment—or the charges may be reduced or allowed to stay at the misdemeanor level and prosecuted in the lower court. The prosecutor may also decide to reject all charges in the case for prosecution.

B. Sample Strata

The sample universe includes:

- Upper-court cases (those that the prosecutor decided to take to the grand jury).

- Lower-court cases (those that the prosecutor decided to prosecute with reduced charges in the lower court).

The sample universe excludes:

- Rejected cases (those for which all charges were dropped for prosecution).

The Queens district attorney's office does not retain either a source for identifying or the case files for cases rejected for prosecution.

C. Sample Universe Charges

The site-specific definitions of burglary and robbery are:

- Burglary: Penal Code 140.30 ("Burglary First Degree"). A person knowingly enters or remains unlawfully in a dwelling with intent to commit a crime therein, and . . . he or another participant in the crime: (1) is armed with explosives or a deadly weapon; (2) causes physical injury to someone not a participant in the crime; (3) uses or threatens to use a dangerous instrument; or (4) displays what appears to be a deadly weapon.

  Penal Code 140.25 ("Burglary Second Degree"). A person knowingly enters or remains unlawfully in a building with intent to commit a crime therein, and . . . he or another participant in the crime: (1) is armed with explosives or a deadly weapon; (2) causes physical injury to someone not a participant in the crime; (3) uses or threatens to use a dangerous instrument; or (4) displays what appears to be a deadly weapon. Or: A person knowingly enters or remains unlawfully in a building with intent to commit a crime therein, and the building is a dwelling.

  This definition does not conform to the project definition of residential burglary.

- Robbery: Penal Code 160.15 ("Robbery First Degree"). A person forcibly steals property and he or another participant in the crime: (1) causes serious physical injury to someone not a participant in the crime; (2) is armed with a deadly weapon; or (3) uses or threatens the immediate use of a dangerous instrument.

Penal Code 160.10 ("Robbery Second Degree"). A person forcibly steals property and: (1) is aided by another person actually present; or (2) in the course of the commission of the crime he or another participant: (a) causes physical injury to someone not a participant in the crime; or (b) displays what appears to be a deadly weapon.

This definition does not conform to the project definition of armed robbery.

II. BUILDING THE SAMPLE FRAME

The sample frame was built from information produced by the prosecutor's automated case-tracking system. This system maintains information about cases filed by the Queens County district attorney in the lower court. The system does not include information about all arrests brought to their office, nor does it include the arrest charges for cases that the prosecutor decided to file. The sample was therefore based on the filing charges of cases in Queens County.

A. Defining Cases for the Sample Frame

The prosecutor's case-tracking system requires that each case represent one criminal incident for a defendant. In a small number of cases, the collected charges in the case represented more than one incident. These multiple incidents could not be identified until the case was selected for coding and the prosecutor's file reviewed.

The sample frame was based on the cases as defined by the automated system, which in most cases were single criminal incidents.

B. Selecting Cases for the Sample Frame

A defendant's case was selected for inclusion in the sample frame if it met the following conditions:

- One of the charges brought by the police was robbery or burglary as defined above.

- The defendant's case was filed by the district attorney's office on or between the dates of January 1, 1986, and December 31, 1986.

III. IDENTIFICATION OF OVERLAPPING CASES

A. Source for Identifying Overlapping Cases

Additional cases against the defendant pending at the same time as the sampled cases were identified through the prosecutor's automated tracking system.

B. Process of Identifying Overlapping Cases

The prosecutor's computer records were queried using the name index, which searched for cases where the defendant's name was the same as or similar to the defendant's name in the sampled case.

In order to determine whether the case with the same or similar defendant name actually belonged to the sampled defendant, date of birth and race were taken into consideration. If the date of birth and race both differed from the sampled defendant's date of birth and race, the defendants were assumed to be different people. If the date of birth was the same and the race different, the case was selected as potentially belonging to the sampled defendant. If race was the same and date of birth was within five to ten years, the case was selected as potentially belonging to the sampled defendant. Once the case file was pulled, it was possible to determine if the defendants in both cases were the same person.

C. Problems with Identifying Overlapping Cases

The prosecutor's computer records did not provide a means of identifying additional cases in the system for the defendant under a different defendant name. Unless the defendant's sampled case file (or another of his case files) gave the abstractor information about other names under which the defendant had been prosecuted, these additional cases were not represented in the set of overlapping cases.

WAYNE COUNTY (DETROIT): SITE 10

I. THE SAMPLE UNIVERSE

A. Sample Universe Background: Case Filing Procedure

The Detroit police bring their arrests to the Wayne County prosecutor's office at the Detroit recorder's court for review and charging decision. This office handles both felonies and misdemeanors. The prosecutor has an "out county" office as well that handles cases brought by the surrounding suburban community police agencies in Wayne County.

The police bring the investigative file to the prosecutor, who decides whether to file as a felony or a misdemeanor or to reject the case for prosecution. If the case is to be filed, a warrant is issued and a complaint filed with the charges being made against the defendant.

B. Sample Strata

The sample universe includes:

- Upper-court cases (those that the prosecutor decided to charge with felony charges).

The sample universe excludes:

- Lower-court cases.

    These cases cannot be identified in this jurisdiction.

- Rejected cases (those for which all charges were dropped for prosecution).

    Rejected cases cannot be identified in this jurisdiction because there is no criminal charge associated with the case if it is rejected and therefore no way to select burglaries or robberies for a sample.

C. Sample Universe Charges

The site-specific definitions of burglary and robbery are:

- Burglary: Penal Code 750.110B ("Burglary of an Occupied Dwelling") (burglary of an inhabitable dwelling)

    This definition conforms to the project definition of a residential burglary.

- Robbery: Penal Code 750.529 ("Armed Robbery") (robbery involving the use or threat of use of a deadly weapon)

    This definition conforms to the project definition of armed robbery.

II. BUILDING THE SAMPLE FRAME

The sample frame was generated from the Detroit recorder's court's automated case-tracking system.

A. Defining Cases for the Sample Frame

If the defendant is charged for multiple criminal incidents at the same time of filing, each is charged in a separate case. Therefore, cases could be sampled based on incident rather than arrest and filing.

B. Selecting Cases for the Sample Frame

A defendant's case was selected for inclusion in the sample frame if it met the following conditions:

- One of the charges named in the complaint was armed robbery or burglary as defined above.

- The defendant's case was brought to the prosecuting attorney's office on or between the dates of January 1, 1986, and December 31, 1986.

- The arrest was brought by the Detroit police department and reviewed at the Wayne County prosecuting attorney's main Detroit branch. Cases handled by the prosecutor's branch offices were not included in the sample frame.

III. IDENTIFICATION OF OVERLAPPING CASES

A. Source for Identifying Overlapping Cases

Additional cases against the defendant pending at the same time as the sampled case were identified through the recorder's court automated case-tracking system.

B. Process of Identifying Overlapping Cases

In order to identify additional cases for the defendant, the court's computer was queried using the defendant identification number, which links a defendant's multiple cases under the same or other names. Additionally, the computer's name index was queried to find cases where the defendant's name was the same as or similar to the defendant's name in the sampled case.

In order to determine whether the case with the same or similar defendant name actually belonged to the sampled defendant in the absence of a defendant identification number, date of birth and race were taken into consideration. If the date of birth and race both differed from the sampled defendant's date of birth and race, the defendants were assumed to be different people. If the date of birth was the same and the race different, the case was selected as potentially belonging to the sampled defendant. If the race was the same and the date of birth was within five to ten years, the case was selected as potentially belonging to the sampled defendant. Once the case file was pulled, it was possible to determine if the defendants in both cases were the same person.

C. Problems with Identifying Overlapping Cases

The Detroit recorder's court does not contain information about cases rejected for prosecution; it was therefore not possible to include a count of rejected cases in the set of overlapping cases.

COOK COUNTY (CHICAGO): SITE 11

I. THE SAMPLE UNIVERSE

A. Sample Universe Background: Case Filing Procedure

The Chicago police bring their arrests to the Cook County prosecutor's Chicago office for review and charging decision. This office handles both felonies and misdemeanors. The prosecutor has several branch offices that handle felony and misdemeanor prosecutions in the outlying suburban areas as well.

The police bring arrests to the prosecutor for review or contact the prosecutor by telephone for consultation on the charging decision and on the appropriate arrest charge(s). If the prosecutor wants to proceed with the case, the arrest charges will be the same as those that appear on the complaint.

B. Sample Strata

The sample universe includes:

- Upper-court cases (those that the prosecutor decided to charge with felony charges).

The sample universe excludes:

- Lower-court cases (those that the prosecutor referred to the city prosecutor).

- Rejected cases (those for which all charges were dropped for prosecution).

  It is not possible to identify rejected cases since the prosecutor's case tracking system (PROMIS) does not contain any record of rejected cases.

C. Sample Universe Charges

The site-specific definitions of burglary and robbery are:

- Burglary: Penal Code 38-19-3 ("Residential Burglary"). Knowingly and without authority entering the dwelling place of another with the intent to commit a felony or theft.

  Penal Code 38-12-11 ("Home Invasion"). Use of force or threat of imminent use of force within a dwelling while armed with a dangerous weapon.

  This definition conforms to the project definition of a residential burglary.

- Robbery: Penal Code 38-18-2 ("Armed Robbery"). Taking property from person or presence of another by use of force or by threatening the imminent use of force while carrying on or about his or her person, or is otherwise armed with, a dangerous weapon.

  This definition conforms to the project definition of armed robbery.

II. BUILDING THE SAMPLE FRAME

The sample frame was generated from the prosecutor's automated case-tracking system (PROMIS).

A. Defining Cases for the Sample Frame

If the defendant is charged for multiple criminal incidents at the time of filing, each is charged in a separate case. Cases could therefore be sampled on the basis of incident rather than arrest and filing.

B. Selecting Cases for the Sample Frame

A defendant's case was selected for inclusion in the sample frame if it met the following conditions:

- One of the charges brought by the police was armed robbery or burglary as defined above.

- The defendant's case was brought to the state attorney's office on or between the dates of January 1, 1986, and December 31, 1986.

- The arrest was brought by the Chicago Police Department and reviewed at the Cook County state attorney's main Chicago branch. Cases handled by the prosecutor's branch offices were not included in the sample frame.

III. IDENTIFICATION OF OVERLAPPING CASES

A. Source for Identifying Overlapping Cases

Additional cases against the defendant pending at the same time as the sampled case were identified through the PROMIS case-tracking system.

B. Process of Identifying Overlapping Cases

PROMIS was queried for additional cases using the defendant's PROMIS identification number. This identification number links a defendant's multiple cases. No other means of identifying additional defendant cases were used.

C. Problems with Identifying Overlapping Cases

PROMIS does not contain information about cases rejected for prosecution; therefore it was not possible to include a count of rejected cases in the set of overlapping cases.

Additional defendant cases not linked by the PROMIS defendant identification number were not included in the set of overlapping cases.

JACKSON COUNTY (KANSAS CITY, MISSOURI): SITE 12

I. THE SAMPLE UNIVERSE

A. Sample Universe Background: Case Filing Procedure

The Jackson County prosecuting attorney's office is located in downtown Kansas City with a branch office in Independence. The downtown office handles only felony cases. The Independence branch handles both felony and misdemeanor cases, prosecuting misdemeanors in the associate circuit (lower) court. Misdemeanors brought by the Kansas City Police Department are screened and handled by the city prosecutor.

The Kansas City Police Department and numerous smaller neighboring police agencies bring their felony arrests to the Jackson County prosecutor for review and charging decision. The prosecutor reviews the police investigation file and decides whether there is justification for obtaining a warrant on felony charges. If so, the prosecutor determines the appropriate charge(s) and obtains a warrant. Until this point, there is no charge formally associated with the defendant's arrest. Otherwise, the prosecutor may refer the case to the city prosecutor or reject it for prosecution altogether.

B. Sample Strata

The sample universe includes:

- Upper-court cases (those that the prosecutor decided to take to preliminary hearing).

The sample universe excludes:

- Lower-court cases (those that the prosecutor referred to the city prosecutor).

    These cases cannot be identified in this jurisdiction. A "lower-court case" is defined by the project as a felony arrest that the prosecutor decided to charge as a misdemeanor. In Jackson County, the police do not charge until the prosecutor has decided the level at which to charge. Cases cannot be reduced at this stage of prosecution, since no charge has yet been attached.

- Rejected cases (those for which all charges were dropped for prosecution).

    The documentation for these cases was not available for coding because the prosecutor does not retain a copy of the police investigative file.

C. Sample Universe Charges

The site-specific definitions of burglary and robbery are:

- Burglary: Penal Code 569.160 ("Burglary First Degree"). Residential or commercial burglary with someone on the premises.

    Penal Code 569.170 ("Burglary Second Degree"). Residential or commercial burglary with no one on the premises.

    This definition does not conform to the project definition of residential burglary. It was possible, however, to distinguish between residential and commercial burglaries at the time of creating the sample frame because the sample source indicated the name of the victim. Where the victim's name was a business or an institution, the case was excluded from the sample frame.

- Robbery: Penal Code 569.020 ("Robbery First Degree"). Weapon used in the commission of a robbery.

This definition conforms to the project definition of armed robbery.

II. BUILDING THE SAMPLE FRAME

The sample frame was constructed from information provided by the prosecuting attorney's daily reports of filed cases. The sample frame was based on these filing charges rather than on the charges brought by the police and reviewed by the prosecutor. This is because no data source exists that records the police charges. The police do not, in effect, charge the defendant until a warrant is obtained from the prosecutor.

A. Defining Cases for the Sample Frame

The prosecutor's office generates daily reports that list the cases for which complaints have been filed. The reports indicate the name of the defendant and the charges included in the complaint. They also include a report number used by the police to distinguish discrete criminal incidents for which the defendant is being charged, since there may be more than one. Unfortunately, there was no way to connect a particular charge with a report number in order to select single incidents filed with a burglary or robbery charge. Therefore, the cases in the sample frame in some instances represented more than a single criminal incident.

B. Selecting Cases for the Sample Frame

A defendant's case was selected for inclusion in the sample frame if it met the following conditions:

- One of the charges brought by the police was armed robbery or burglary as defined above.

- The defendant's case was brought to the prosecuting attorney's office on or between the dates of January 1, 1986, and December 31, 1986.

- The arrest was brought to the Jackson County prosecutor's downtown office. Cases handled by the Independence branch of the attorney's office were not included in the sample frame.

III. IDENTIFICATION OF OVERLAPPING CASES

A. Source for Identifying Overlapping Cases

Additional cases against the defendant pending at the same time as the sampled case were identified through the Jackson County court's automated case management system.

B. Process of Identifying Overlapping Cases

The court's records were queried using the name index, which searched for cases where the defendant's name was the same as or similar to the defendant's name in the sampled case. The name index also linked cases where the defendant used a name differing from that used in the sampled case.

In order to determine whether the case with the same or similar defendant name actually belonged to the sampled defendant, date of birth and race were taken into consideration. If the date of birth and race both differed from the sampled defendant's date of birth and race, the defendants were assumed to be different people. If the date of birth was the same and the race different, the case was selected as potentially belonging to the sampled defendant. If race was the same and date of birth was within five to ten years, the case was selected as potentially belonging to the sampled defendant. Once the case file was pulled, it was possible to determine if the defendants in both cases were the same person.

C. Problems with Identifying Overlapping Cases

The court's record system does not contain information about cases rejected for prosecution; therefore it was not possible to include a count of rejected cases in the set of overlapping cases.

SAINT LOUIS: SITE 13

I. THE SAMPLE UNIVERSE

A. Sample Universe Background: Case Filing Procedure

The Saint Louis City circuit attorney prosecutes both felonies and misdemeanors.

Saint Louis police officers bring their misdemeanor and felony arrests to the prosecutor for review and charging decision. If the case warrants felony charges, the prosecutor will take it to the upper court through preliminary hearing or grand jury indictment— or the charges may be reduced or allowed to stay at the misdemeanor level and prosecuted in the lower court. The prosecutor may also decide to reject all charges in the case for prosecution.

B. Sample Strata

The sample universe includes:

- Upper-court cases (those that the prosecutor decided to take to preliminary hearing or the grand jury).

- Lower-court cases (those that the prosecutor decided to prosecute with reduced charges in the lower court).

The sample universe excludes:

- Rejected cases (those for which all charges were dropped for prosecution).

    The documentation for these cases was not available for coding, since the circuit attorney does not create a case in the automated record system or retain the investigative file brought by the police in rejected cases.

C. Sample Universe Charges

The site-specific definitions of burglary and robbery are:

- Burglary: Penal Code 569.160 ("Burglary First Degree"). Residential or commercial burglary with someone on the premises.

    Penal Code 569.170 ("Burglary Second Degree"). Residential or commercial burglary with no one on the premises.

    This definition does not conform to the project definition of residential burglary.

- Robbery: Penal Code 569.020 ("Robbery First Degree"). Weapon used in the commission of a robbery.

    This site does provide a definition that conforms to the project definition of armed robbery.

II. BUILDING THE SAMPLE FRAME

The sample frame was constructed from information provided by the circuit attorney's hard-copy log of charges brought by the police seeking prosecution. The log includes a notation on the outcome of the attorney case-screening process for each charge in the case.

A. Defining Cases for the Sample Frame

The circuit attorney's log of incoming cases from the police is arranged chronologically, showing all defendants brought each day and each charge against a defendant listed separately. A defendant is often charged with multiple incidents at the time he is brought to the prosecutor. There is a unique arrest identifier for each set of charges associated with a single criminal incident, however, which allowed us to build the sample frame on the basis of criminal incidents (rather than defendants).

Therefore, in the sample frame, a case is defined as a single criminal incident.

B. Selecting Cases for the Sample Frame

A defendant's case was selected for inclusion in the sample frame if it met the following conditions:

- One of the charges brought by the police was armed robbery or burglary as defined above.

- The defendant's case was brought to the circuit attorney's office on or between the dates of January 1, 1986, and December 31, 1986.

III. IDENTIFICATION OF OVERLAPPING CASES

A. Source for Identifying Overlapping Cases

Additional cases against the defendant pending at the same time as the sampled case were identified through the prosecutor's automated management information system.

The Saint Louis circuit attorney's office uses PROMIS to track their cases from the point that the prosecutor decides to file charges. Cases rejected for prosecution are not contained in the system.

B. Process of Identifying Overlapping Cases

PROMIS records were queried using the name index, which searched for cases where the defendant's name was the same as or similar to the defendant's name in the sampled case. The name index also linked cases where the defendant used a name different from that used in the sampled case.

In order to determine whether the case with the same or similar defendant name actually belonged to the sampled defendant, date of birth and race were taken into consideration. If the date of birth and race both differed from the sampled defendant's date of birth and race, the defendants were assumed to be different people. If the date of birth was the same and the race different, the case was selected as potentially belonging to the sampled defendant. If race was the same and date of birth was within five to ten years, the case was selected as potentially belonging to the sampled defendant. Once the case file was pulled, it was possible to determine if the defendants in both cases were the same person.

C. Problems Identifying Overlapping Cases

The Saint Louis circuit attorney's PROMIS system does not contain information about cases rejected for prosecution; therefore it was not possible to include a count of rejected cases in the set of overlapping cases.

ATLANTA: SITE 14

I. THE SAMPLE UNIVERSE

A. Sample Universe Background: Case Filing Procedure

The Fulton County prosecutor handles only felony cases.

All arrests are brought by the police to the lower court for a probable cause hearing before a magistrate with the city solicitor representing the state. The county prosecutor is not involved at this stage. Cases that are bound over with felony charges are sent to the prosecutor, who decides whether to present the charges to the grand jury. The case may also be referred back to the lower court for prosecution as a misdemeanor or rejected for prosecution altogether.

B. Sample Strata

The sample universe includes:

- Upper-court cases (those bound over from the lower court with felony charges, which the prosecutor decided to present to the grand jury).

- Rejected cases (those bound over from the lower court with felony charges, which the prosecutor decided to reject for prosecution altogether).

The sample universe excludes:

- Lower-court cases (those bound over from the lower court with felony charges, which the prosecutor decided to refer back to the lower court for prosecution on misdemeanor charges).

Because these cases are not within the jurisdiction of the county prosecutor's office, the case files were not available for coding, and therefore the cases were excluded from the sample universe.

C. Sample Universe Charges

The site-specific definitions of robbery and burglary are:

- Burglary: Penal Code 16.7.1 ("Burglary")

"A person commits the offense of burglary when, without authority and with the intent to commit felony or theft therein, he enters or remains within the dwelling house of another or any building, vehicle, railroad car, watercraft, or other such structure designed for use as the dwelling of another or enters or remains within any other building, railroad car, aircraft, or any room or any part thereof."

This definition does not conform to the project definition of residential burglary.

- Robbery: Penal Code 16.8.41 ("Armed Robbery")

"A person commits the offense of armed robbery when, with intent to commit theft, he takes property of another from the person or the immediate presence of another by use of an offensive weapon or any replica, article, or device having the appearance of such weapon."

This definition conforms to the project definition of armed robbery.

II. BUILDING THE SAMPLE FRAME

The sample frame was constructed from information provided by the prosecutor's card file record of defendant commitments to custody of the county jail following bindover on felony charges from the lower court to the upper court.

A. Defining Cases for the Sample Frame

For the purpose of sampling, each defendant commitment was treated as a single sampling unit, although it was possible that multiple criminal incidents were represented by one commitment.

B. Selecting Cases for the Sample Frame

A defendant's case was selected for inclusion in the sample frame if it met the following conditions:

- One of the charges on which the defendant was bound over by the magistrate was armed robbery or burglary as defined above.

- The arrest was made by the Atlanta Police Department. (Around 80 percent of Fulton County's cases come from Atlanta arrests. The court's jurisdiction extends beyond Atlanta to several suburban Atlanta communities whose arrests were not included in the sample.)

- The defendant was committed to custody of the Fulton County Jail between the dates of January 1, 1986, and December 31, 1986.

III. IDENTIFICATION OF OVERLAPPING CASES

A. Source for Identifying Overlapping Cases

The prosecutor's office maintains a hard-copy file of defendants who have been bound over on felony charges in the lower court to be prosecuted in the upper court by the district attorney.

Each document in the file records information for an individual defendant's commitment to custody of the county jail following bindover. The card can contain charges for one or more criminal incidents.

The card is used by the prosecutor to record the screening decision on all cases.

B. Process of Identifying Overlapping Cases

The cards are filed alphabetically by defendant name within each year.

Additional cases for the defendant were generally identified as those with a defendant whose name was the same as or close to the sampled defendant's and with the same date of birth. The card file listed a defendant alias, if any, which was also used for looking up additional cases. Cases were not identified as belonging to the defendant strictly by date of birth, however. Multiple reported birthdates were known for some defendants through review of the sampled incident case file, and could therefore be taken into consideration when identifying additional cases.

Additional cases for the defendant were searched for in each year's records starting with 1986 and going back to 1985. If the sampled incident was disposed after the beginning of 1987, then the 1987 files and, if necessary, the 1988 files were searched for potential additional cases that were pending at the time of the sampled incident case.

C. Problems with Identifying Overlapping Cases

The Fulton County district attorney's office does not use a defendant identification number. The cases of defendants in the card files under multiple names without a cross-referencing alias were not identifiable as additional cases. The number of such unidentified cases is estimated to be very small.

Appendix B

DATA COLLECTION FORMS

DMF
Form 3.1

CRIMINAL JUSTICE POLICIES AND OUTCOMES

Defendant Main Form
February 1988

| BATCH/D.E. #: | ☐☐☐☐ | *001/* |

| RAND I.D. #: | | *002/* |

| INCIDENT #: | 1 1 | *0021/* |

SITE 1 2   *003/*

ABSTRACTOR I.D.: ☐☐☐   *004/*

DATE FORM COMPLETED: ☐☐☐☐ 8 8   *005/*
MO DAY YR

THE **RAND** CORPORATION

1700 Main Street, PO Box 2138
Santa Monica, CA 90406-2138

Attn: Nora Fitzgerald

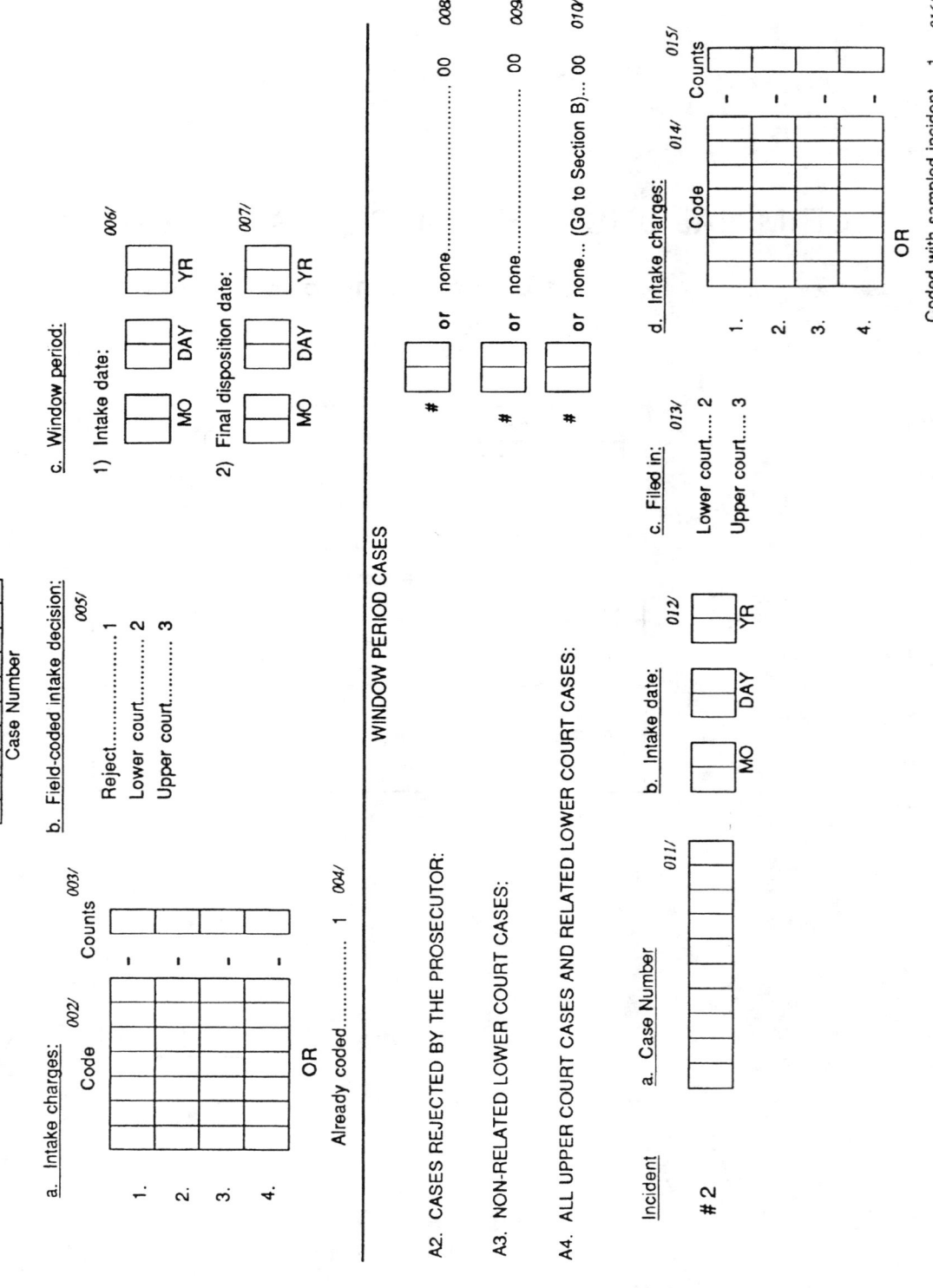

A4. (continued):

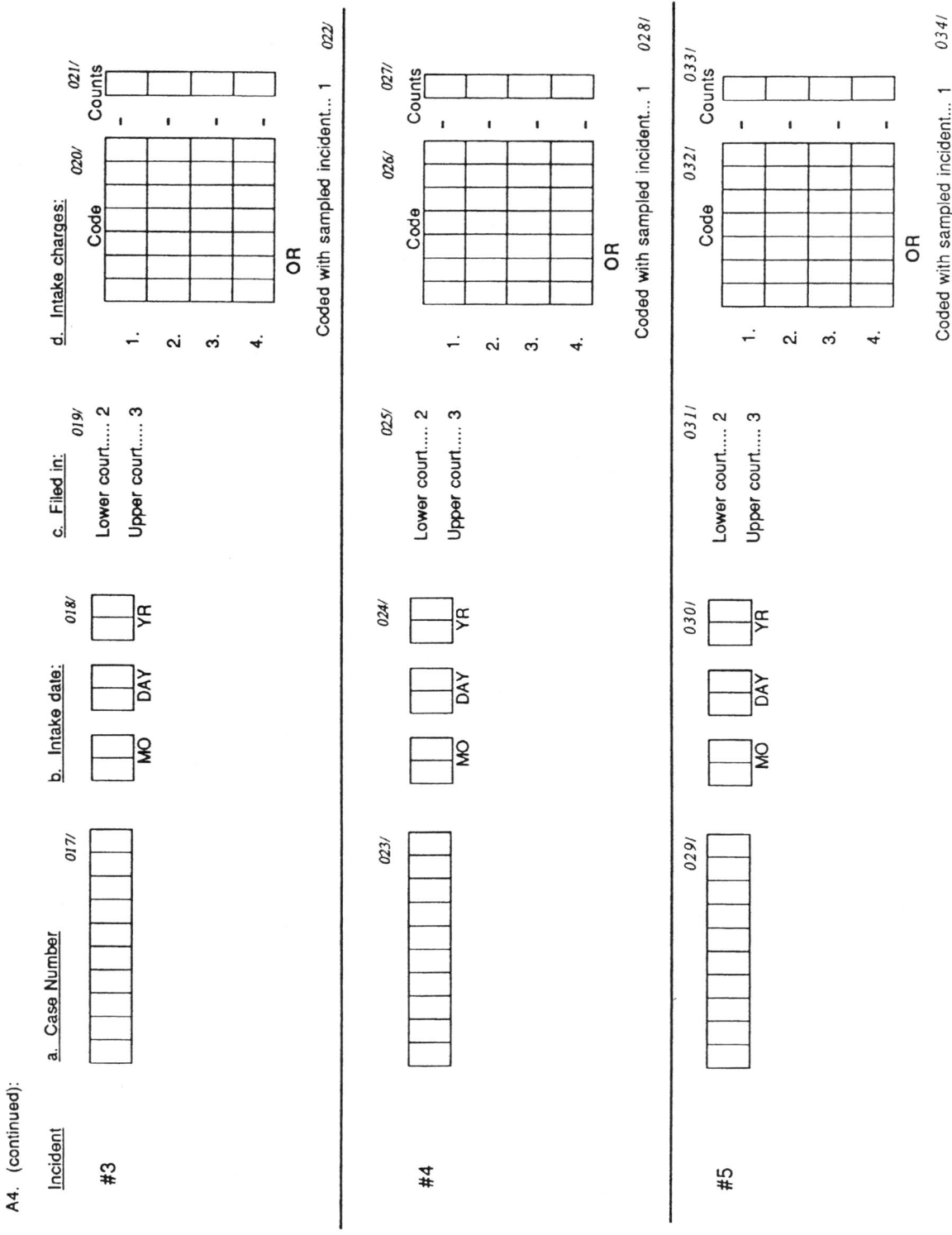

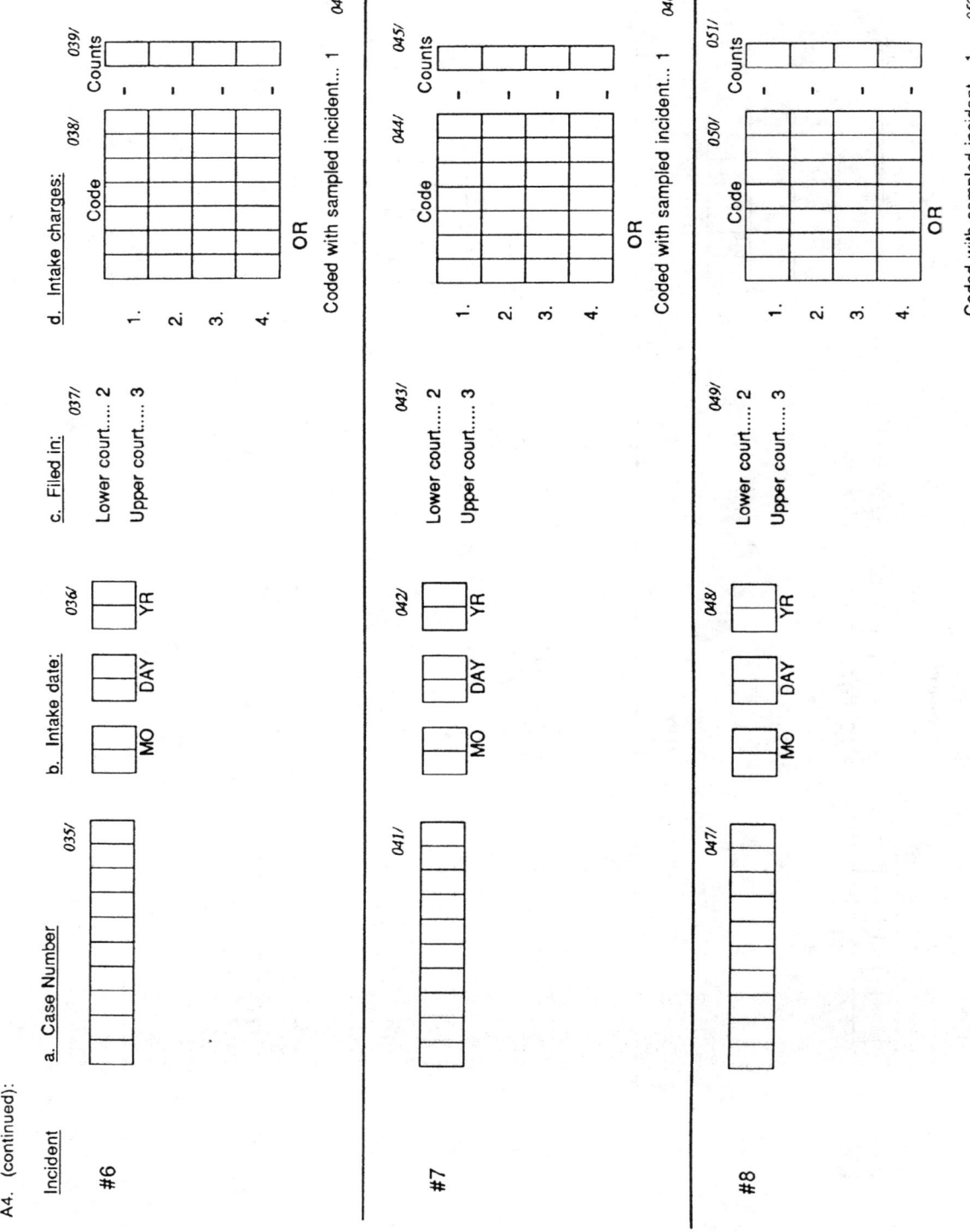

A5. SELECTION DECISION:

Sampled incident was...

1) Rejected for prosecution, select all upper court cases listed in A4. If no upper court cases listed, select all lower court cases in A4.
2) Filed in the lower court, select all upper court cases listed in A4. If no upper court cases listed, select all lower court cases in A4.
3) Filed in the upper court, select all upper court cases listed in A4.

NUMBER OF CASES SELECTED FOR SUPPLEMENTAL CODING:

☐☐ # or none......... 00   053/

A6. NON-SELECTED LOWER COURT CASES:

☐☐ # or none... (Go to Section B).... 00   054/

a. Incident #: ☐ 055/

b. Date of final disposition:
- Mo ☐☐ 056/
- Day ☐☐
- Yr ☐☐ 057/

OR

Pending...(go to next incident or Section B).... 1

c. Outcome: 058/

1.				059/
2.			
3.			
4.			

d. Disposition charges: 060/

Same as intake..... 1

Code 061/				Cts. 062/
1.				☐-☐
2.				☐-☐
3.				☐-☐
4.				☐-☐

e. Sentencing:

- Status ☐ 063/
- Type ☐ 064/
- Length ☐☐ 065/
- Period ☐ 066/

Status:
- Not sentenced/pending............1
- To be served/paid..................2
- Entire sentence suspended.....3
- Not reported...........................9

Type (of most severe):
- Prison................1
- Jail....................2
- Sentence suspended, probation.........3
- Probation...........4
- Fine...................5
- Restitution.........6
- Community service......7
- Other.................8

Period:
- Days..........1
- Months.......2
- Years..........3
- Weekends....4

101

A6. (continued):

a. Incident #: 067/

b. Date of final disposition:
- Mo 068/
- Day
- Yr 069/
- OR
- Pending...(go to next incident or Section B)... 1

c. Outcome: 070/ 071/
1.
2.
3.
4.

d. Disposition charges:
Same as intake..... 1
Code 072/ 073/ — Cts. 074/
1.
2.
3.
4.

e. Sentencing:
- Status 075/
- Type 076/
- Length 077/
- Period 078/

---

a. Incident #: 079/

b. Date of final disposition:
- Mo 080/
- Day
- Yr 081/
- OR
- Pending...(go to next incident or Section B)... 1

c. Outcome: 082/ 083/
1.
2.
3.
4.

d. Disposition charges:
Same as intake..... 1
Code 084/ 085/ — Cts. 086/
1.
2.
3.
4.

e. Sentencing:
- Status 087/
- Type 088/
- Length 089/
- Period 090/

---

a. Incident #: 091/

b. Date of final disposition:
- Mo 092/
- Day
- Yr 093/
- OR
- Pending...(go to next incident or Section B)... 1

c. Outcome: 094/ 095/
1.
2.
3.
4.

d. Disposition charges:
Same as intake..... 1
Code 096/ 097/ — Cts. 098/
1.
2.
3.
4.

e. Sentencing:
- Status 099/
- Type 100/
- Length 101/
- Period 102/

B. Criminal Incident Description
(for sampled incident)

B1. Case number: ⬜⬜⬜⬜⬜⬜⬜⬜   *001/*

B2. Police arrest charges:

                                                  (Circle One)

                           Same as intake charges 1   *002/*
                           Not reported 9

                                    (OR)

      003/   Code   Cts   *004/*

1. ⬜⬜⬜⬜⬜ - ⬜
2. ⬜⬜⬜⬜⬜ - ⬜
3. ⬜⬜⬜⬜⬜ - ⬜
4. ⬜⬜⬜⬜⬜ - ⬜

                  If more than four charges, total # ⬜⬜   *005/*

B3. Date of arrest: ⬜⬜ ⬜⬜ ⬜⬜   *006/*
                          MO DAY YR

                  Not reported 9   *007/*

B4. Date of sampled incident: ⬜⬜ ⬜⬜ ⬜⬜   *008/*
                                  MO DAY YR
                                   (OR)

                  Same as date of arrest 1   *009/*
                  No specific incident date...
                  (Go to B20) 2
                  Not reported 9

B5. Time between incident and arrest:

                                                      (Circle One)

Arrest at the scene	1	010/
Within 24 hours	2	
More than 24 hours	3	
Not reported	9	

B6. Time of day incident occurred:

                                                      (Circle One)

Day...(6:00 am - 5:59 pm)	1	011/
Night...(6:00 pm - 5:59 am)	2	
Not reported	9	

B7. Location of incident:

                                                      (Circle One)

Bar, restaurant, night club	01	012/
Bank	02	
Gas station/convenience store	03	
Other commercial	06	
Street/Out of doors	07	
Residence/dwelling	08	
Miscellaneous	09	
Not reported	99	

B8. Number of individual victims:

Number of victims: ☐☐ 013/
None...*(Go to B16)*................ 00

Code up to 3 victims in this incident, starting with the most seriously injured.

Victim #1

B9. Victim's relationship to defendant: (Circle One)

014/

Neighbor/co-worker/acquaintance 04
Stranger 05
Peace officer 06
Not reported 07

B10. Race/descent of victim: (Circle One)

White 1 015/
Black 2
Hispanic 3
Asian 4
Other 5
Not reported 9

B11. Victim's sex: (Circle One)

Female 1 016/
Male 2
Not reported 9

B12. Report of special victim vulnerability:

Not reported 9 017/

OR
(Circle All That Apply)

Handicapped 1 018/
Elderly...(over 65) 2 019/
Juvenile...(under 16) 3 020/
Other 4 021/
(Specify)_____

B13. Report of victim injury: (Circle One)

Yes, major 1 022/
Yes, minor 2
Not reported 9

| Victim #2 | Victim #3 |

Victim #2

(Circle One)   023/

Neighbor/co-worker/acquaintance	04
Stranger	05
Peace officer	06
Not reported	07

(Circle One)   024/

White	1
Black	2
Hispanic	3
Asian	4
Other	5
Not reported	9

(Circle One)   025/

Female	1
Male	2
Not reported	9

Not reported ... 9   026/

OR

(Circle All That Apply)

Handicapped	1	027/
Elderly...(over 65)	2	028/
Juvenile...(under 16)	3	029/
Other	4	030/
(Specify)_____		

(Circle One)   031/

Yes, major	1
Yes, minor	2
Not reported	9

Victim #3

(Circle One)   032/

Neighbor/co-worker/acquaintance	04
Stranger	05
Peace officer	06
Not reported	07

(Circle One)   033/

White	1
Black	2
Hispanic	3
Asian	4
Other	5
Not reported	9

(Circle One)   034/

Female	1
Male	2
Not reported	9

Not reported ... 9   035/

OR

(Circle All That Apply)

Handicapped	1	036/
Elderly...(over 65)	2	037/
Juvenile...(under 16)	3	038/
Other	4	039/
(Specify)_____		

(Circle One)   040/

Yes, major	1
Yes, minor	2
Not reported	9

B14. Weapon present at the incident:

None...*(Go to B16)*	0	*041/*
Not reported	9	

(OR)
(Circle All That Apply)

a.	Handgun (pistol, revolver, etc.)	1	*042/*
b.	Other gun (rifle, shotgun, etc.)	2	*043/*
c.	Knife, pointed object	3	*044/*
d.	Blunt object	4	*045/*
e.	Other - (specify)_____	5	*046/*

B15. Sampled defendant used, threatened to use, or possessed a weapon:

(Circle One on Each Line)

	Used	Threatened	Possessed	Not Reported	
a. Handgun (pistol, revolver, etc.)	1	2	3	9	*047/*
b. Other gun (rifle, shotgun, etc.)	1	2	3	9	*048/*
c. Knife, pointed object	1	2	3	9	*049/*
d. Blunt object	1	2	3	9	*050/*
e. Other	1	2	3	9	*051/*

(specify)_____

B16. Accomplices:

(Circle One)

None	0	*052/*
One	1	
Two or more	2	
Not reported	9	

B17. Police obtained eyewitness account from someone other than the police or victim:

(Circle One)

No	0	*053/*
Yes	1	
Not reported	9	

B18. Police obtained physical evidence:

        Not reported 9   *054/*

        OR

        (Circle All That Apply)

    a. Victim property 1   *055/*
    b. Weapon 2   *056/*
    c. Fingerprints 3   *057/*
    d. Defendant confession 5   *0571/*
    e. Other tangible evidence 6   *058/*

B19. Defendant under the influence of drugs or alcohol at time of incident:

        (Circle One)

    Drugs/narcotics 1   *059/*
    Alcohol 2
    Both drugs and alcohol 3
    Not reported 9

B20. Defendant's criminal history records contained in this file:

    None 0   *060/*

    OR

    (Circle All That Apply)

    a. PSI/Probation report 1   *061/*
    b. Local rap sheet 2   *062/*
    c. State rap sheet 3   *063/*
    d. Federal rap sheet 4   *064/*
    e. Non-site local rap sheet 5   *065/*
    f. Non-site state rap sheet 6   *066/*

C. Adjudication Process
(for sampled incident)

C1. Release status before sentencing:

                                                           (Circle One)

    Not released...*(Go to C3)* 0   *001/*
    Released on bond 1
    Released without bond...*(Go to C3)* 2
    Released, bond status not reported...*(Go to C3)* 3
    Not reported...*(Go to C3)* 9

C2. Amount of bond released on in this case:

                                                  $ ☐☐☐ , ☐☐☐   *002/*

                                                            (OR)

                                   Not reported 9   *003/*

C3. Case rejected by the prosecutor:

                                                           (Circle One)

    No...*(Go to C6)* 0   *004/*
    Yes 1

C4. Date case was rejected:

                                                       ☐☐ ☐☐ ☐☐   *005/*
                                                        MO   DAY   YR

                                 Not reported 9   *006/*

C5. Reason case was rejected:

        Not reported 99   *007/*

        OR   (Circle All That Apply)

- a. In favor of another case/charge 01   *008/*
- b. Insufficient evidence/lack of corpus 02   *009/*
- c. Victim unwilling to prosecute 03   *010/*
- d. Victim unavailable 04   *011/*
- e. Witness unwilling to testify 05   *012/*
- f. Witness unavailable 06   *013/*
- g. Inadmissible search and seizure 07   *014/*
- h. Defendant placed in pretrial diversion program 08   *015/*
- i. Further investigation 09   *016/*
- j. Extradited/declined in favor of another jurisdiction 10   *017/*
- k. Transferred to juvenile court 11   *018/*
- l. Other 12   *019/*
  (specify) _____
- m. Other 13   *020/*
  (specify) _____

Go To Section D

C6. Legal representation:

Not reported 9
Not represented 0   *021/*
(OR)
(Code All That Apply)

	Event	Attorney Type Code	
a.	at arraignment	☐	*022/*
b.	at preliminary hearing	☐	*023/*
c.	at entry of plea	☐	*024/*
d.	at trial	☐	*025/*
e.	at sentencing	☐	*026/*
f.	other/don't know	☐	*027/*

Attorney Type Codes

Public defender .... = 1
Private counsel .... = 2
Court appointed
  private attorney ..... = 3
Type unknown .... = 4

C7a. Charges filed by the prosecutor:

Same as intake charges ...... 0 ⎫ Go to C7b
Not reported .... 9 ⎭   *0271/*

(OR)

0272/   Code   Cts   *0273/*
1. ☐☐☐☐☐☐ ☐☐
2.
3.
4.

If more than four charges, total # ☐☐   *0274/*

C7b. Charges filed in the upper court:

Same as charges filed by the prosecutor .... 0 ⎫
Charges not filed in the upper court .... 1 ⎬ Go to C8
Not reported .... 9 ⎭   *028/*

(OR)

029/   Code   Cts   *030/*
1. ☐☐☐☐☐☐ ☐☐
2.
3.
4.

If more than four charges, total # ☐☐   *031/*

C8. Adjudication Events and Outcomes:

	A. Event	B. Date	C. Outcome Code
1.	☐☐ 032/	☐☐ Mo ☐☐ Day ☐☐ Yr 033/	☐☐☐ 034/
2.	☐☐ 035/	☐☐ Mo ☐☐ Day ☐☐ Yr 036/	☐☐☐ 037/
3.	☐☐ 038/	☐☐ Mo ☐☐ Day ☐☐ Yr 039/	☐☐☐ 040/
4.	☐☐ 041/	☐☐ Mo ☐☐ Day ☐☐ Yr 042/	☐☐☐ 043/
5.	☐☐ 044/	☐☐ Mo ☐☐ Day ☐☐ Yr 045/	☐☐☐ 046/
6.	☐☐ 047/	☐☐ Mo ☐☐ Day ☐☐ Yr 048/	☐☐☐ 049/
7.	☐☐ 050/	☐☐ Mo ☐☐ Day ☐☐ Yr 051/	☐☐☐ 052/
8.	☐☐ 053/	☐☐ Mo ☐☐ Day ☐☐ Yr 054/	☐☐☐ 055/
9.	☐☐ 056/	☐☐ Mo ☐☐ Day ☐☐ Yr 057/	☐☐☐ 058/
10.	☐☐ 059/	☐☐ Mo ☐☐ Day ☐☐ Yr 060/	☐☐☐ 061/

C9. Disposition charges and outcomes:

    A. Same as charges filed in the highest court, and same outcome for all charges... 1   062/

        OR

    Outcome not the same for all charges:

B. Outcome Code 063/	C. Charge Code 064/	D. Counts 065/
1.		-
2.		-
3.		-
4.		-
5.		-
6.		-
7.		-
8.		-

C10. Defendant sentenced for this incident:

    No, acquitted/dismissed/dropped... *(Go To Section D)* 0   066/

    Yes 1

    Disposition or sentencing pending... *(Go to Section D)* 2

    Not reported...*(Go to Section D)* 9

C11. Date of sentencing: MO DAY YR   067/

    Not reported 9   068/

C12. Type of incarceration imposed (before reductions):

                                            (Circle One)

- None...*(Go to C18)* 0   *069/*
- Prison 1
- Jail 2
- Prison suspended/jail imposed 3
- Young adult authority 4
- Juvenile authority 5

C13. Length of incarceration imposed (before reductions):

                                            (Circle One)

    A. Type: Life/life plus 1   *070/*
                                  Death 2
                                  Not reported 9

                                   (OR)

	YEARS	MONTHS	WEEKS	DAYS	
B. Minimum:					*071/ 072/ 073/ 074/*
C. Maximum:					*075/ 076/*

C14. Length of incarceration term suspended:

                            None...*(Go to C16)* 0   *077/*
                            All 1
                             (OR)

YEARS	MONTHS	WEEKS	DAYS	
				078/ 079/ 080/ 081/

C15. Net imposed after reduction for full or partial suspension:

    A.   None 0   *082/*

                                  (OR)

	YEARS	MONTHS	WEEKS	DAYS	
B. Minimum:					*083/ 084/ 085/ 086/*
C. Maximum:					*087/ 088/*

C16. Credit for time served/unsentenced time:

None...*(Go to C18)* 0   *089/*
Not reported...*(Go to C18)* 9

OR

YEARS	MONTHS	WEEKS	DAYS

090/
091/
092/
093/

C17. Net length of incarceration to be served:

None   0
Not reported   9   *094/*

OR

YEARS	MONTHS	WEEKS	DAYS

095/
096/
097/
098/

C18. Probation term:

None   0   *099/*
Not reported   9

OR

YEARS	MONTHS	WEEKS	DAYS

100/
101/
102/
103/

C19. Additional sentence ordered:

(Circle One On Each Line)

	No	Yes	NR	
a. Restitution.............................	0	1	9	*104/*
b. Fine...	0	1	9	*105/*
c. Drug/alcohol treatment.............	0	1	9	*106/*
d. Community service...................	0	1	9	*107/*

C20. This sentence concurrent with sentences arising from other incidents?

		(Circle One)	
a.	No/no other incidents	0	108/
	Yes, concurrent with all other incidents	1	
	Not reported	9	

OR

b. Sentence concurrent with incident #: ☐ 109/

c. Sentence concurrent with incident #: ☐ 110/

d. Sentence concurrent with incident #: ☐ 111/

e. Sentence concurrent with incident #: ☐ 112/

D. Defendant's Personal Background

D1. Date of birth: ☐☐ ☐☐ ☐☐ 001/
                                       Mo Day Yr

D2. Address at time of arrest:

Non-site state _____ ☐☐ 002/
OR
                      (Circle One)

Site state 1   003/
Foreign country 2
Transient 3
Not reported 9

D3. Illegal alien:

                      (Circle One)

Yes 1   004/
Not reported 9

D4. Race/Descent:

                      (Circle One)

White 1   005/
Black 2
Hispanic 3
Asian 4
Other 5
Not reported 9

D5. Employment status at time of arrest:

                      (Circle One)

Employed 1   006/
Unemployed 2
Other 3
Not reported 9

E. Criminal History Record

E1. Juvenile criminal (non-traffic) arrest:

                                                   (Circle One)

- No...*(Go to E8)* 0   *001/*
- Yes 1
- Not reported...*(Go to E8)* 9

E2. Age or year of first arrest on criminal (non-traffic) charge:

                            Age   ☐☐ *002/*

                            (OR)

                          Year 19 ☐☐ *003/*

- Not reported 9 *004/*

E3. Age or year of first juvenile arrest for an index crime:

                          Age   ☐☐ *005/*

                        (OR)

                      Year 19 ☐☐ *006/*

- None 00 *007/*
- Not reported 99

INDEX CRIMES

Murder/non-negligent manslaughter   Burglary
Forcible rape   Larceny-theft
Robbery   Motor-vehicle theft
Aggravated assault   Arson

E4. Defendant convicted as a juvenile:

                                                   (Circle One)

- No...*(Go to E8)* 0   *008/*
- Yes 1
- Not reported...*(Go to E8)* 9

E5. Defendant served time while a juvenile:

                                                        (Circle One)

No...*(Go to E8)* 0   *009/*
Yes 1
Not reported...*(Go to E8)* 9

E6. Number of commitments:

(Circle One On Each Line)

	None	One	Two	Three or More	At Least One, DK If More	Not Reported	
a. Local facility............	0	1	2	3	4	9	*010/*
b. State facility............	0	1	2	3	4	9	*011/*

E7. Age or year of first incarceration:

                                                  Age   ☐☐ *012/*

                                                  (OR)

                                                  Year   19 ☐☐ *013/*

                                Not reported 9   *014/*

E8. Prior adult criminal arrest:

                                                        (Circle One)

No......*(Go to E15)* 0   *015/*
Yes 1
Not reported...*(Go to E15)* 9

E9. Age or year of first adult arrest on a criminal (non-traffic) charge:

                                                  Age   ☐☐ *016/*

                                                  (OR)

                                                Year   19 ☐☐ *017/*

                                Not reported 9   *018/*

E10. Prior adult conviction:

        (Circle One)

No......*(Go to E15)* 0   *019/*
Yes 1
Not reported...*(Go to E15)* 9

E11. Defendant served time as an adult:

        (Circle One)

No..*(Go to E15)* 0   *020/*
Yes 1
Not reported *(Go to E15)* 9

E12. Number of incarcerations:

(Circle One On Each Line)

	None	One	Two	Three or More	At Least One, DK If More	Not Reported	
a. Local facility............	0	1	2	3	4	9	*021/*
b. State facility............	0	1	2	3	4	9	*022/*

E13. Age or year of first adult incarceration:

Age   ☐☐   *023/*

(OR)

Year 19   ☐☐   *024/*

Not reported 9   *025/*

E14. Date of release from last incarceration:

☐☐ ☐☐ ☐☐   *026/*
MO DAY YR

Not reported 9   *027/*

E15. Release status at time of arrest for sampled incident:

(Circle One)

None	0	028/
Probation	1	
Parole	2	
Furlough/Work release	3	
Escape from jail or prison	4	
Not reported	9	

E16. History of drug abuse:

Not reported	9	029/

(OR)

(Circle All That Apply)

In drug treatment or diversion program at time of arrest	1	030/
Prior commitment to drug treatment or diversion program	2	031/
Prior arrest for possession of drugs	3	032/
Defendant's self-report of history of drug abuse	5	0321/
Other	4	033/
(specify)_____		

E17. History of alcohol abuse:

Not reported	9	034/

(OR)

(Circle All That Apply)

In alcohol treatment program at time of arrest	1	035/
Prior commitment to alcohol treatment program	2	036/
Defendant's self-report of history of alcohol abuse	4	0361/
Other	3	037/
(specify) _____		

SIF
Form 2.2a

CRIMINAL JUSTICE POLICIES AND OUTCOMES

Supplemental Incident Form
February 1988

| BATCH/D.E. #: | ☐☐☐☐ | 001/ |

| RAND I.D. #: | | 002/ |

| INCIDENT #: | ☐ — ☐ | 0021/ |

SITE: 13 003/

ABSTRACTOR I.D.: ☐☐☐ 004/

DATE FORM COMPLETED: ☐☐☐☐88 005/
MO DAY YR

THE RAND CORPORATION
1700 Main Street, PO Box 2138
Santa Monica, CA 90406-2138
Attn: Nora Fitzgerald

This form does not contain Section A.

B. Criminal Incident Description

B1. Case number: ⬜⬜⬜⬜⬜⬜⬜⬜ *001/*

B2. Police arrest charges:

(Circle One)

Included in and same as intake charges
 for this case 1 *002/*
Included in arrest charges for this case 2
Not arrested for this incident...*(Go to B4)* 7
Not reported 9

OR

003/ **Code**   Cts *004/*

1.
2.
3.
4.

If more than four charges, total # ⬜⬜ *005/*

B3. Date of arrest: ⬜⬜ ⬜⬜ ⬜⬜ *006/*
 MO DAY YR

Not reported 9 *007/*
Not arrested 7

B4. Date of incident:

☐☐ ☐☐ ☐☐ *008/*
MO DAY YR

OR

Same as date of arrest 1 *009/*
No specific incident date...
 (Go to B20) 2
Not reported 9

B5. Time between incident and arrest:

(Circle One)

Arrest at the scene 1 *010/*
Within 24 hours 2
More than 24 hours 3
Not reported 9

B6. Time of day incident occurred:

(Circle One)

Day...(6:00 am - 5:59 pm) 1 *011/*
Night...(6:00 pm - 5:59 am) 2
Not reported 9

B7. Location of incident:

(Circle One)

Bar, restaurant, night club 01 *012/*
Bank 02
Gas station/convenience store 03
Other commercial 06
Street/Out of doors 07
Residence/dwelling 08
Miscellaneous 09
Not reported 99

B8. Number of individual victims:

Number of victims: ☐☐ *013/*

None...*(Go to B16)* 00

Code up to 3 victims in this incident, starting with the most seriously injured.

Victim #1

B9. Victim's relationship to defendant: (Circle One)

Family/ex-family	01
Domestic partners/roommates/people living together	02
Criminal cohort/accomplice	03
Neighbor/co-worker/acquaintance	04
Stranger	05
Peace officer	06
Not reported	07

014/

B10. Race/descent of victim: (Circle One)

White	1
Black	2
Hispanic	3
Asian	4
Other	5
Not reported	9

015/

B11. Victim's sex: (Circle One)

Female	1
Male	2
Not reported	9

016/

B12. Report of special victim vulnerability:

Not reported 9 *017/*

OR

(Circle All That Apply)

Handicapped	1	*018/*
Elderly...(over 65)	2	*019/*
Juvenile...(under 16)	3	*020/*
Other	4	*021/*
(Specify)_____		

B13. Report of victim injury: (Circle One)

Yes, major	1
Yes, minor	2
Not reported	9

022/

Victim #2

(Circle One)

Family/ex-family	01 *023/*
Domestic partners/roommates/ people living together	02
Criminal cohort/accomplice	03
Neighbor/co-worker/acquaintance	04
Stranger	05
Peace officer	06
Not reported	07

(Circle One)

White	1 *024/*
Black	2
Hispanic	3
Asian	4
Other	5
Not reported	9

(Circle One)

Female	1 *025/*
Male	2
Not reported	9

Not reported	9

OR

(Circle All That Apply)

Handicapped	1
Elderly...(over 65)	2
Juvenile...(under 16)	3
Other	4
(Specify)_____	

(Circle One)

Yes, major	1 *031/*
Yes, minor	2
Not reported	9

Victim #3

(Circle One)

Family/ex-family	01 *032/*
Domestic partners/roommates/ people living together	02
Criminal cohort/accomplice	03
Neighbor/co-worker/acquaintance	04
Stranger	05
Peace officer	06
Not reported	07

(Circle One)

White	1 *033/*
Black	2
Hispanic	3
Asian	4
Other	5
Not reported	9

(Circle One)

Female	1 *034/*
Male	2
Not reported	9

Not reported	9 *035/*

OR

(Circle All That Apply)

Handicapped	1
Elderly...(over 65)	2
Juvenile...(under 16)	3
Other	4
(Specify)_____	

(Circle One)

Yes, major	1 *040/*
Yes, minor	2
Not reported	9

B14. Weapon present at the incident:

	None...*(Go to B16)* 0	*041/*
	Not reported 9	
	OR	
	(Circle All That Apply)	
a.	Handgun (pistol, revolver, etc.) 1	*042/*
b.	Other gun (rifle, shotgun, etc.) 2	*043/*
c.	Knife, pointed object 3	*044/*
d.	Blunt object 4	*045/*
e.	Other - (specify)_____ 5	*046/*

B15. Sampled defendant used, threatened to use, or possessed a weapon:

(Circle One on Each Line)

	Used	Threatened	Possessed	Not Reported	
a. Hand gun (pistol, revolver, etc.)	1	2	3	9	*047/*
b. Other gun (rifle, shotgun, etc.)...............	1	2	3	9	*048/*
c. Knife, pointed object............................	1	2	3	9	*049/*
d. Blunt object...	1	2	3	9	*050/*
e. Other...	1	2	3	9	*051/*

(specify)_____

B16. Accomplices:

(Circle One)

None	 0	*052/*
One	 1	
Two or more	 2	
Not reported	 9	

B17. Police obtained eyewitness account from someone other than the police or victim:

(Circle One)

No	 0	*053/*
Yes	 1	
Not reported	 9	

B18. Police obtained physical evidence:

	Not reported 9	*054/*
	OR	
	(Circle All That Apply)	
a.	Victim property 1	*055/*
b.	Weapon 2	*056/*
c.	Fingerprints 3	*057/*
d.	Other tangible evidence 6	*058/*
e.	Defendant confession 7	*0581/*

B19. Defendant under the influence of drugs or alcohol at time of incident:

(Circle One)

Drugs/narcotics 1	*059/*
Alcohol 2	
Both drugs and alcohol 3	
Not reported 9	

B20. Defendant's criminal history records contained in this file:

	None 0	*060/*
	OR	
	(Circle All That Apply)	
a.	PSI/Probation report 1	*061/*
b.	Local rap sheet 2	*062/*
c.	State rap sheet 3	*063/*
d.	Federal rap sheet 4	*064/*
e.	Non-site local rap sheet 5	*065/*
f.	Non-site state rap sheet 6	*066/*

SCF
Form 3.2

CRIMINAL JUSTICE POLICIES AND OUTCOMES

Supplemental Case Form
February 1988

BATCH/D.E. #: ☐☐☐☐   *001/*

RAND I.D. #:   *002/*

INCIDENT #: ☐–☐   *0021/*

SITE: |1 3| *003/*

ABSTRACTOR I.D.: ☐☐☐   *004/*

DATE FORM COMPLETED: ☐☐|☐☐|8 8| *005/*
MO DAY YR

THE **RAND** CORPORATION
1700 Main Street, PO Box 2138
Santa Monica, CA 90406-2138

Attn: Nora Fitzgerald

> This form does not contain Section A.

B. Criminal Incident Description
(for sampled incident)

B1. Case number: ☐☐☐☐☐☐☐ *001/*

B2. Police arrest charges:

                                              (Circle One)

Same as intake charges 1   *002/*
Not reported 9

OR

003/   Code   Cts   *004/*

1. ☐☐☐☐☐☐ - ☐
2. ☐☐☐☐☐☐ - ☐
3. ☐☐☐☐☐☐ - ☐
4. ☐☐☐☐☐☐ - ☐

If more than four charges, total # ☐☐   *005/*

B3. Date of arrest: ☐☐ ☐☐ ☐☐   *006/*
                     MO DAY YR

Not reported 9   *007/*

B4. Date of sampled incident: ☐☐ ☐☐ ☐☐   *008/*
                                  MO DAY YR

OR

Same as date of arrest 1   *009/*
No specific incident date...
  (Go to B20) 2
Not reported 9

B5. Time between incident and arrest:

                                            (Circle One)

Arrest at the scene	1	010/
Within 24 hours	2	
More than 24 hours	3	
Not reported	9	

B6. Time of day incident occurred:

                                              (Circle One)

Day...(6:00 am - 5:59 pm)	1	011/
Night...(6:00 pm - 5:59 am)	2	
Not reported	9	

B7. Location of incident:

                                              (Circle One)

Bar, restaurant, night club	01	012/
Bank	02	
Gas station/convenience store	03	
Other commercial	06	
Street/Out of doors	07	
Residence/dwelling	08	
Miscellaneous	09	
Not reported	99	

B8. Number of individual victims:

Number of victims: .... ☐☐   013/
None...*(Go to B16)*................................ 00

Code up to 3 victims in this incident, starting with the most seriously injured.

Victim #1

B9. Victim's relationship to defendant: (Circle One)

014/

Neighbor/co-worker/acquaintance 04
Stranger 05
Peace officer 06
Not reported 07

B10. Race/descent of victim: (Circle One)

White 1   015/
Black 2
Hispanic 3
Asian 4
Other 5
Not reported 9

B11. Victim's sex: (Circle One)

Female 1   016/
Male 2
Not reported 9

B12. Report of special victim vulnerability:

Not reported 9   017/

OR
(Circle All That Apply)

Handicapped 1   018/
Elderly...(over 65) 2   019/
Juvenile...(under 16) 3   020/
Other 4   021/
(Specify)_____

B13. Report of victim injury: (Circle One)

Yes, major 1   022/
Yes, minor 2
Not reported 9

Victim #2	Victim #3
(Circle One)	(Circle One)

	Victim #2		Victim #3	
		023/		032/
Neighbor/co-worker/acquaintance	04		04	
Stranger	05		05	
Peace officer	06		06	
Not reported	07		07	
	(Circle One)		(Circle One)	
White	1	024/	1	033/
Black	2		2	
Hispanic	3		3	
Asian	4		4	
Other	5		5	
Not reported	9		9	
	(Circle One)		(Circle One)	
Female	1	025/	1	034/
Male	2		2	
Not reported	9		9	
Not reported	9	026/	9	035/
OR				
(Circle All That Apply)				
Handicapped	1	027/	1	036/
Elderly...(over 65)	2	028/	2	037/
Juvenile...(under 16)	3	029/	3	038/
Other	4	030/	4	039/
(Specify)_____				
	(Circle One)		(Circle One)	
Yes, major	1	031/	1	040/
Yes, minor	2		2	
Not reported	9		9	

B14. Weapon present at the incident:

None...*(Go to B16)*	0	041/
Not reported	9	

OR

(Circle All That Apply)

a.	Handgun (pistol, revolver, etc.)	1	042/
b.	Other gun (rifle, shotgun, etc.)	2	043/
c.	Knife, pointed object	3	044/
d.	Blunt object	4	045/
e.	Other - (specify)_____	5	046/

B15. Sampled defendant used, threatened to use, or possessed a weapon:

(Circle One on Each Line)

	Used	Threatened	Possessed	Not Reported	
a. Handgun (pistol, revolver, etc.)	1	2	3	9	047/
b. Other gun (rifle, shotgun, etc.)	1	2	3	9	048/
c. Knife, pointed object	1	2	3	9	049/
d. Blunt object	1	2	3	9	050/
e. Other	1	2	3	9	051/

(specify)_____

B16. Accomplices:

(Circle One)

None	0	052/
One	1	
Two or more	2	
Not reported	9	

B17. Police obtained eyewitness account from someone other than the police or victim:

(Circle One)

No	0	053/
Yes	1	
Not reported	9	

B18. Police obtained physical evidence:

		Not reported 9	054/
		OR	
		(Circle All That Apply)	
	a.	Victim property 1	055/
	b.	Weapon 2	056/
	c.	Fingerprints 3	057/
	d.	Other tangible evidence 6	058/
	e.	Defendant confession 7	0581/

B19. Defendant under the influence of drugs or alcohol at time of incident:

	(Circle One)	
Drugs/narcotics 1		059/
Alcohol 2		
Both drugs and alcohol 3		
Not reported 9		

B20. Defendant's criminal history records contained in this file:

		None 0	060/
		OR	
		(Circle All That Apply)	
	a.	PSI/Probation report 1	061/
	b.	Local rap sheet 2	062/
	c.	State rap sheet 3	063/
	d.	Federal rap sheet 4	064/
	e.	Non-site local rap sheet 5	065/
	f.	Non-site state rap sheet 6	066/

C. Adjudication Process
(for sampled incident)

C1. Release status before sentencing:

                                                        (Circle One)

    Not released...*(Go to C3)* 0   *001/*
    Released on bond 1
    Released without bond...*(Go to C3)* 2
    Released, bond status not reported...*(Go to C3)* 3
    Not reported...*(Go to C3)* 9

C2. Amount of bond released on in this case:

                                                            $ ☐☐☐ , ☐☐☐   *002/*

                                                                              OR

            Not reported 9   *003/*

C3. Case rejected by the prosecutor:

                                                           (Circle One)

    No...*(Go to C6)* 0   *004/*
    Yes 1

C4. Date case was rejected:

                                                            ☐☐ ☐☐ ☐☐   *005/*
                                                             MO   DAY   YR

            Not reported 9   *006/*

C5. Reason case was rejected:

	Not reported 99	007/
	OR	
	(Circle All That Apply)	
a.	In favor of another case/charge 01	008/
b.	Insufficient evidence/lack of corpus 02	009/
c.	Victim unwilling to prosecute 03	010/
d.	Victim unavailable 04	011/
e.	Witness unwilling to testify 05	012/
f.	Witness unavailable 06	013/
g.	Inadmissable search and seizure 07	014/
h.	Defendant placed in pretrial diversion program 08	015/
i.	Further investigation 09	016/
j.	Extradited/declined in favor of another jurisdiction 10	017/
k.	Transferred to juvenile court 11	018/
l.	Other .... 12 (specify) _____	019/
m.	Other .... 13 (specify) _____	020/

Go To Section D

C6. Legal representation:

Not reported 9
Not represented 0   *C21/*

OR
(Code All That Apply)

Attorney Type Codes

Public defender .... = 1
Private counsel .... = 2
Court appointed
  private attorney ..... = 3
Type unknown .... = 4

Event	Attorney Type Code	
a. at arraignment	☐	*022/*
b. at preliminary hearing	☐	*023/*
c. at entry of plea	☐	*024/*
d. at trial	☐	*025/*
e. at sentencing	☐	*026/*
f. other/don't know	☐	*027/*

C7. Charges filed by the prosecutor:

Same as intake charges ...... 0 ⎫
                                 ⎬ Go to C8
Not reported .... 9 ⎭   *0271/*

OR

0272/

	Code					Cts
1.						
2.						
3.						
4.						

0273/

If more than four charges, total # ☐☐   *0274/*

C8. Charges filed in the upper court:

Same as charges filed by the prosecutor .... 0 ⎫
Charges not filed in the upper court .... 1 ⎬ Go to C9
Not reported .... 9 ⎭   *028/*

OR

029/

	Code					Cts
1.						
2.						
3.						
4.						

030/

If more than four charges, total # ☐☐   *031/*

C9. Adjudication Events and Outcomes:

	A. Event	B. Date (Mo / Day / Yr)	C. Outcome Code
1.	☐☐ *032/*	☐☐ ☐☐ ☐☐ *033/*	☐☐☐ *034/*
2.	☐☐ *035/*	☐☐ ☐☐ ☐☐ *036/*	☐☐☐ *037/*
3.	☐☐ *038/*	☐☐ ☐☐ ☐☐ *039/*	☐☐☐ *040/*
4.	☐☐ *041/*	☐☐ ☐☐ ☐☐ *042/*	☐☐☐ *043/*
5.	☐☐ *044/*	☐☐ ☐☐ ☐☐ *045/*	☐☐☐ *046/*
6.	☐☐ *047/*	☐☐ ☐☐ ☐☐ *048/*	☐☐☐ *049/*
7.	☐☐ *050/*	☐☐ ☐☐ ☐☐ *051/*	☐☐☐ *052/*
8.	☐☐ *053/*	☐☐ ☐☐ ☐☐ *054/*	☐☐☐ *055/*
9.	☐☐ *056/*	☐☐ ☐☐ ☐☐ *057/*	☐☐☐ *058/*
10.	☐☐ *059/*	☐☐ ☐☐ ☐☐ *060/*	☐☐☐ *061/*

C10. Disposition charges and outcomes:

    A. Same as charges filed in the highest court, and same outcome for all charges... 1   062/

OR

Outcome not the same for all charges:

B. Outcome Code 063/	C. Charge Code 064/	D. Counts 065/
1.		-
2.		-
3.		-
4.		-
5.		-
6.		-
7.		-
8.		-

C11. Defendant sentenced for this incident:

    No, acquitted/dismissed/dropped... *(Go To Section D)* 0   066/
    Yes 1
    Disposition or sentencing pending... *(Go to Section D)* 2
    Not reported...*(Go to Section D)* 9

C12. Date of sentencing: MO DAY YR   067/

    Not reported 9   068/

C12a. Concurrent sentence:

    No 0   0681/
    Yes, sentence coded for this incident 1

OR

    Yes, concurrent with sentence coded for incident #

C13. Type of incarceration imposed (before reductions):

                                                    (Circle One)
             None...*(Go to C17)* 0   *069/*
             Prison 1
             Jail 2
             Prison suspended/jail imposed 3
             Young adult authority 4
             Juvenile authority 5

C14. Length of incarceration imposed (before reductions):

    A. Type: (Circle One)
                               Life/life plus 1   *070/*
                               Death 2
                               Not reported 9
                                       OR

	YEARS	MONTHS	WEEKS	DAYS
B. Minimum:							
C. Maximum:							

    071/
    072/
    073/
    074/
    075/
    076/

C15. Length of incarceration term suspended:

                               None...*(Go to C17)* 0   *077/*
                               All 1
                                       OR

	YEARS	MONTHS	WEEKS	DAYS

    078/
    079/
    080/
    081/

C16. Net imposed after reduction for full or partial suspension:

    A.   None 0   *082/*
                                       OR

	YEARS	MONTHS	WEEKS	DAYS
B. Minimum:							
C. Maximum:							

    083/
    084/
    085/
    086/
    087/
    088/

C17. Credit for time served/unsentenced time:

None...*(Go to C19)* 0 *089/*
Not reported...*(Go to C19)* 9

OR

YEARS		MONTHS		WEEKS		DAYS	

090/
091/
092/
093/

C18. Net length of incarceration to be served:

None 0
Not reported 9   *094/*

OR

YEARS		MONTHS		WEEKS		DAYS	

095/
096/
097/
098/

C19. Probation term:

None 0   *099/*
Not reported 9

OR

YEARS		MONTHS		WEEKS		DAYS	

100/
101/
102/
103/

C20. Additional sentence ordered:

(Circle One On Each Line)

	No	Yes	NR	
a. Restitution....................	0	1	9	*104/*
b. Fine............................	0	1	9	*105/*
c. Drug/alcohol treatment..........	0	1	9	*106/*
d. Community service...............	0	1	9	*107/*

C21. This sentence concurrent with sentences arising from other incidents?

		(Circle One)	
a.	No/no other incidents	0	108/
	Yes, concurrent with all other incidents	1	
	Not reported	9	

OR

b.	Sentence concurrent with incident #:	☐	109/
c.	Sentence concurrent with incident #:	☐	110/
d.	Sentence concurrent with incident #:	☐	111/
e.	Sentence concurrent with incident #:	☐	112/

Appendix C

VARIABLE NAMES

To be consistent with the variable names in the public-use files for this project, the term "clutch" is used as a variable name. This term is synonymous with "overlapping" in this report.

OUTCOME MEASURES

The six major outcome variables that were studied were as follows:

PLEAD	Did offender plead guilty to either the sampled case or the clutch case (or both)?
FOUND	If the offender did not plead guilty to any case, was he found guilty at a trial to some case?
CONVICTD	Was the offender convicted *either* because he pleaded guilty or was found guilty? (This outcome combines the two above.)
INCARC	If the offender was convicted, was he sentenced to a state (prison) or local (jail) institution?
LONGSENT	If the offender was sentenced to either jail or prison, was the total sentence for all incidents above the median length for the sampled offense and state?
LONGTIME	Was total case-processing time (defined as the length of time from the beginning of the earliest sampled or clutch case to the disposition of the latest) above the median level for this offense (over all states)?

We defined each outcome measure with respect to the sampled case *and* any clutch cases (including extra cases). Thus, an offender is convicted if he is convicted of *at least one* incident—either the sampled case or any clutch cases.

For some cases, we could not determine the outcome (for example, some cases had not been completed when we investigated them). Such cases were dropped from the analysis of the corresponding outcome, but they were not dropped from the analysis of *other* outcomes if these other outcomes could be determined.

If an outcome could be determined, we coded it as a zero-one variable, with the usual meaning: outcome = 1: outcome occurred; or outcome = 0: outcome did not occur.

PREDICTOR VARIABLES

We defined nine *predictor classes* of independent (predictor) variables. Each class *included* every variable in the previous class. The nine classes were:

1. Random: a class consisting of a single variable (called FUZZ), set equal to a pseudorandom number uniformly distributed on the interval between 0 and 0.01.

2. Incidence:

ACCOMP	Did offender have an accomplice?
COUNTS	Were there multiple counts charged?
FEMALVIC	Were there any female victims?
MAJORINJ	Did any victim suffer a major injury?
MULTVIC	Was there more than one victim?
VICTVUL	Were there any "vulnerable" victims (old, young)?
NITETIME	Did incident happen at night?
WEAPTHRT	Did offender threaten to use a weapon?

3. Evidence:

EYEWIT	Were there any eyewitnesses to the incident?
FINGER	Were fingerprints entered as evidence?
PROPER	Was victim property recovered and used as evidence?
WEAPEVID	Was a weapon used as evidence?

4. Arrest:

ATSCENE	Was offender arrested at scene of crime?
DELAYED	Was there more than a 24-hour delay before arrest?
DRUGS	Was offender under the influence of drugs at the time of arrest?

5. Clutch:

CLUTCH1	Exactly one clutch case?
CLUTCH2	Two or more clutch cases?
EXTRA1	Exactly one extra case?
EXTRA2	Two or more extra cases?
CLU_EXT	At least one clutch case and one extra case?

6. Priors:

ARREST	Did offender have prior adult arrest?
CONVICT	Did offender have prior adult conviction?
PRISON	Did offender have prior adult prison term?
JUVPRIS	Did offender have prior juvenile incarceration?
PROBSTAT	Was offender on probation or parole when arrested?

7. Offender:

BLACK	Was offender black?
HISPANIC	Was offender Hispanic?
WHITE	Was offender white?
NOJOB	Was offender unemployed at time of arrest?
NONSTATE	Was offender resident of another state?

8. State:

GA	Georgia?
IL	Illinois?
MD	Maryland?
MI	Michigan?

MO	Missouri?
NY	New York?
TX	Texas?

9. Site:

SDGO	San Diego?
SACR	Sacramento?
FTWO	Fort Worth?
MONT	Montgomery County?
KANC	Kansas City?
MANH	Manhattan?

As with the outcome measures, we defined each of the predictor variables as a characteristic of the entire set of incidents analyzed, including both the sampled incident and any clutch cases. For example, the variable ACCOMP was coded "yes" if the offender had an accomplice for at least one incident. It is therefore possible for two apparently exclusive predictors to occur simultaneously; for example, it is possible that a case is characterized by *both* an ATSCENE arrest *and* a DELAYED arrest.

Unlike the outcome measures, we *always* coded a predictor variable. If for some reason the data needed to code a predictor were missing or incomplete, we coded the variable as though the corresponding characteristic were not present. Each predictor variable (except for FUZZ), was coded in the usual way: 1 = characteristic was present and 0 = not present. A more complete description of the database is presented in Abrahamse, Ebener, and Klein (1990).

Appendix D

SITE CHARACTERISTICS

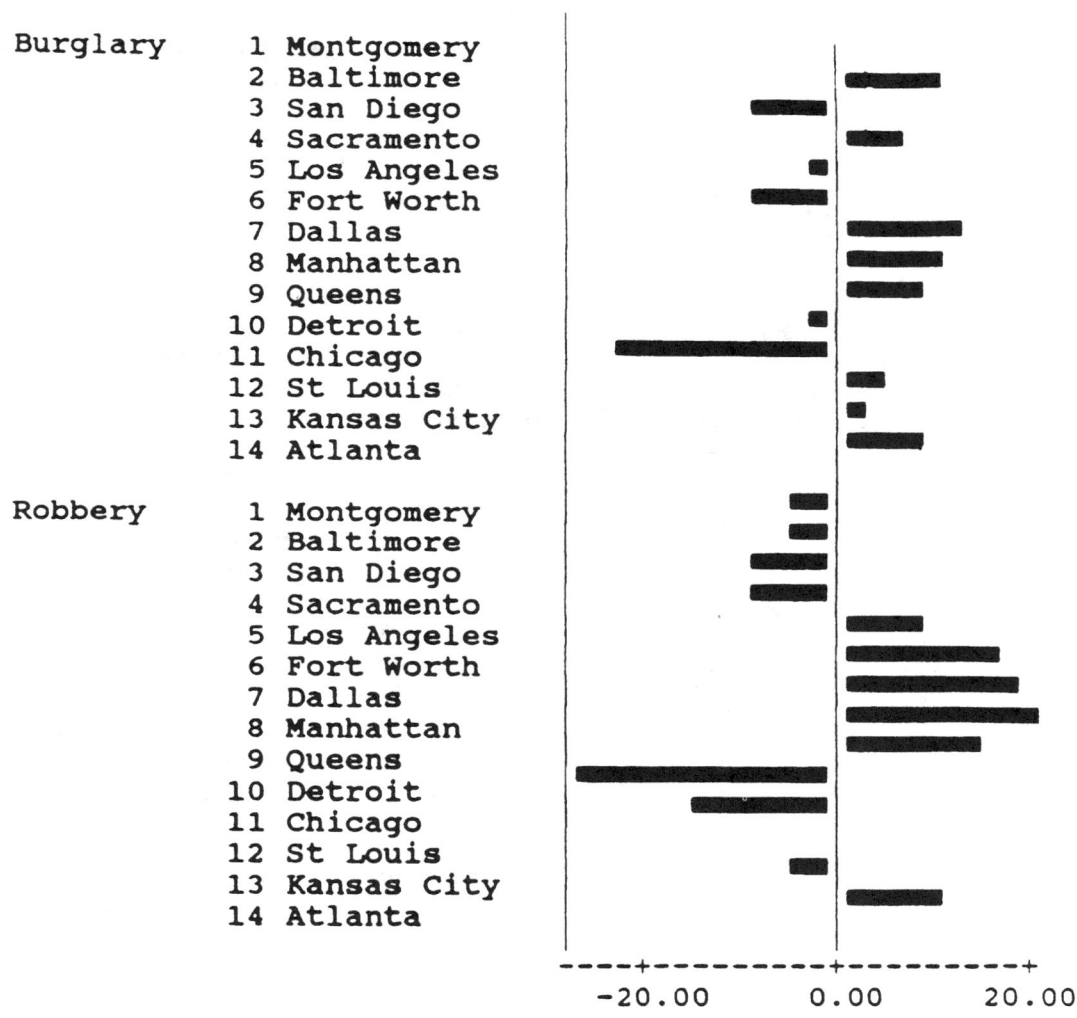

Fig. D.1—Site comparisons: pleaded guilty?

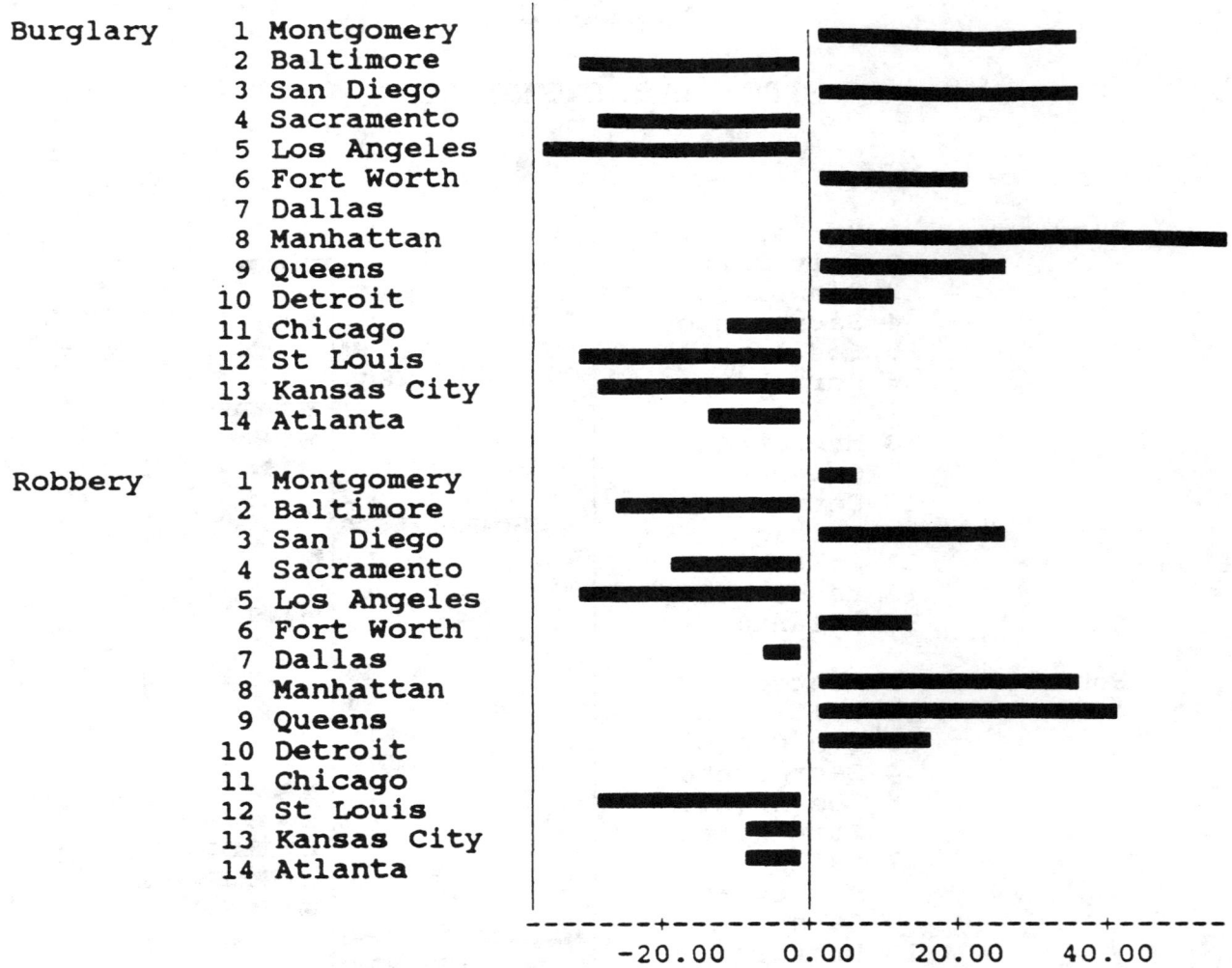

Fig. D.2—Site comparisons: found guilty at trial?

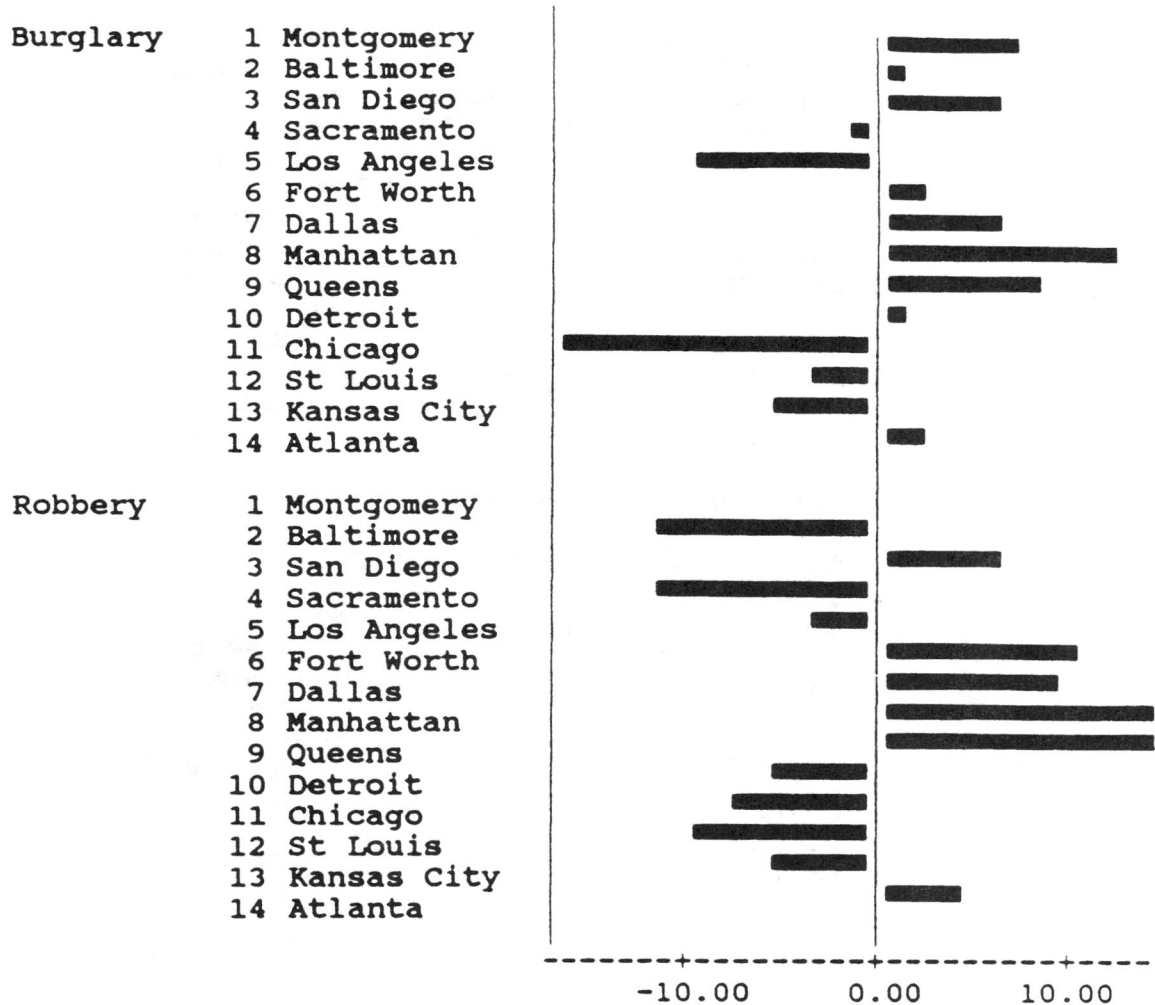

Fig. D.3—Site comparisons: convicted?

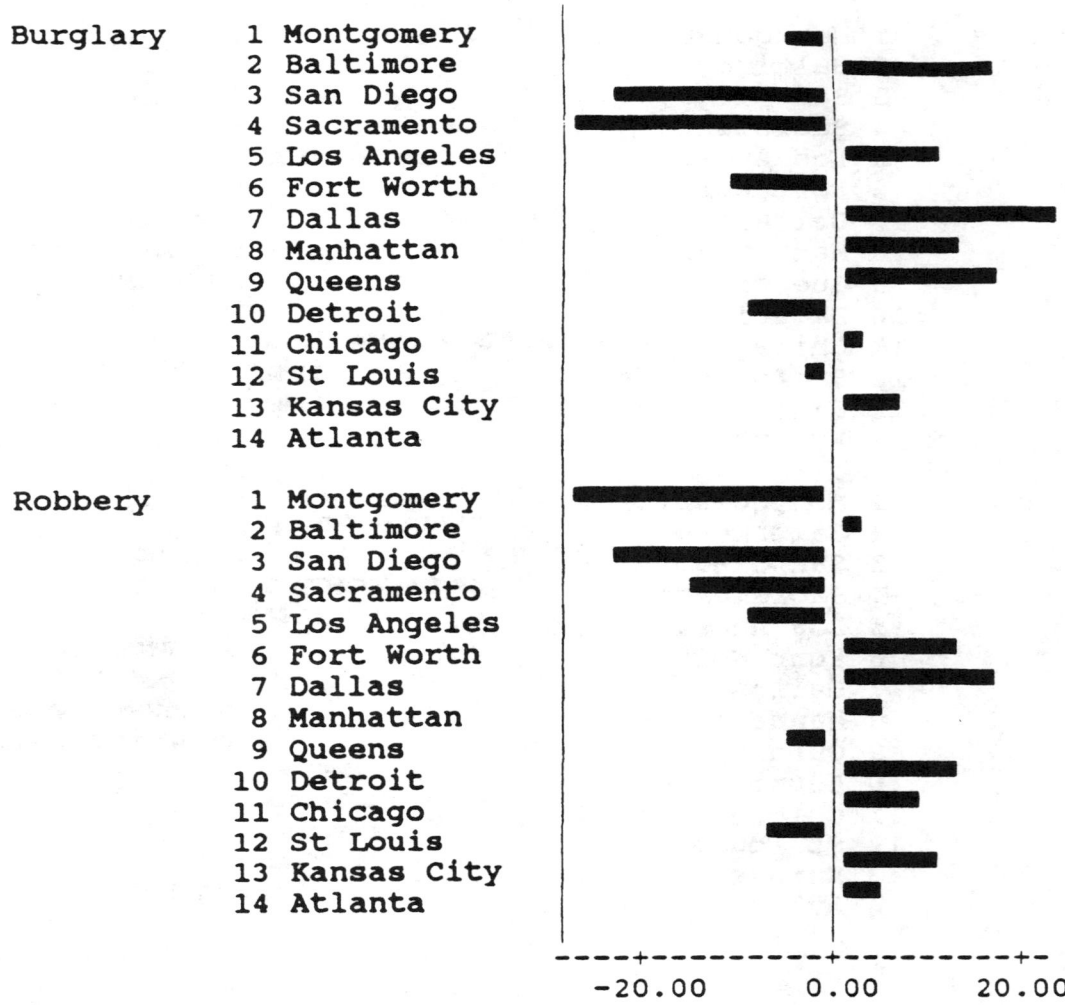

Fig. D.4—Site comparisons: sent to prison?

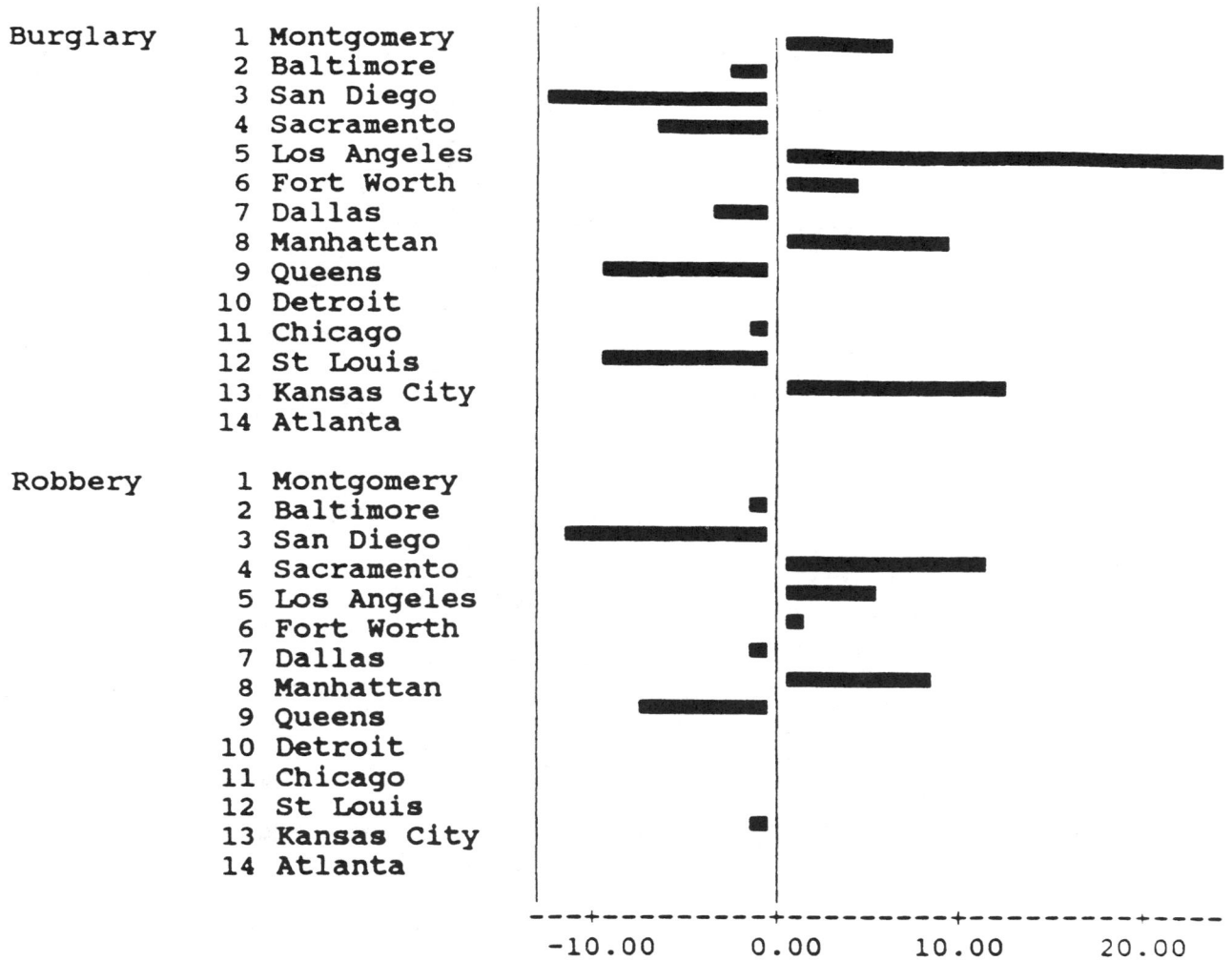

Fig. D.5—Site comparisons: relatively long sentence?

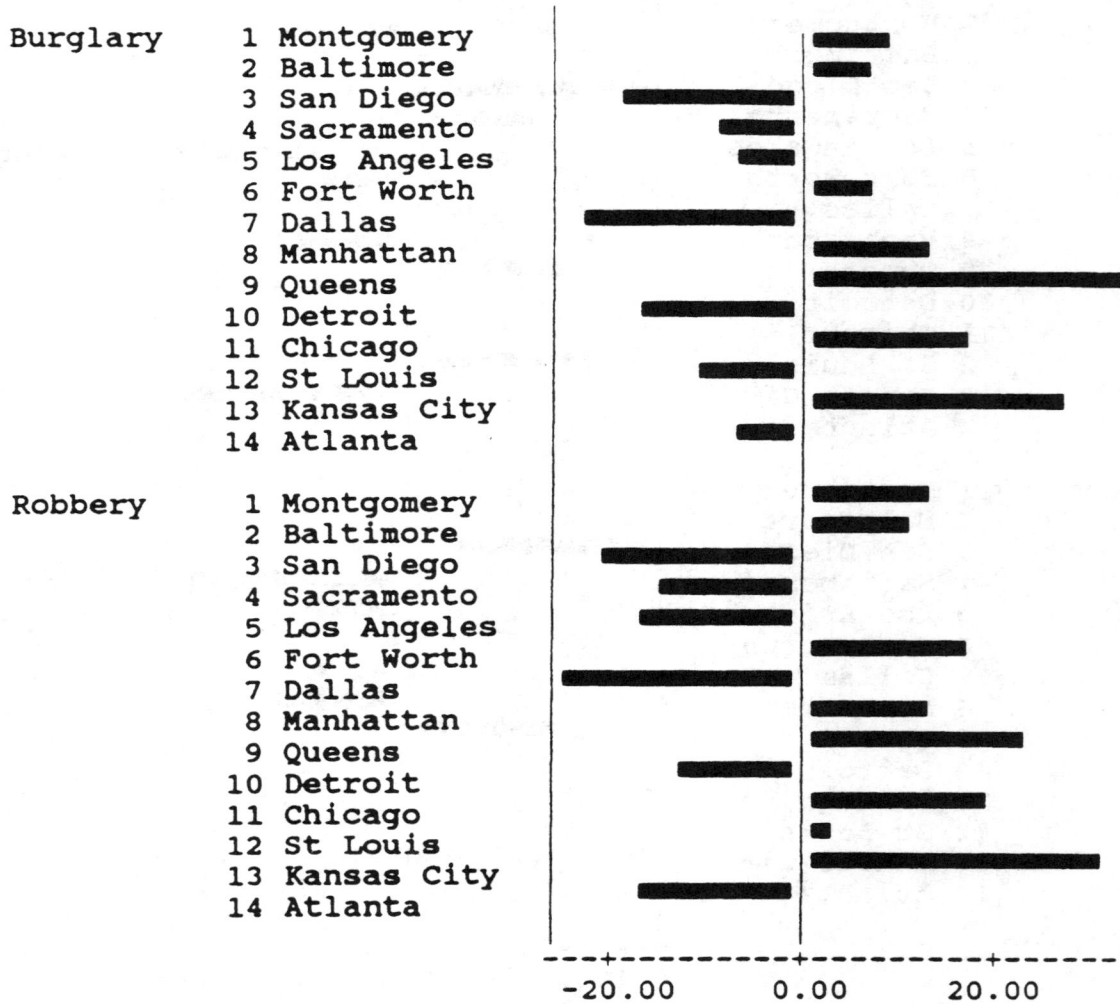

Fig. D.6—Site comparisons: long disposition time?

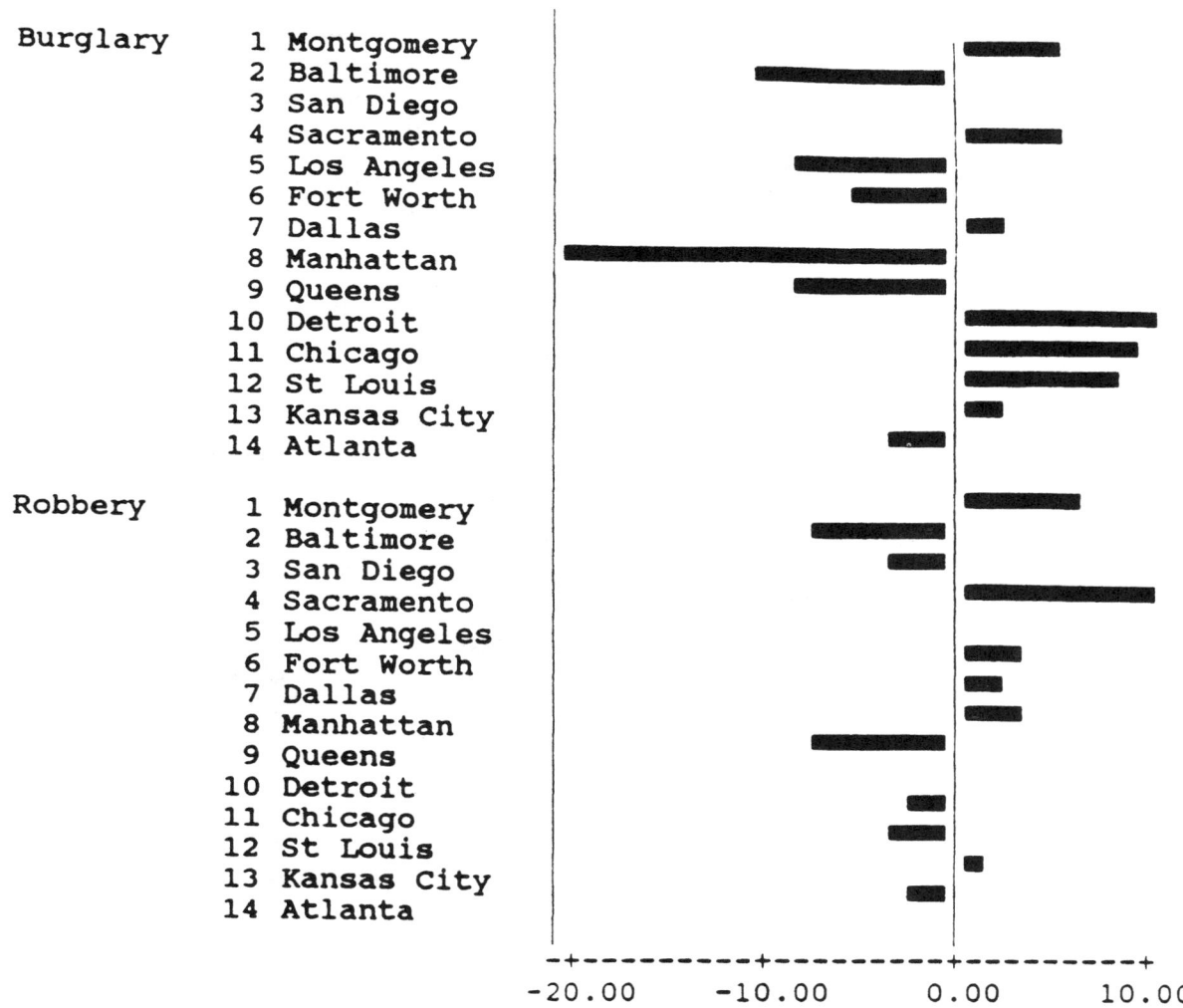

Fig. D.7—Site comparisons: had an accomplice?

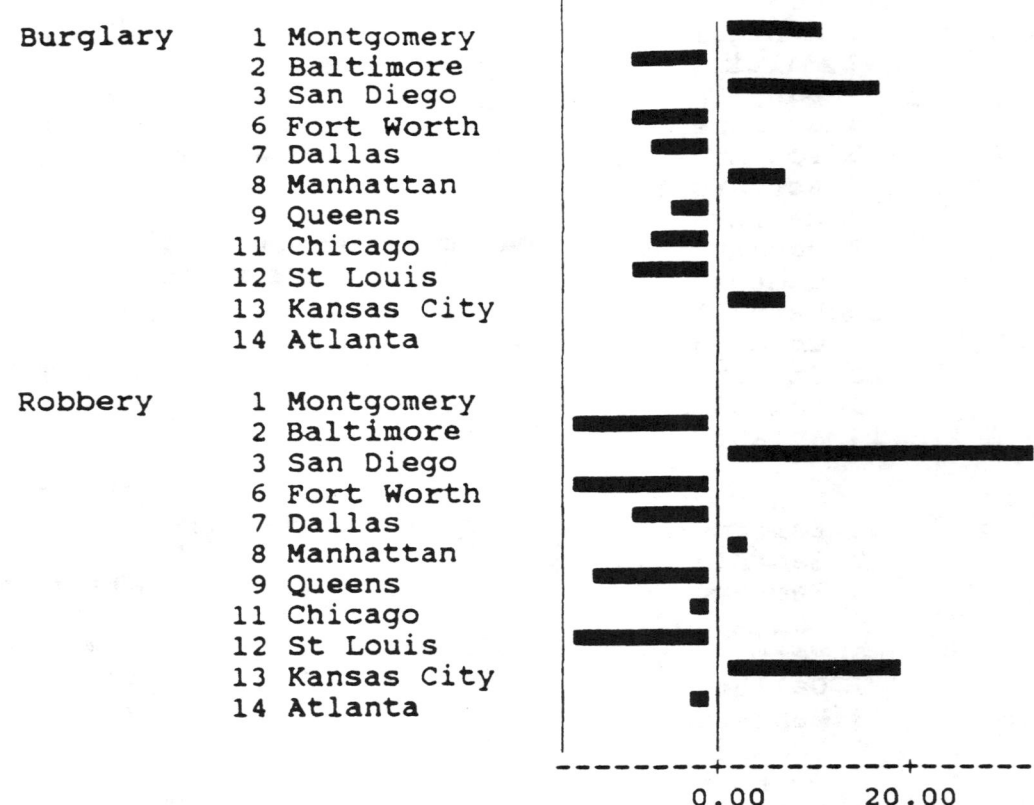

Fig. D.8—Site comparisons: multiple sample counts?

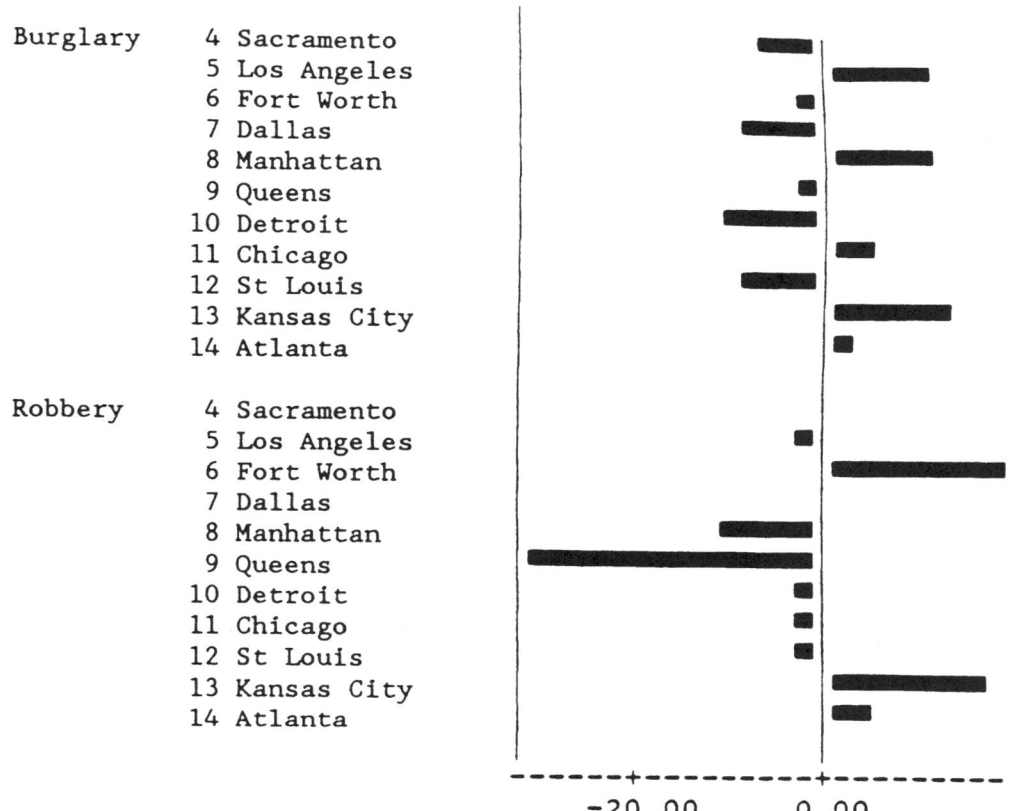

Fig. D.9—Site comparisons: any victim a female?

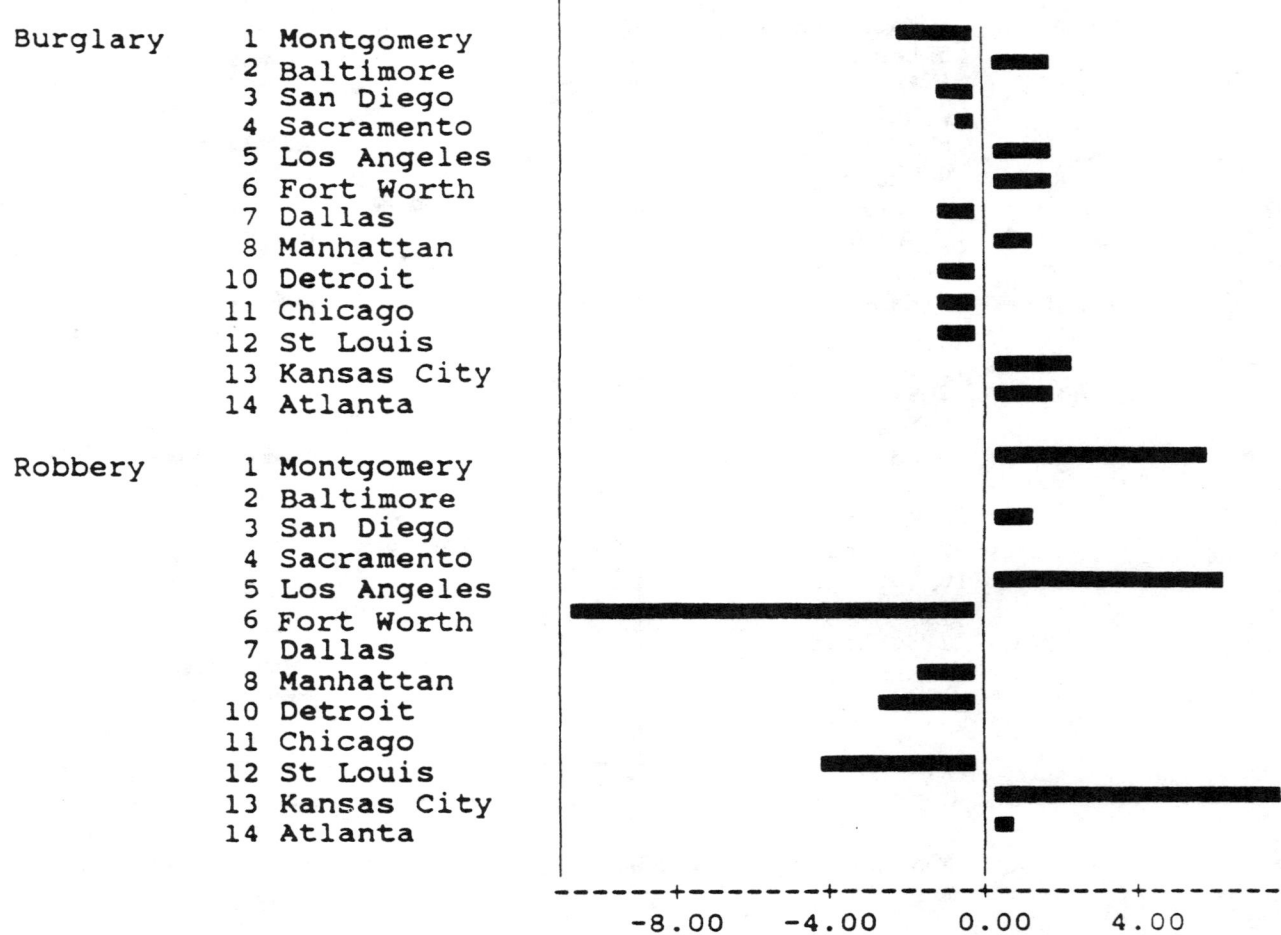

Fig. D.10—Site comparisons: major victim injury?

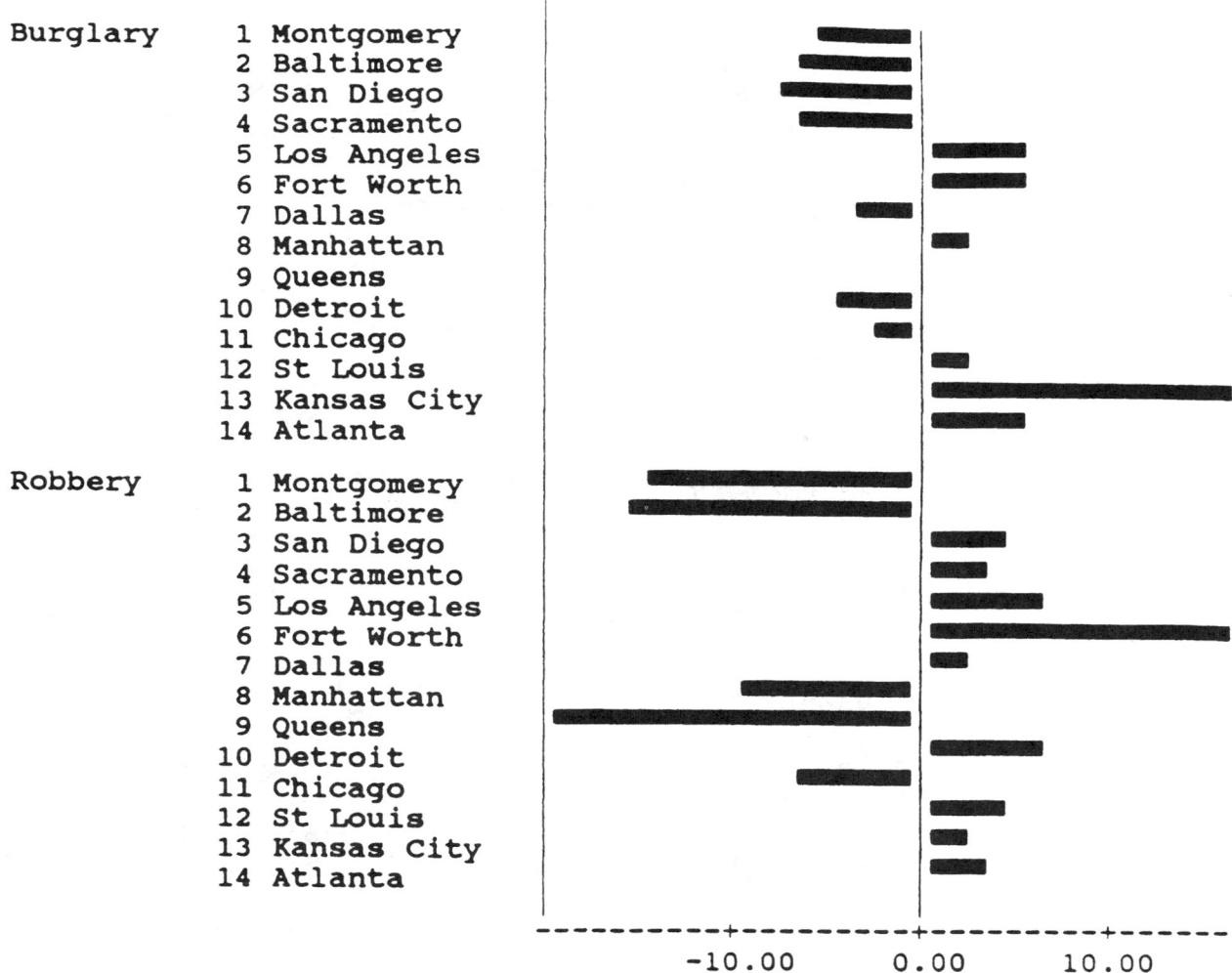

Fig. D.11—Site comparisons: two or more victims?

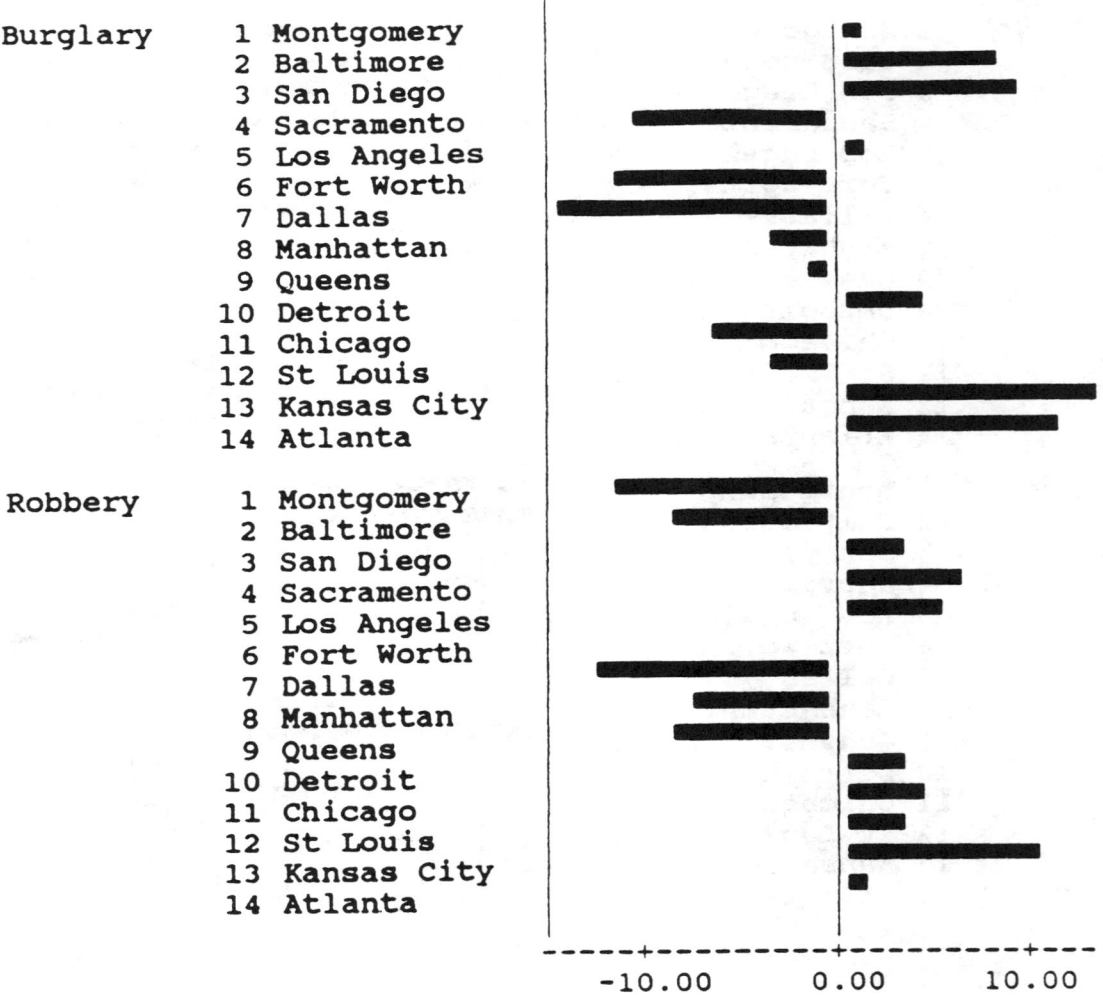

Fig. D.12—Site comparisons: nighttime arrests?

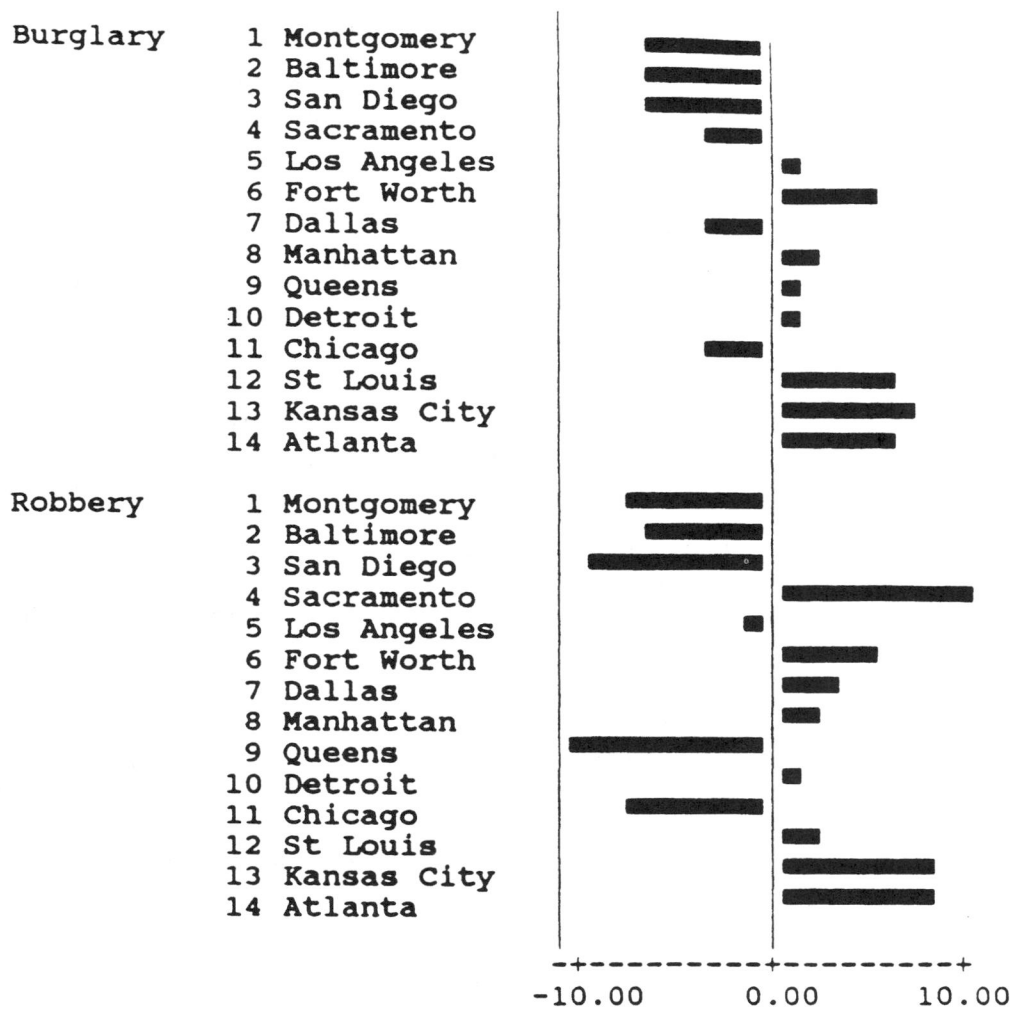

Fig. D.13—Site comparisons: vulnerable victim?

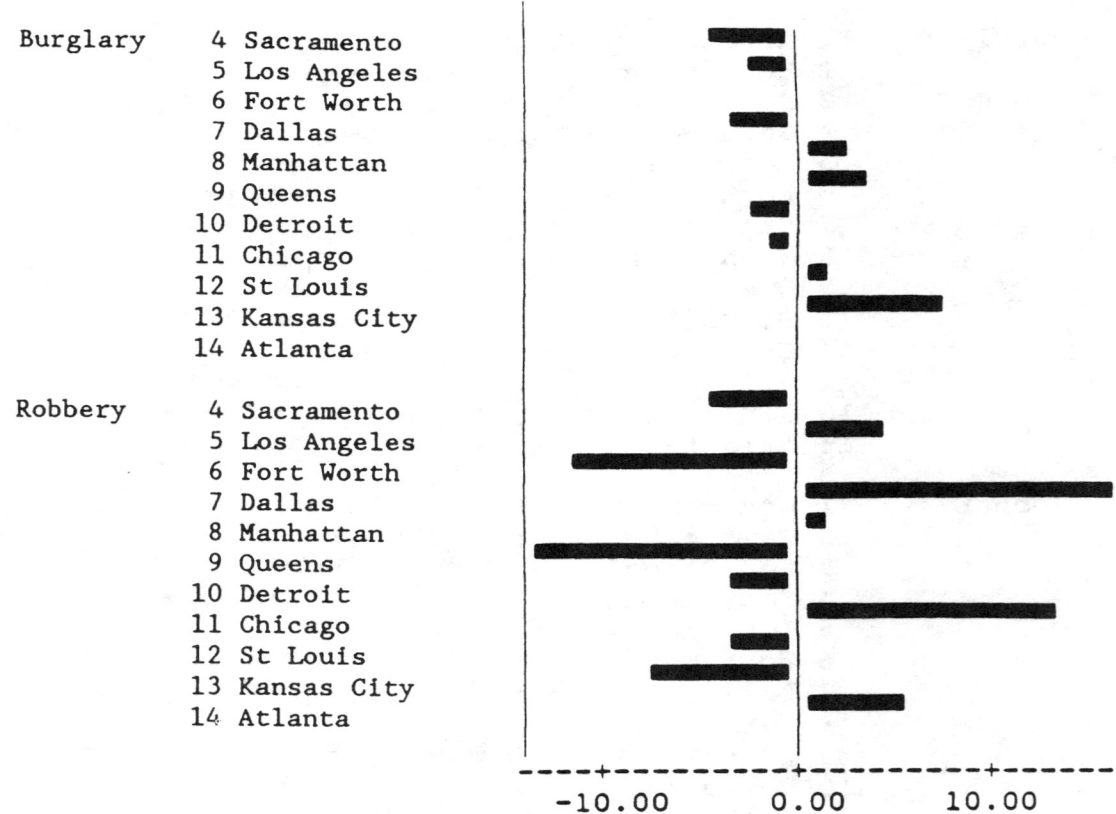

Fig. D.14—Site comparisons: did offender threaten use of weapon?

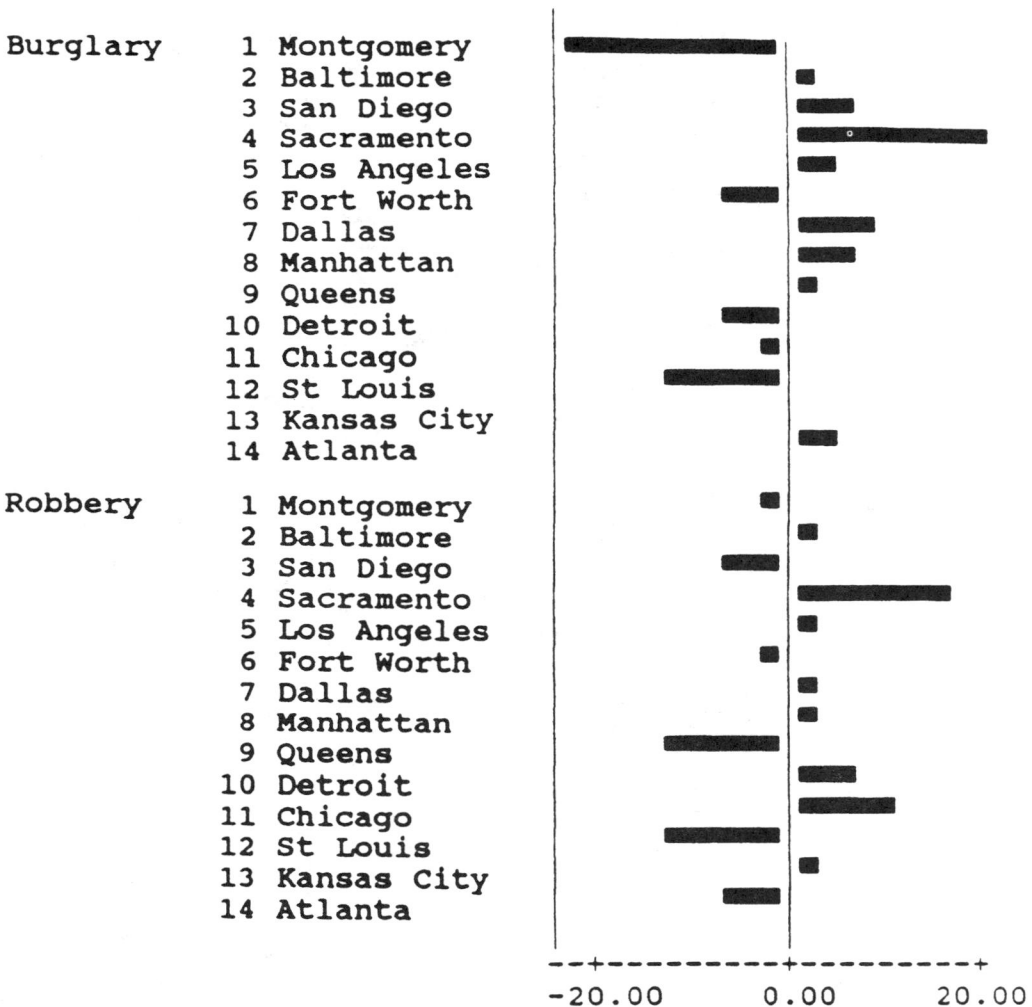

Fig. D.15—Site comparisons: eyewitness?

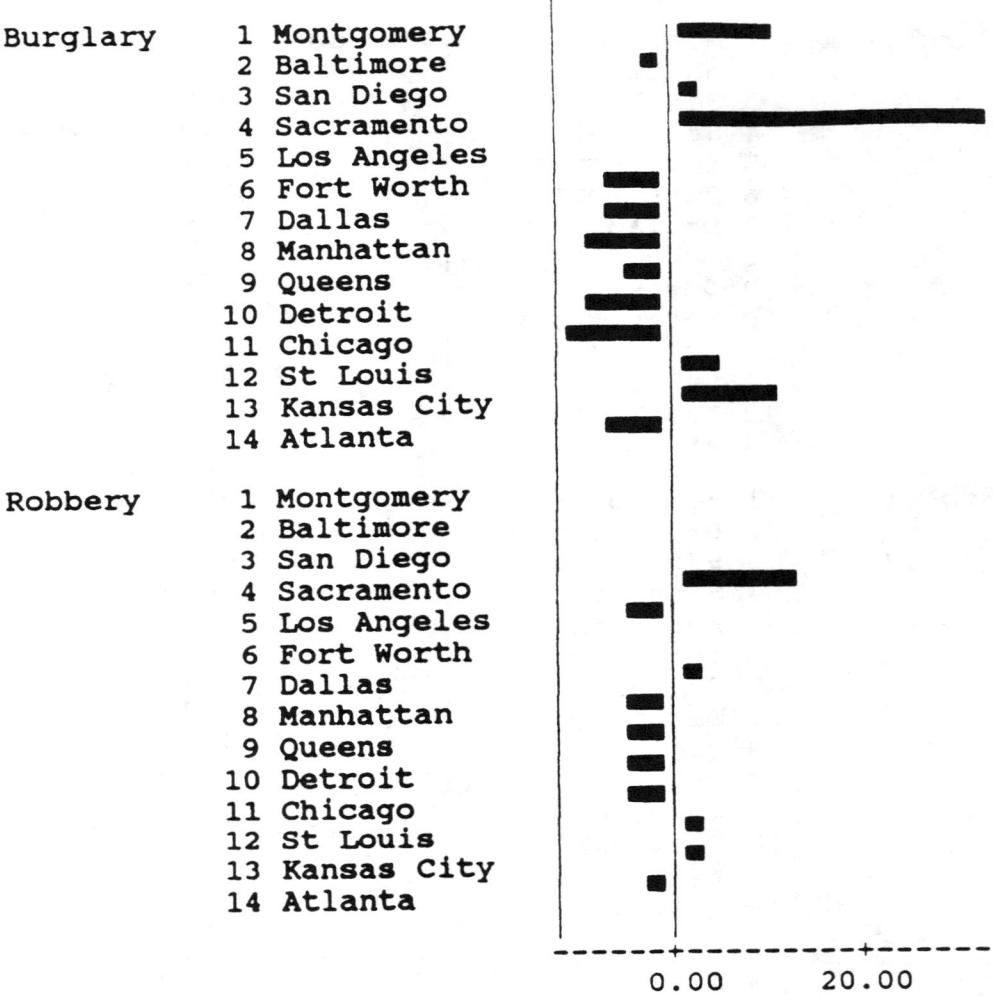

Fig. D.16—Site comparisons: fingerprints?

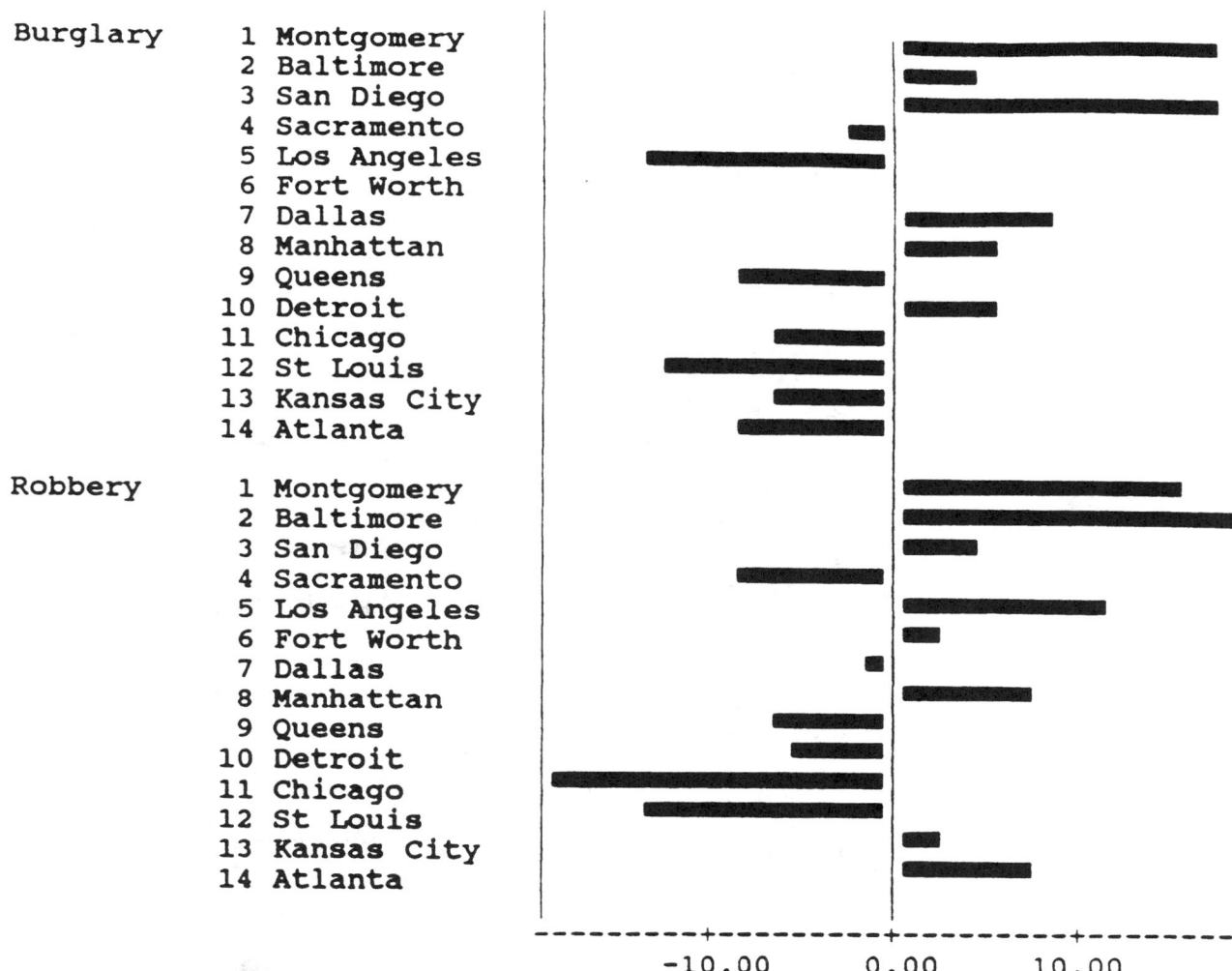

Fig. D.17—Site comparisons: property recovered?

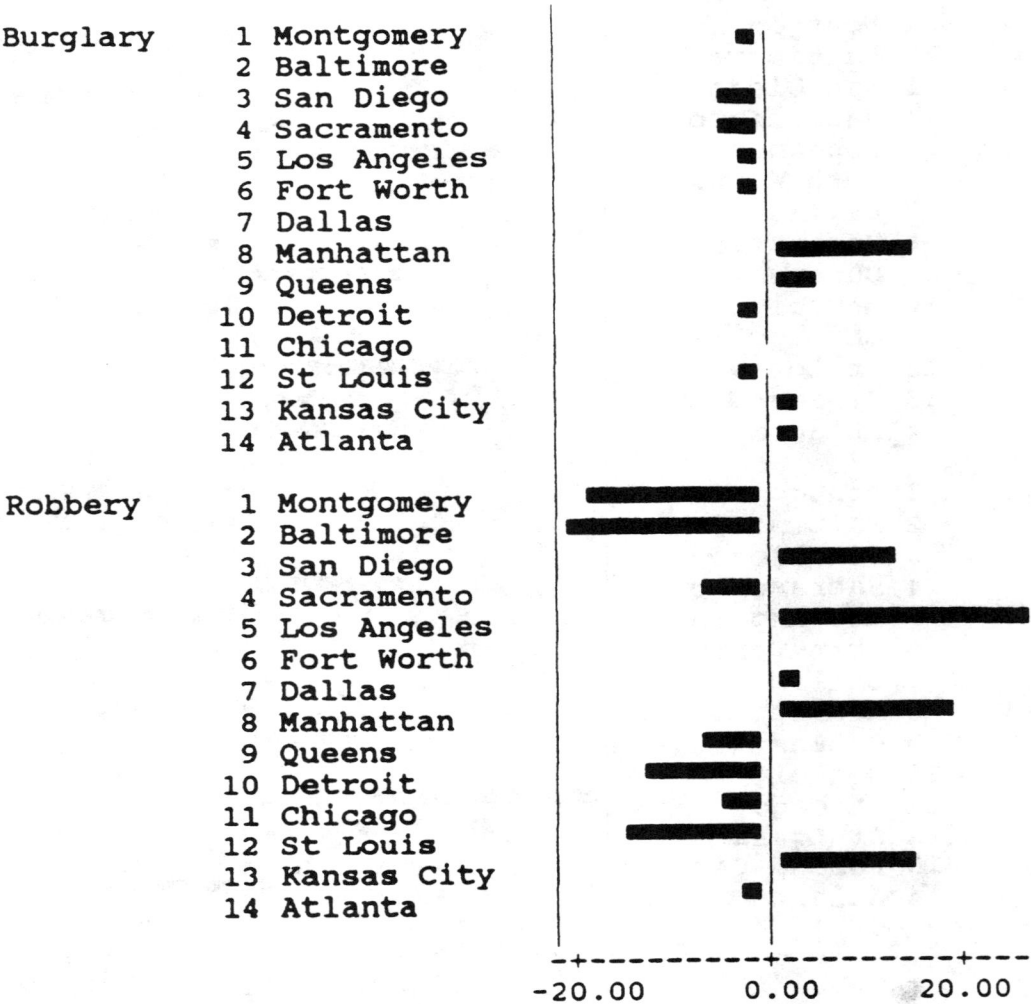

Fig. D.18—Site comparisons: weapon as evidence?

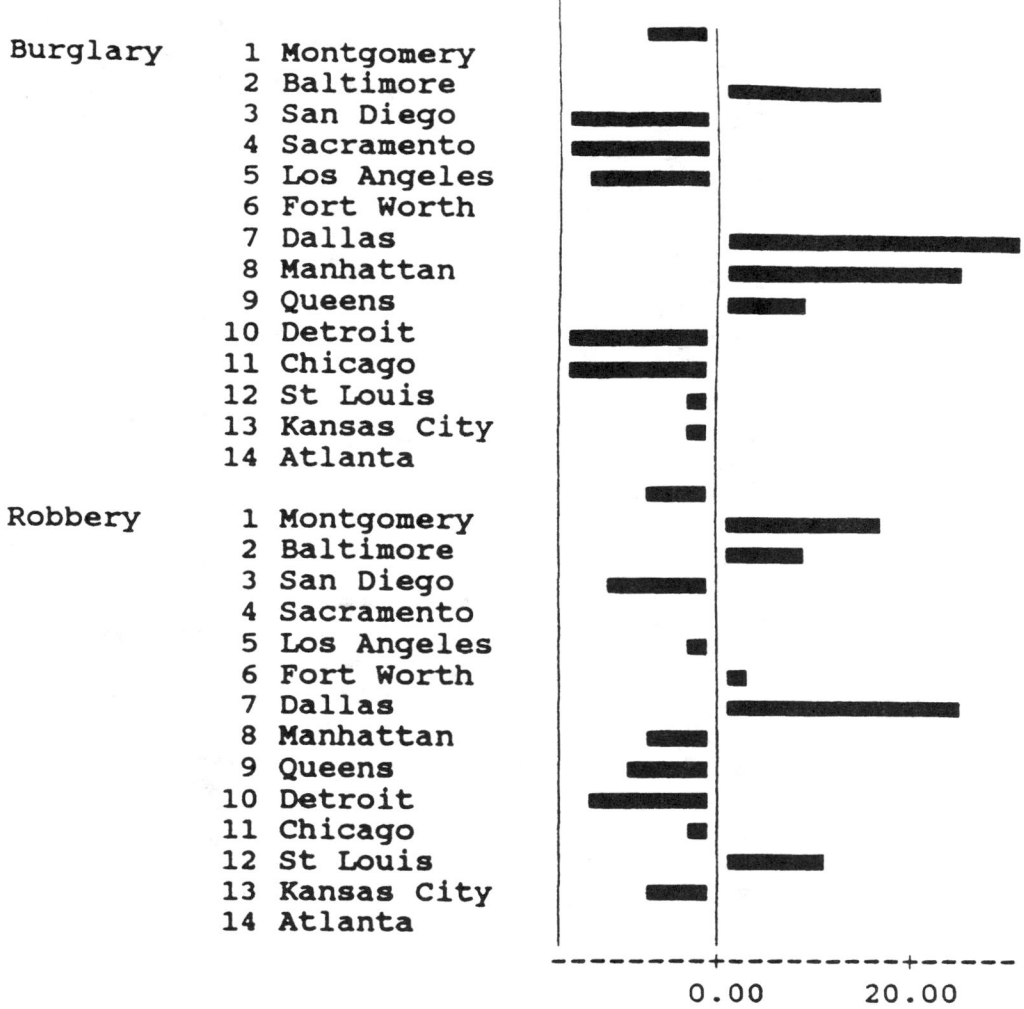

Fig. D.19—Site comparisons: arrested at scene?

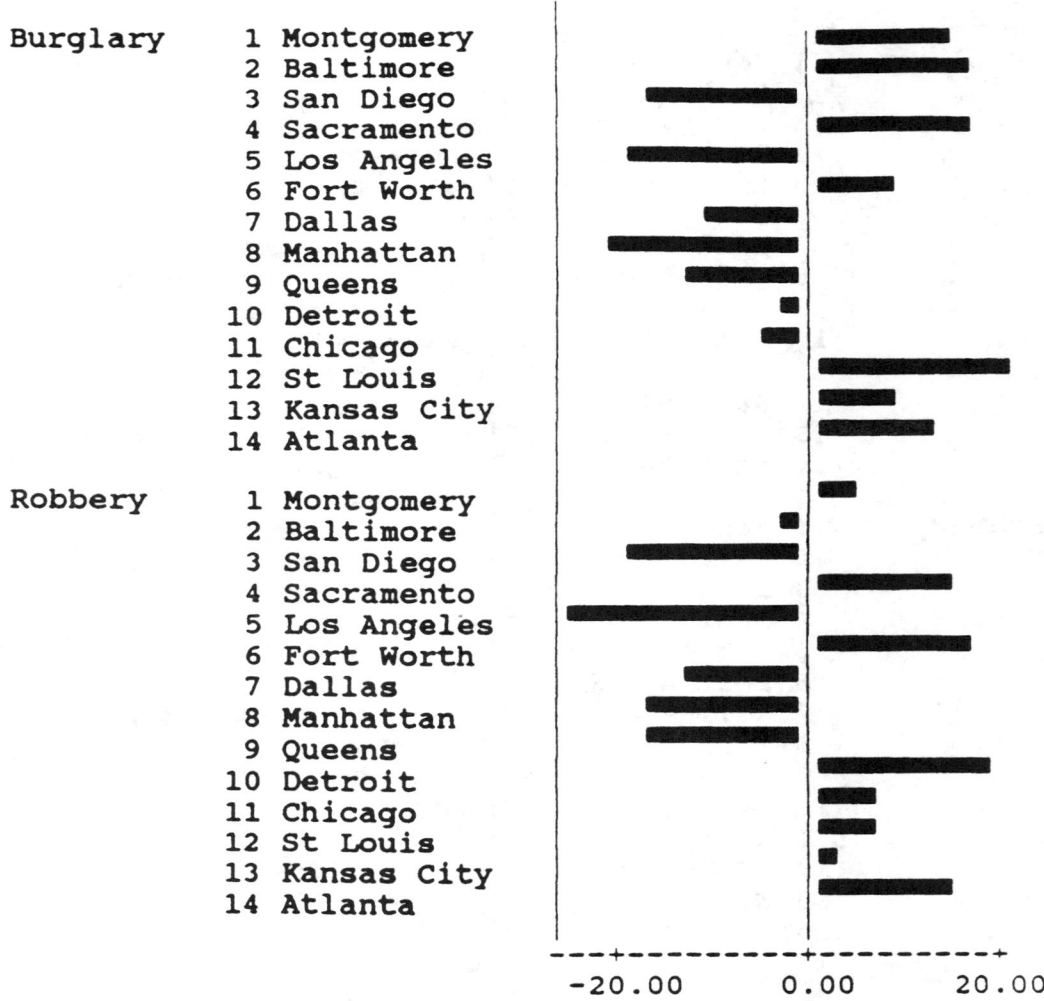

Fig. D.20—Site comparisons: arrested after 24 hours?

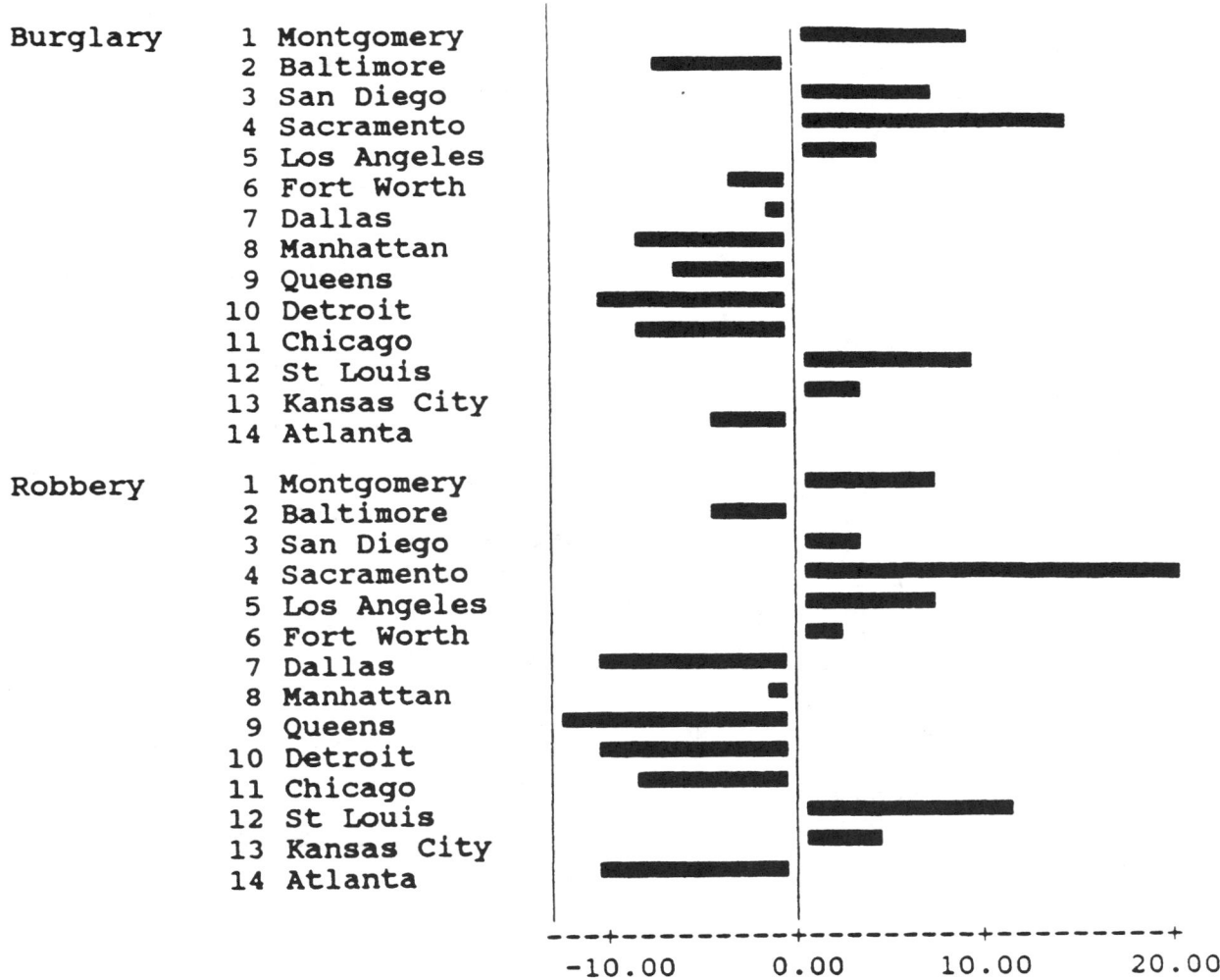

Fig. D.21—Site comparisons: under influence of drugs at arrest?

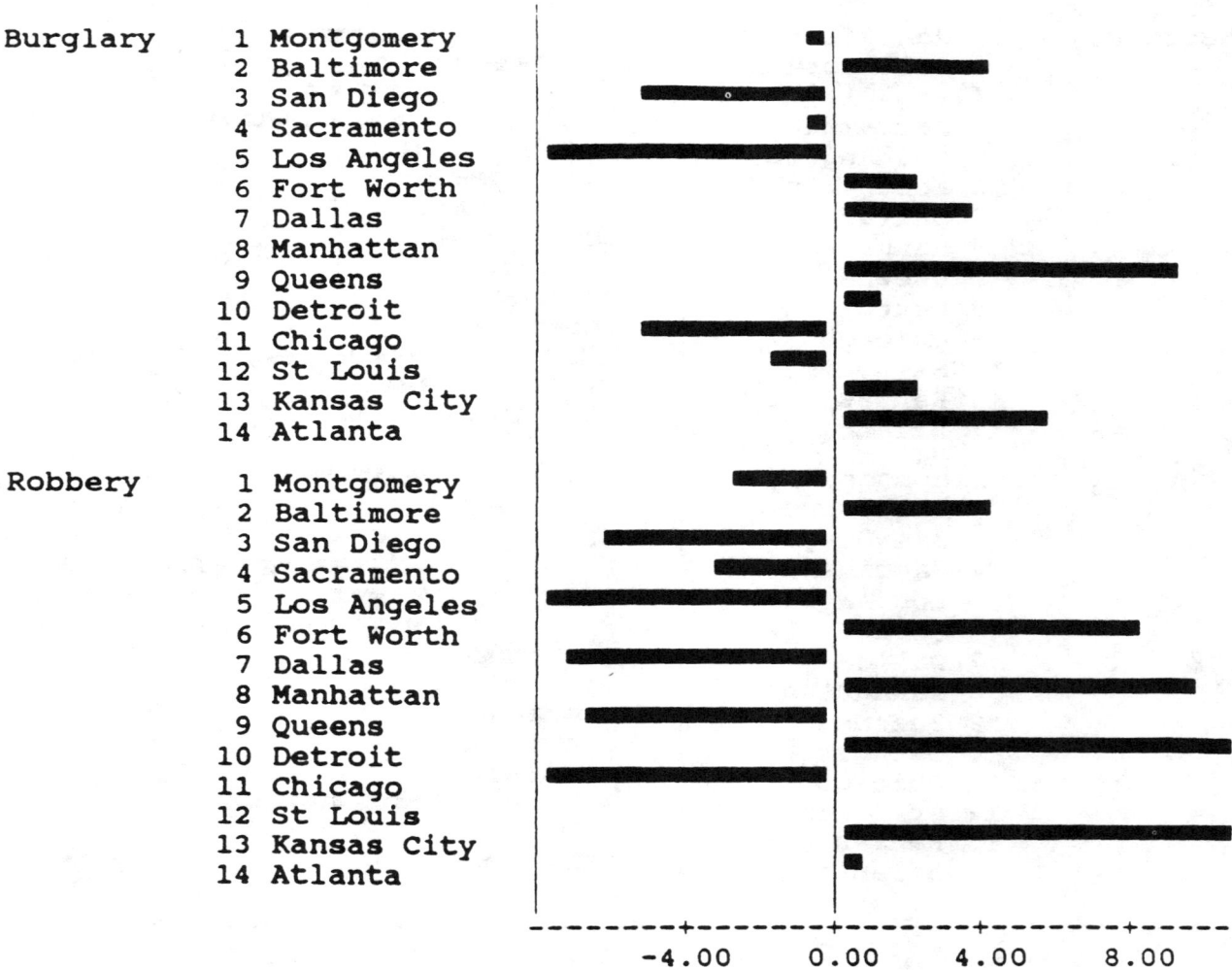

Fig. D.22—Site comparisons: exactly one overlapping case?

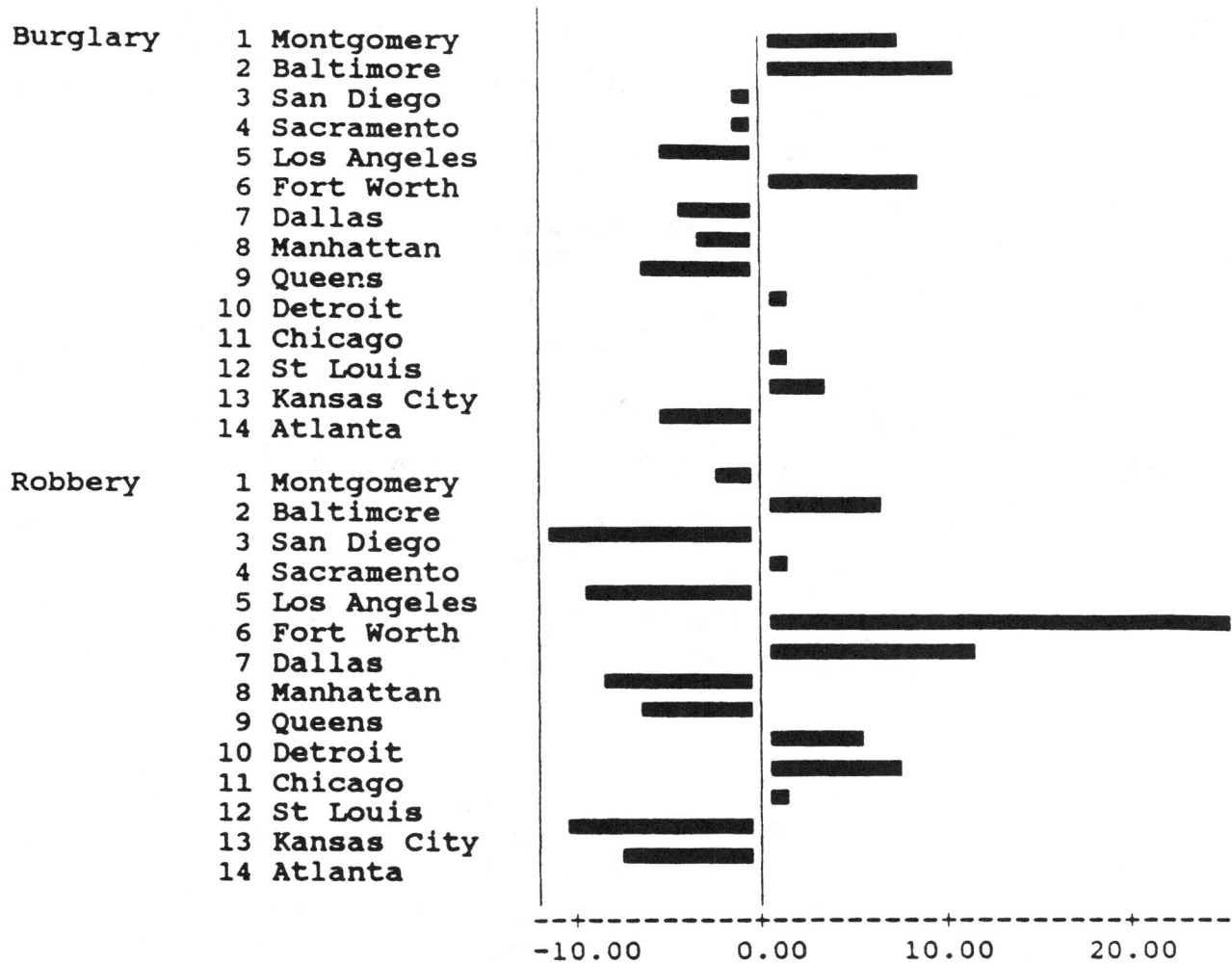

Fig. D.23—Site comparisons: two or more overlapping cases?

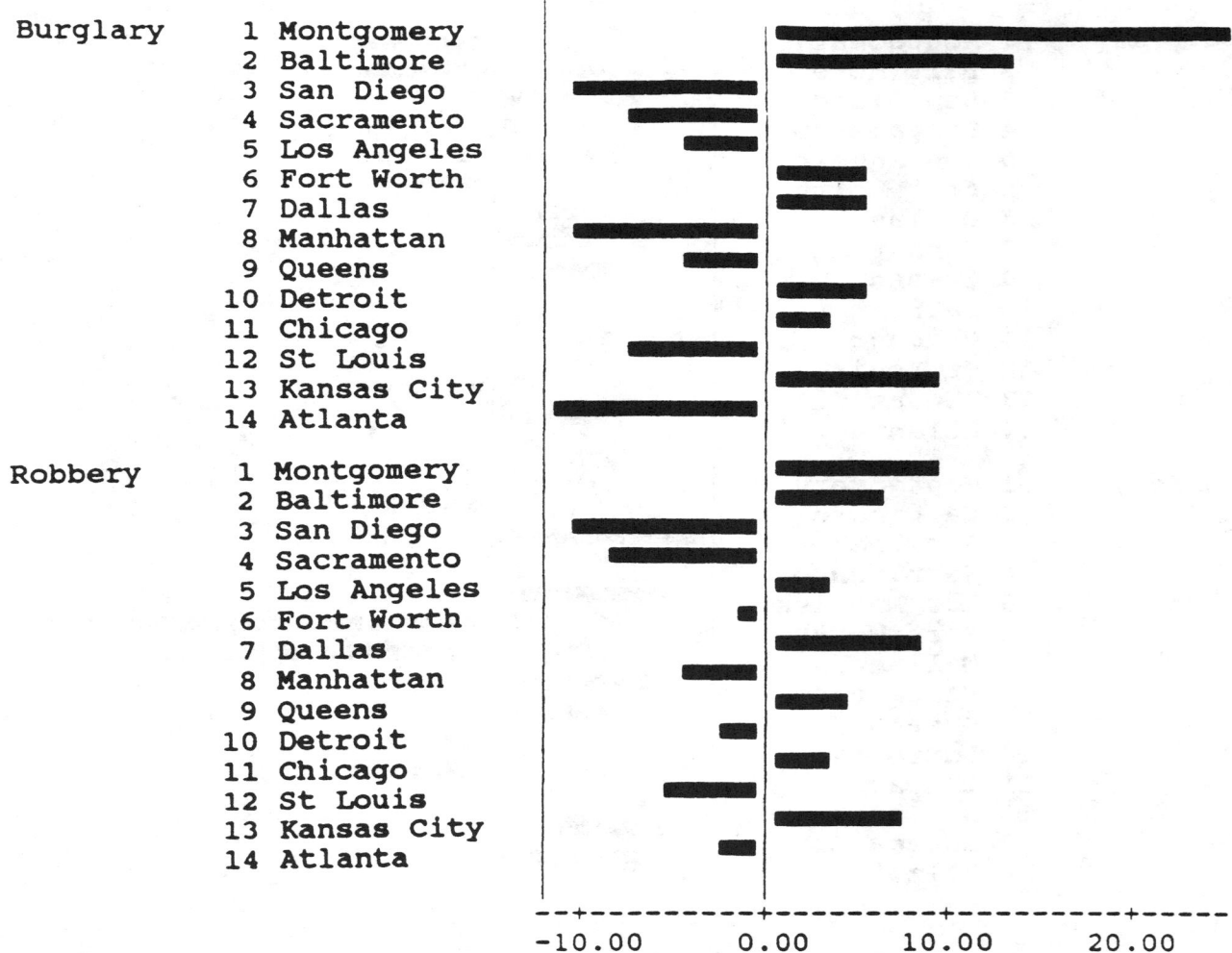

Fig. D.24—Site comparisons: prior adult arrest?

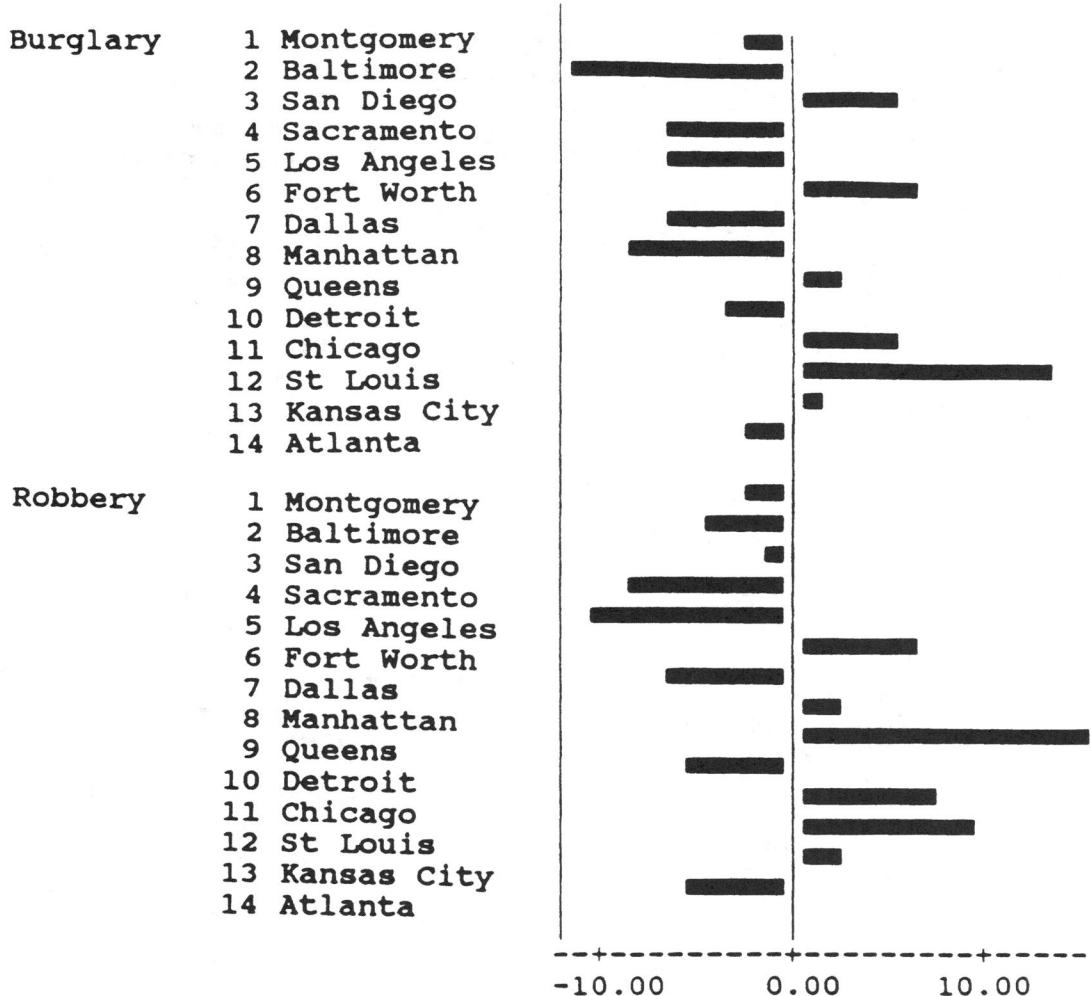

Fig. D.25—Site comparisons: prior adult conviction?

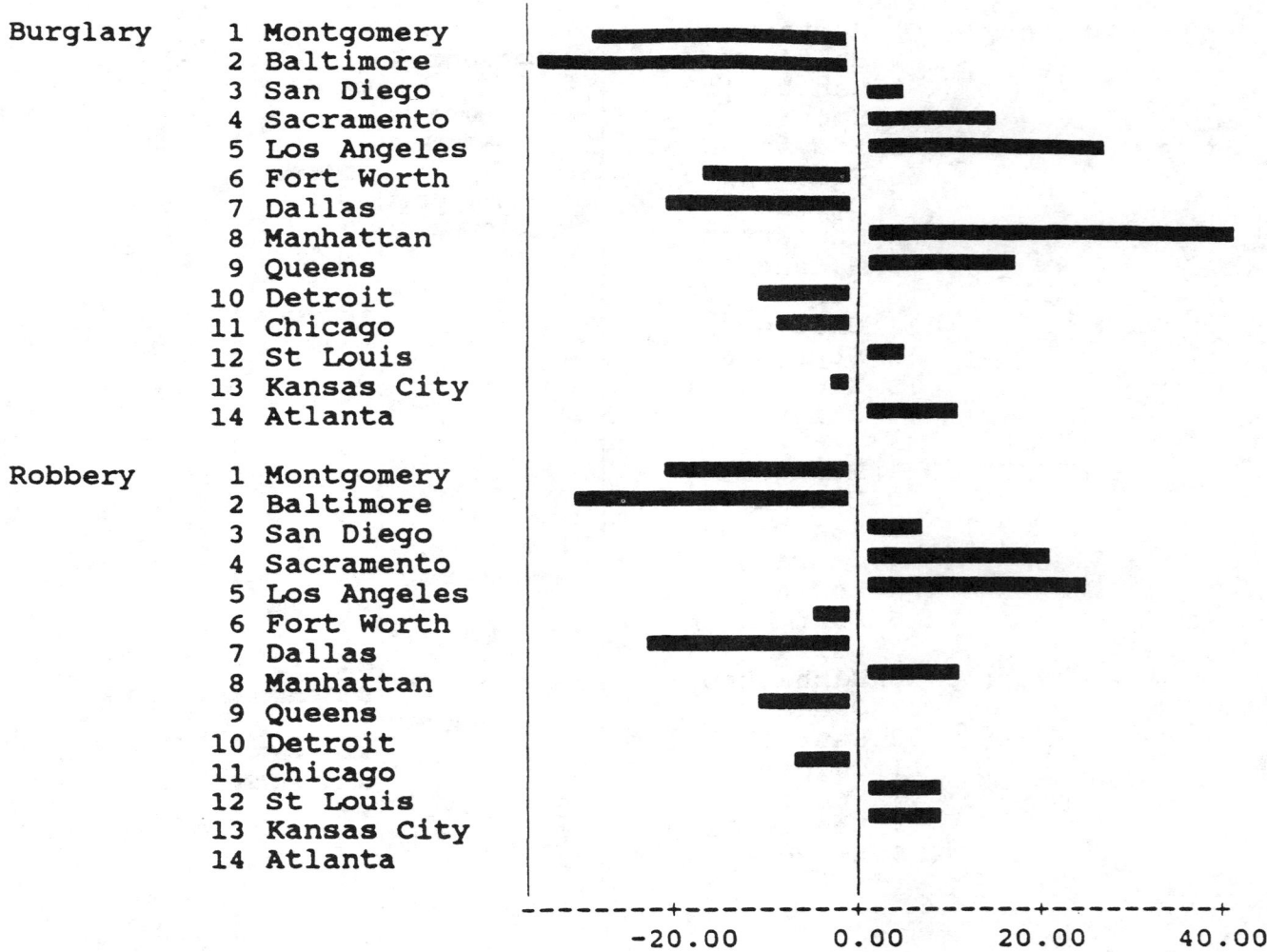

Fig. D.26—Site comparisons: prior adult incarceration?

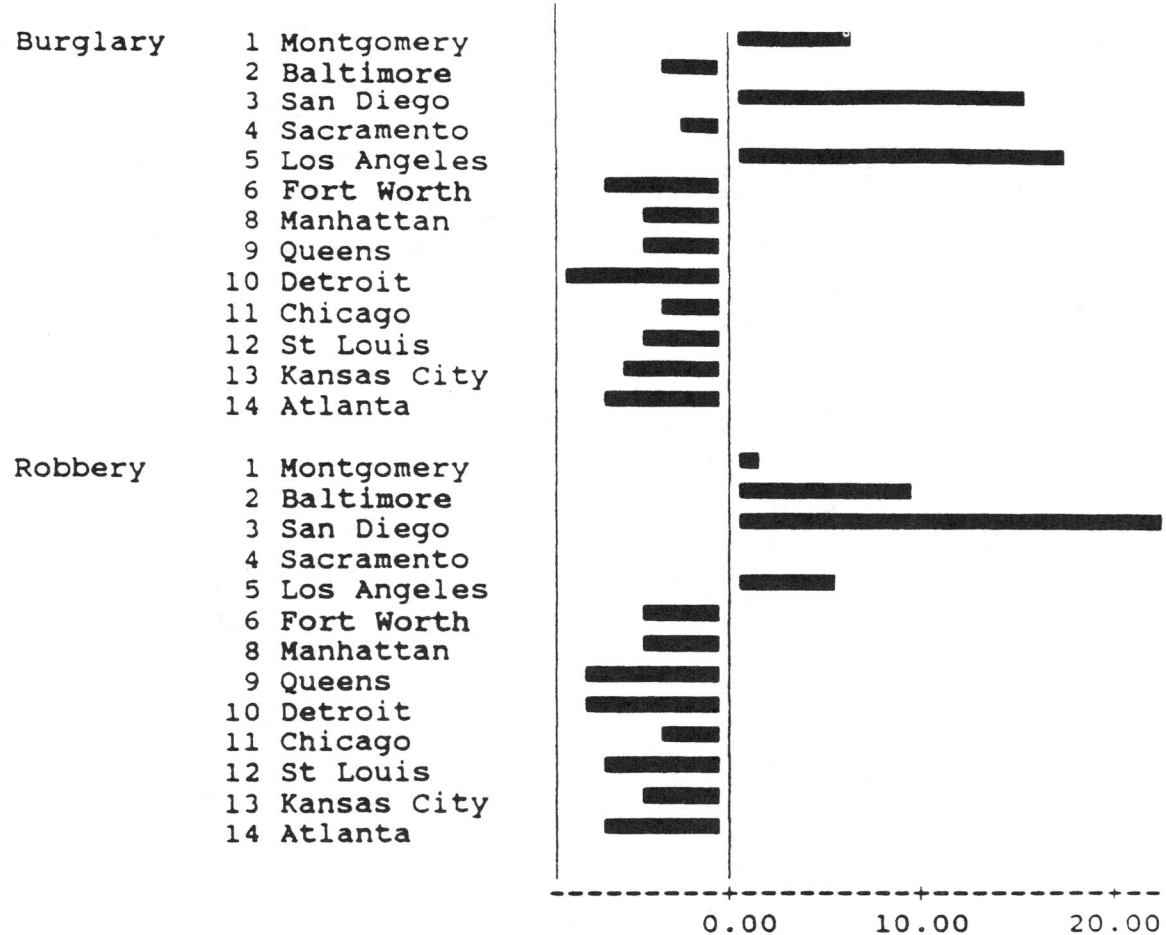

Fig. D.27—Site comparisons: prior juvenile arrest?

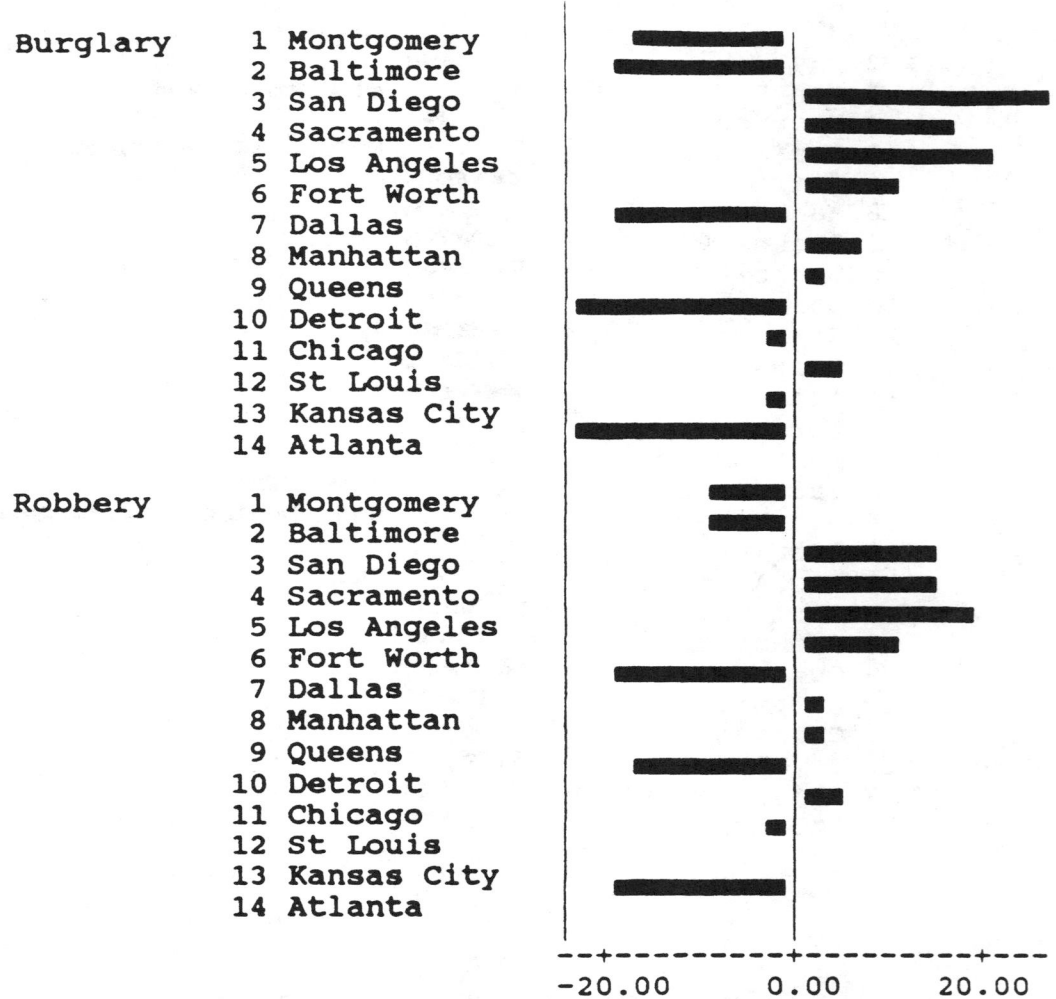

Fig. D.28—Site comparisons: probation/parole/escape at arrest?

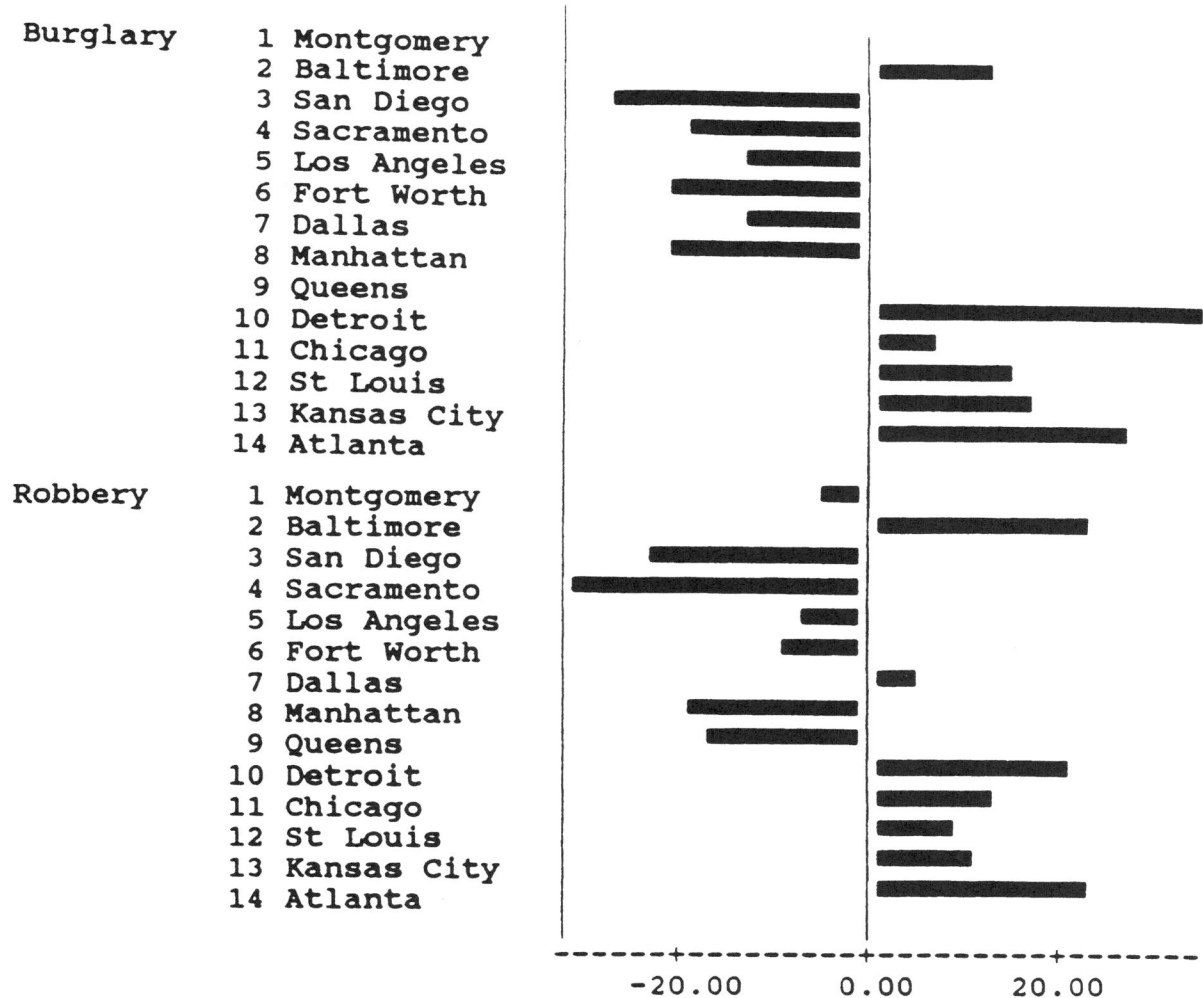

Fig. D.29—Site comparisons: defendant black?

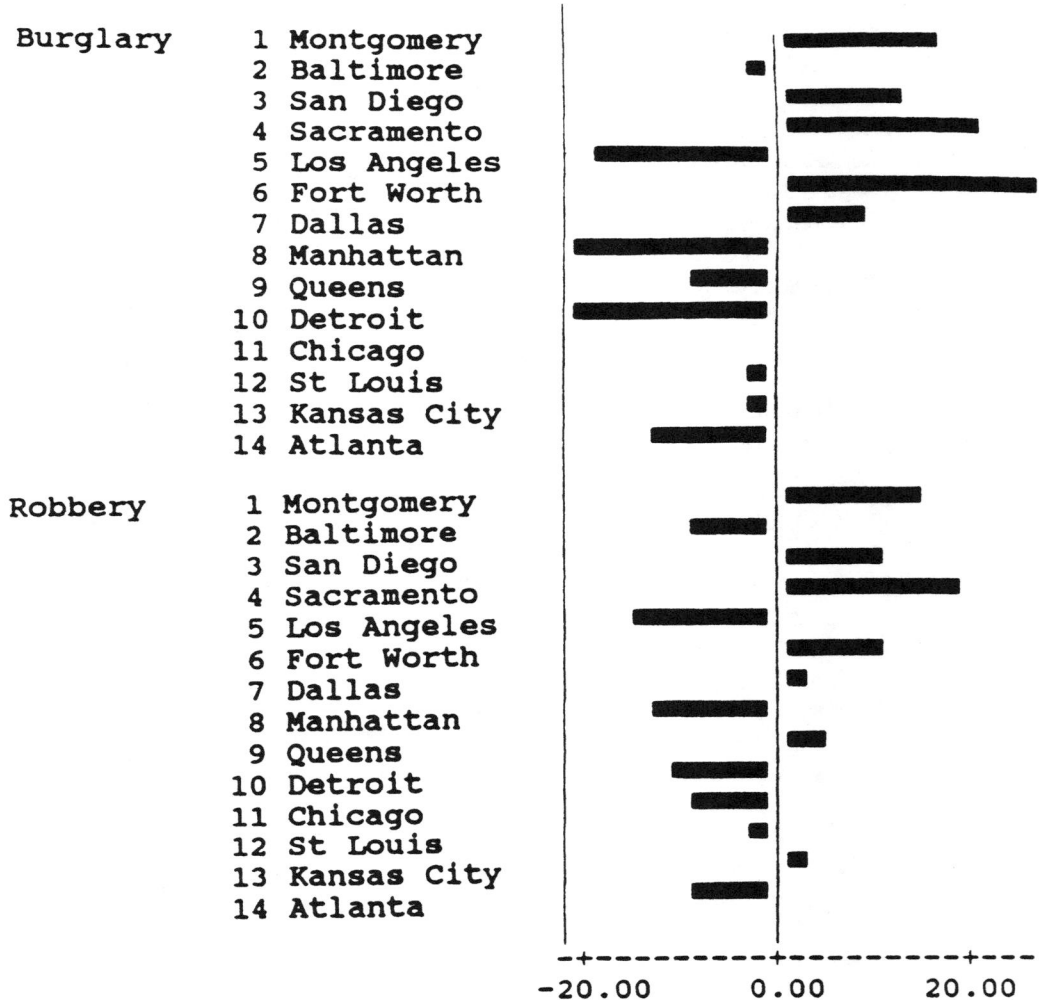

Fig. D.30—Site comparisons: defendant white?

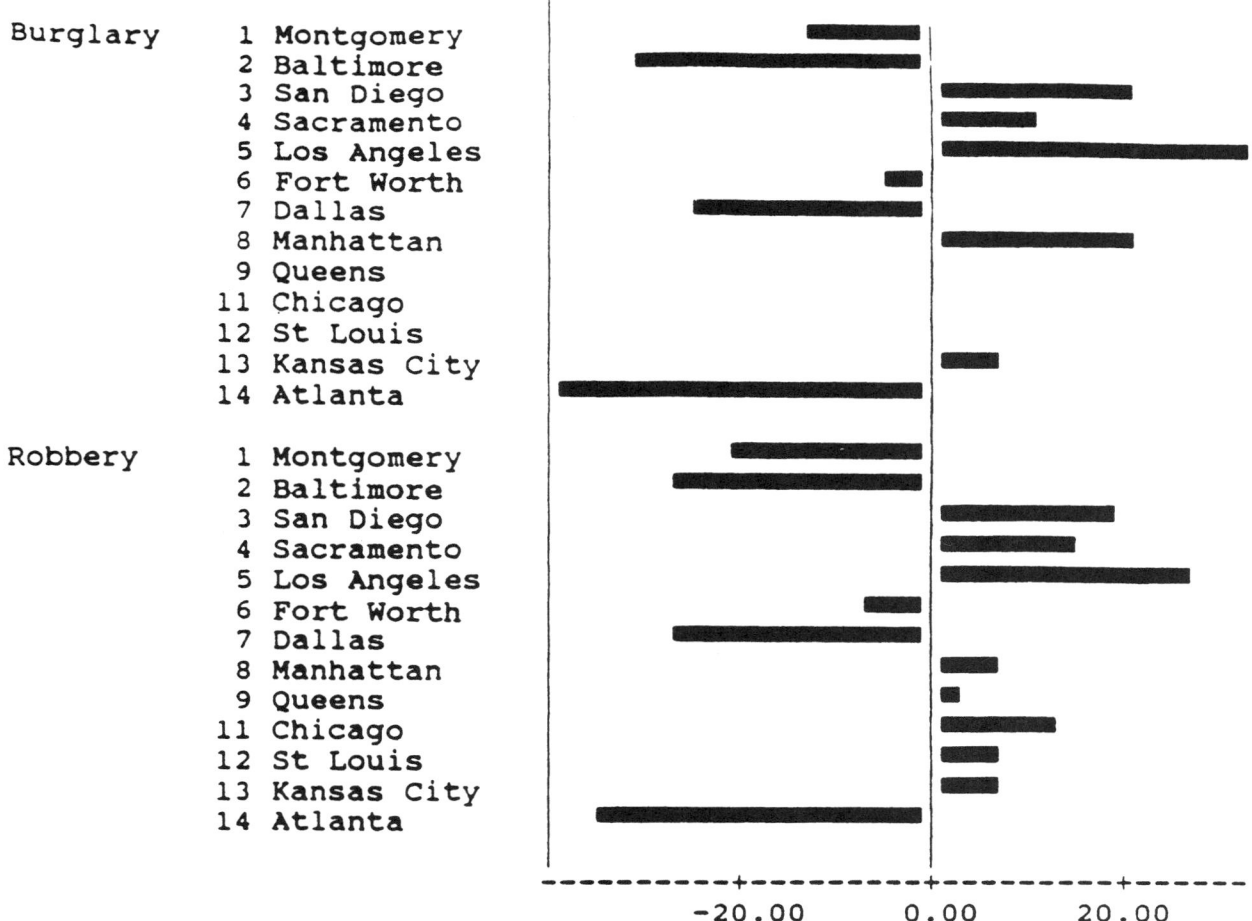

Fig. D.31—Site comparisons: defendant unemployed?

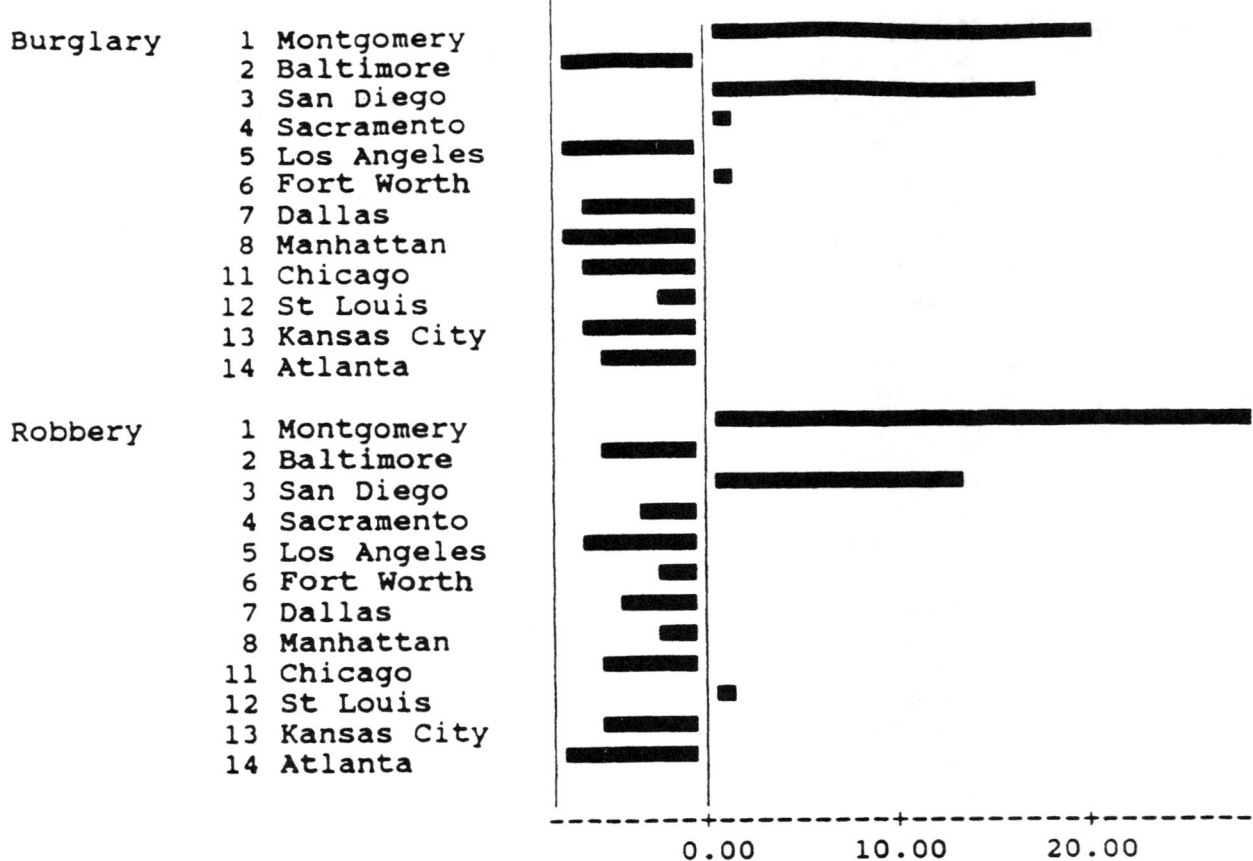

Fig. D.32—Site comparisons: defendant from out of state?

Appendix E

RELATIONSHIP OF OUTCOME VARIABLES TO CASE AND DEFENDANT CHARACTERISTICS

CORRELATES OF CASE OUTCOMES

Table E.1 shows the relationship between each of the major outcome variables and the various incident characteristics for those defendants whose sampled cases involved burglary. The first row for each outcome variable in this table shows the rate across all burglary defendants (i.e., regardless of site). Thus, it shows that 77.9 percent of the 1,115 burglary defendants pleaded guilty. Under the "Factor Present" column, we see that 76.7 percent of the defendants who did *not* have an accomplice pleaded guilty, whereas a plea was entered in 79.2 percent of cases in which there was an accomplice. The two columns under the word "Difference" show how these rates differ from the overall average rate of 77.9 percent. The pluses and minuses in the last two columns show the degree to which the absence or presence of a characteristic corresponded with a higher or lower plea rate. Each plus or minus sign corresponds to one standard error. An asterisk means that the difference was less than one standard error.

In these comparisons, a "standard error" relates to the probability that an observed difference between two percentages arose by chance. Specifically, was the observed percentage when the factor was present really different from the percentage when it was not present? The larger the number of standard errors, the less likely that chance was the source of the difference. A difference of two standard errors corresponds to a likelihood of about 5 in 100 that the observed difference was due to chance. Because so many comparisons were made, however, some of the differences that were two or more standard errors apart may be due to chance. We therefore recommend a more conservative test for deciding whether two percentages really differed from each other—namely, that they are at least three standard errors apart. Finally, even if a difference between two percentages meets this test, it does not indicate that they differ by as many percentage points as are observed.

An inspection of the "Major injury?" row in the "Pleaded guilty?" section of Table E.1 shows that when there was major injury, defendants were less likely to plead than when there was no injury. Similarly, they were somewhat more likely to plead when the incident took place at night than when it did not (there was one plus sign for a "Yes" response to this question and one minus sign for a "No").

Tables E.2 through E.12 provide the corresponding information for all the outcome variables under investigation for each of the six categories of variables listed in Table 6.1.

Table E.1

RELATIONSHIP BETWEEN OUTCOME AND CASE CHARACTERISTICS
INCIDENT OFFENSE: BURGLARY

Outcome	Factor	Factor Present (%)?		Difference (%)		Strength	
		No	Yes	No	Yes	No	Yes
Pleaded guilty?	All cases	77.9	77.9				
	Accomplice?	76.7	79.2	−1.2	1.3	−	+
	Multiple counts?	78.0	76.2	0.1	−1.7	*	−
	Female victim?	78.6	75.2	0.7	−2.7	*	− −
	Major injury?	78.0	73.7	0.1	−4.3	*	− − − −
	2+ victims?	78.1	76.9	0.1	−1.1	*	−
	Nighttime incident?	76.9	79.1	−1.1	1.2	−	+
	Vulnerable victim?	78.2	74.3	0.3	−3.6	*	− − −
	Weapon threatened?	78.3	70.7	0.4	−7.2	*	− − − − − − −
Found guilty?	All cases	45.5	45.5				
	Accomplice?	46.3	44.6	0.7	−0.9	*	*
	Multiple counts?	42.4	93.3	−3.1	47.8	− − −	++++++++++
	Female victim?	46.1	43.6	0.5	−1.9	*	−
	Major injury?	44.8	80.0	−0.7	34.5	*	++++++++++
	2+ victims?	46.2	40.0	0.6	−5.5	*	− − − − −
	Nighttime incident?	47.8	42.9	2.2	−2.7	++	− −
	Vulnerable victim?	47.6	21.1	2.0	−24.5	++	− − − − − − − − − −
	Weapon threatened?	45.9	41.2	0.3	−4.4	*	− − − −
Convicted?	All cases	88.0	88.0				
	Accomplice?	87.5	88.5	−0.5	0.5	*	*
	Multiple counts?	87.4	98.4	−0.6	10.4	*	++++++++++
	Female victim?	88.5	86.0	0.5	−1.9	*	−
	Major injury?	87.9	94.7	−0.1	6.8	*	++++++
	2+ victims?	88.2	86.1	0.2	−1.9	*	−
	Nighttime incident?	87.9	88.1	−0.1	0.1	*	*
	Vulnerable victim?	88.6	79.7	0.6	−8.3	*	− − − − − − − −
	Weapon threatened?	88.3	82.8	0.3	−5.2	*	− − − − −
Incarcerated?	All cases	84.0	84.0				
	Accomplice?	85.3	82.6	1.3	−1.4	+	−
	Multiple counts?	83.2	95.2	−0.8	11.2	*	++++++++++
	Female victim?	83.9	84.3	−0.1	0.3	*	*
	Major injury?	83.8	94.4	−0.2	10.4	*	++++++++++
	2+ victims?	83.8	86.0	−0.2	2.0	*	++
	Nighttime incident?	83.7	84.3	−0.3	0.3	*	*
	Vulnerable victim?	84.3	79.7	0.3	−4.3	*	− − − −
	Weapon threatened?	83.5	93.8	−0.5	9.8	*	+++++++++
Long time?	All cases	50.0	50.0				
	Accomplice?	49.7	50.3	−0.2	0.3	*	*
	Multiple counts?	49.1	62.5	−0.9	12.5	*	++++++++++
	Female victim?	47.2	61.7	−2.8	11.7	− −	++++++++++
	Major injury?	49.5	71.4	−0.4	21.5	*	++++++++++
	2+ victims?	48.1	67.0	−1.9	17.0	−	++++++++++
	Nighttime incident?	46.8	53.2	−3.1	3.3	− − −	+++
	Vulnerable victim?	49.4	57.7	−0.5	7.8	*	++++++
	Weapon threatened?	49.3	61.4	−0.6	11.4	*	++++++++++
Sentence?	All cases	49.8	49.8				
	Accomplice?	49.3	50.3	−0.5	0.5	*	*
	Multiple counts?	49.9	48.3	0.1	−1.5	*	−
	Female victim?	47.8	57.6	−1.9	7.8	−	+++++++
	Major injury?	48.9	93.3	−0.8	43.6	*	++++++++++
	2+ victims?	48.9	57.7	−0.9	7.9	*	+++++++
	Nighttime incident?	48.6	51.0	−1.2	1.3	−	+
	Vulnerable victim?	48.7	67.4	−1.1	17.6	−	++++++++++
	Weapon threatened?	48.0	81.4	−1.8	31.6	−	++++++++++

NOTE: Each plus and minus sign indicates one standard error, and an asterisk indicates less than one standard error.

Table E.2

RELATIONSHIP BETWEEN OUTCOME AND CASE CHARACTERISTICS
INCIDENT OFFENSE: ROBBERY

Outcome	Factor	Factor Present (%)?		Difference (%)		Strength	
		No	Yes	No	Yes	No	Yes
Pleaded guilty?	All cases	68.2	68.2				
	Accomplice?	67.7	68.5	−0.6	0.3	*	*
	Multiple counts?	67.9	70.7	−0.3	2.5	*	++
	Female victim?	64.0	74.6	−4.2	6.4	− − − −	++++++
	Major injury?	69.2	60.0	1.0	−8.2	+	− − − − − − − −
	2+ victims?	65.9	71.6	−2.3	3.4	− −	+++
	Nighttime incident?	64.0	70.1	−4.2	1.9	− − − −	+
	Vulnerable victim?	68.3	67.2	0.1	−1.1	*	−
	Weapon threatened?	61.0	71.5	−7.3	3.3	− − − − − −	+++
Found guilty?	All cases	49.9	49.9				
	Accomplice?	49.6	50.0	−0.2	0.1	*	*
	Multiple counts?	47.2	71.8	−2.6	21.9	− −	++++++++++
	Female victim?	47.2	55.7	−2.7	5.8	− −	+++++
	Major injury?	48.6	58.0	−1.3	8.1	−	++++++++
	2+ victims?	47.5	54.3	−2.4	4.4	− −	++++
	Nighttime incident?	44.2	53.0	−5.7	3.1	− − − − −	+++
	Vulnerable victim?	49.1	55.6	−0.8	5.7	*	+++++
	Weapon threatened?	46.8	51.8	−3.1	1.9	− − −	+
Convicted?	All cases	84.1	84.1				
	Accomplice?	83.7	84.3	−0.4	0.2	*	*
	Multiple counts?	83.1	91.7	−1.0	7.7	−	+++++++
	Female victim?	81.0	88.7	−3.1	4.7	− − −	++++
	Major injury?	84.2	83.2	0.1	−0.9	*	*
	2+ victims?	82.1	87.0	−2.0	3.0	−	++
	Nighttime incident?	79.9	85.9	−4.2	1.9	− − − −	+
	Vulnerable victim?	83.9	85.4	−0.2	1.3	*	+
	Weapon threatened?	79.2	86.2	−4.8	2.2	− − − −	++
Incarcerated?	All cases	92.5	92.5				
	Accomplice?	93.2	92.2	0.7	−0.4	*	*
	Multiple counts?	91.7	98.4	−0.8	5.8	*	+++++
	Female victim?	91.5	94.0	−1.1	1.5	−	+
	Major injury?	91.9	98.1	−0.7	5.5	*	+++++
	2+ victims?	90.3	95.7	−2.2	3.2	− −	+++
	Nighttime incident?	94.1	91.9	1.5	−0.6	+	*
	Vulnerable victim?	92.1	95.7	−0.4	3.2	*	+++
	Weapon threatened?	89.0	94.0	−3.5	1.5	− − −	+
Long time?	All cases	50.0	50.0				
	Accomplice?	49.5	50.2	−0.5	0.2	*	*
	Multiple counts?	48.8	58.6	−1.1	8.7	−	++++++++
	Female victim?	44.5	58.9	−5.5	8.9	− − − − −	++++++++
	Major injury?	49.2	55.7	−0.7	5.8	*	+++++
	2+ victims?	47.5	53.7	−2.5	3.8	− −	+++
	Nighttime incident?	45.8	51.9	−4.2	2.0	− − − −	+
	Vulnerable victim?	48.8	58.8	−1.2	8.9	−	++++++++
	Weapon threatened?	46.1	51.9	−3.8	1.9	− − −	+
Sentence?	All cases	49.8	49.8				
	Accomplice?	52.0	48.7	2.1	−1.2	++	−
	Multiple counts?	48.6	57.9	−1.2	8.1	−	++++++++
	Female victim?	37.8	66.8	−12.0	16.9	− − − − − − − − − −	++++++++++
	Major injury?	49.0	56.4	−0.8	6.6	*	++++++
	2+ victims?	42.2	60.4	−7.6	10.6	− − − − − −	++++++++++
	Nighttime incident?	51.0	49.3	1.1	−0.5	+	*
	Vulnerable victim?	47.9	63.8	−1.9	14.0	−	++++++++++
	Weapon threatened?	40.0	53.7	−9.8	3.9	− − − − − − − −	+++

NOTE: Each plus and minus sign indicates one standard error, and an asterisk indicates less than one standard error.

Table E.3

RELATIONSHIP BETWEEN OUTCOME AND CASE CHARACTERISTICS
EVIDENCE OFFENSE: BURGLARY

Outcome	Factor	Factor Present (%)? No	Factor Present (%)? Yes	Difference (%) No	Difference (%) Yes	Strength No	Strength Yes
Pleaded guilty?	All cases	77.9	77.9				
	Eyewitness?	75.7	80.1	-2.3	2.2	- -	++
	Fingerprints?	77.7	79.3	-0.2	1.3	*	+
	Property?	70.7	82.8	-7.2	4.9	- - - - - - -	++++
	Weapon?	77.9	78.7	-0.1	0.7	*	*
Found guilty?	All cases	45.5	45.5				
	Eyewitness?	37.6	54.9	-7.9	9.3	- - - - - - -	+++++++++
	Fingerprints?	43.3	62.1	-2.2	16.5	- -	++++++++++
	Property?	39.4	52.6	-6.1	7.1	- - - - - -	+++++++
	Weapon?	43.9	68.8	-1.6	23.2	-	++++++++++
Convicted?	All cases	88.0	88.0				
	Eyewitness?	84.8	91.0	-3.2	3.0	- - -	+++
	Fingerprints?	87.4	92.1	-0.6	4.2	*	++++
	Property?	82.3	91.9	-5.7	3.9	- - - - -	+++
	Weapon?	87.6	93.3	-0.4	5.4	*	+++++
Incarcerated?	All cases	84.0	84.0				
	Eyewitness?	80.2	87.4	-3.8	3.4	- - -	+++
	Fingerprints?	83.0	90.7	-1.0	6.7	-	++++++
	Property?	79.8	86.6	-4.2	2.6	- - - -	++
	Weapon?	83.2	94.3	-0.8	10.3	*	++++++++++
Long time?	All cases	50.0	50.0				
	Eyewitness?	46.5	53.3	-3.4	3.3	- - -	+++
	Fingerprints?	48.5	59.2	-1.4	9.2	-	+++++++++
	Property?	52.0	48.6	2.1	-1.4	++	-
	Weapon?	48.4	70.9	-1.6	20.9	-	++++++++++
Sentence?	All cases	49.8	49.8				
	Eyewitness?	46.2	52.8	-3.6	3.0	- - -	+++
	Fingerprints?	47.5	63.2	-2.2	13.4	- -	++++++++++
	Property?	47.1	51.3	-2.7	1.5	- -	+
	Weapon?	47.2	79.7	-2.6	29.9	- -	++++++++++

NOTE: Each plus and minus sign indicates one standard error, and an asterisk indicates less than one standard error.

Table E.4

RELATIONSHIP BETWEEN OUTCOME AND CASE CHARACTERISTICS
EVIDENCE OFFENSE: ROBBERY

Outcome	Factor	Factor Present (%)? No	Factor Present (%)? Yes	Difference (%) No	Difference (%) Yes	Strength No	Strength Yes
Pleaded guilty?	All cases	68.2	68.2				
	Eyewitness?	64.6	74.5	−3.6	6.3	− − −	++++++
	Fingerprints?	67.6	78.3	−0.6	10.1	*	++++++++++
	Property?	63.0	73.9	−5.2	5.7	− − − − −	+++++
	Weapon?	65.8	72.7	−2.4	4.5	− −	++++
Found guilty?	All cases	49.9	49.9				
	Eyewitness?	45.0	61.7	−4.9	11.8	− − − −	++++++++++
	Fingerprints?	49.1	69.2	−0.7	19.4	*	++++++++++
	Property?	44.6	58.0	−5.3	8.2	− − − − −	++++++++
	Weapon?	47.1	56.4	−2.8	6.5	− −	++++++
Convicted?	All cases	84.1	84.1				
	Eyewitness?	80.5	90.2	−3.5	6.2	− − −	++++++
	Fingerprints?	83.5	93.3	−0.5	9.3	*	+++++++++
	Property?	79.5	89.1	−4.6	5.0	− − − −	++++
	Weapon?	81.9	88.1	−2.2	4.0	− −	++++
Incarcerated?	All cases	92.5	92.5				
	Eyewitness?	91.5	94.2	−1.1	1.6	−	+
	Fingerprints?	92.3	96.4	−0.2	3.9	*	+++
	Property?	92.5	92.6	−0.1	0.1	*	*
	Weapon?	92.1	93.2	−0.4	0.7	*	*
Long time?	All cases	50.0	50.0				
	Eyewitness?	47.8	53.6	−2.2	3.6	− −	+++
	Fingerprints?	50.0	48.4	0.1	−1.6	*	−
	Property?	47.9	52.2	−2.1	2.2	− −	++
	Weapon?	50.5	48.9	0.6	−1.1	*	−
Sentence?	All cases	49.8	49.8				
	Eyewitness?	44.1	58.3	−5.7	8.5	− − − − −	++++++++
	Fingerprints?	48.1	76.9	−1.7	27.1	−	++++++++++
	Property?	47.3	52.3	−2.5	2.4	− −	++
	Weapon?	47.6	53.6	−2.2	3.8	− −	+++

NOTE: Each plus and minus sign indicates one standard error, and an asterisk indicates less than one standard error.

Table E.5

RELATIONSHIP BETWEEN OUTCOME AND CASE CHARACTERISTICS
PROCESS OFFENSE: BURGLARY

		Factor Present (%)?		Difference (%)		Strength	
Outcome	Factor	No	Yes	No	Yes	No	Yes
Pleaded guilty?	All cases	77.9	77.9				
	At scene?	74.4	83.2	−3.5	5.2	− − −	+++++
	Delayed?	74.3	83.1	−3.6	5.1	− − −	+++++
	Drugs?	77.6	80.9	−0.3	2.9	*	++
Found guilty?	All cases	45.5	45.5				
	At scene?	38.0	62.7	−7.5	17.1	− − − − − − −	++++++++++
	Delayed?	47.0	42.3	1.5	−3.2	+	− − −
	Drugs?	42.0	81.8	−3.6	36.3	− − −	++++++++++
Convicted?	All cases	88.0	88.0				
	At scene?	84.2	93.7	−3.8	5.7	− − −	+++++
	Delayed?	86.4	90.2	−1.6	2.3	−	++
	Drugs?	87.0	96.5	−1.0	8.5	*	++++++++
Incarcerated?	All cases	84.0	84.0				
	At scene?	79.9	89.5	−4.1	5.5	− − − −	+++++
	Delayed?	84.4	83.4	0.4	−0.6	*	*
	Drugs?	83.7	86.5	−0.3	2.5	*	++
Time?	All cases	50.0	50.0				
	At scene?	49.2	51.1	−0.8	1.1	*	+
	Delayed?	46.7	54.4	−3.2	4.5	− − −	++++
	Drugs?	49.7	52.1	−0.3	2.1	*	++
Sentence?	All cases	49.8	49.8				
	At scene?	47.8	52.1	−1.9	2.3	−	++
	Delayed?	44.5	56.9	−5.3	7.1	− − − − −	+++++++
	Drugs?	49.0	55.3	−0.7	5.6	*	+++++

NOTE: Each plus and minus sign indicates one standard error, and an asterisk indicates less than one standard error.

Table E.6

RELATIONSHIP BETWEEN OUTCOME AND CASE CHARACTERISTICS
PROCESS OFFENSE: ROBBERY

Outcome	Factor	Factor Present (%)?		Difference (%)		Strength	
		No	Yes	No	Yes	No	Yes
Pleaded guilty?	All cases	68.2	68.2				
	At scene?	65.3	78.9	−2.9	10.7	− −	++++++++++
	Delayed?	68.0	68.4	−0.2	0.2	*	*
	Drugs?	67.4	74.3	−0.8	6.1	*	++++++
Found guilty?	All cases	49.9	49.9				
	At scene?	49.0	54.9	−0.8	5.0	*	+++++
	Delayed?	49.2	50.6	−0.7	0.7	*	*
	Drugs?	49.8	50.0	−0.0	0.1	*	*
Convicted?	All cases	84.1	84.1				
	At scene?	82.3	90.5	−1.7	6.4	−	++++++
	Delayed?	83.7	84.4	−0.3	0.3	*	*
	Drugs?	83.6	87.1	−0.4	3.1	*	+++
Incarcerated?	All cases	92.5	92.5				
	At scene?	91.7	95.4	−0.9	2.9	*	++
	Delayed?	90.8	94.3	−1.7	1.8	−	+
	Drugs?	92.5	92.6	−0.0	0.1	*	*
Time?	All cases	50.0	50.0				
	At scene?	48.8	54.3	−1.2	4.3	−	++++
	Delayed?	42.6	57.6	−7.4	7.6	− − − − − − −	+++++++
	Drugs?	50.6	44.9	0.7	−5.1	*	− − − − −
Sentence?	All cases	49.8	49.8				
	At scene?	52.3	41.7	2.5	−8.2	++	− − − − − − − −
	Delayed?	37.1	62.7	−12.8	12.9	− − − − − − − − − −	++++++++++
	Drugs?	49.3	53.2	−0.5	3.4	*	+++

NOTE: Each plus and minus sign indicates one standard error, and an asterisk indicates less than one standard error.

Table E.7

RELATIONSHIP BETWEEN OUTCOME AND CASE CHARACTERISTICS
OVERLAPPING OFFENSE: BURGLARY

Outcome	Factor	Factor Present (%)? No	Factor Present (%)? Yes	Difference (%) No	Difference (%) Yes	Strength No	Strength Yes
Pleaded guilty?	All cases	77.9	77.9				
	Exactly one?	75.1	90.0	−2.8	12.1	− −	++++++++++
	Two or more?	76.5	96.4	−1.5	18.4	−	++++++++++
	One extra?	77.2	91.5	−0.8	13.6	*	++++++++++
	2+ extra?	77.6	86.0	−0.3	8.1	*	++++++++
	Overlapping and extra?	77.2	95.7	−0.8	17.7	*	++++++++++
Found guilty?	All cases	45.5	45.5				
	Exactly one?	43.1	71.4	−2.4	25.9	− −	++++++++++
	Two or more?	44.9	100.0	−0.7	54.5	*	++++++++++
	One extra?	45.2	60.0	−0.3	14.5	*	++++++++++
	2+ extra?	44.2	100.0	−1.4	54.5	−	++++++++++
	Overlapping and extra?	45.1	100.0	−0.4	54.5	*	++++++++++
Convicted?	All cases	88.0	88.0				
	Exactly one?	85.8	97.2	−2.1	9.2	− −	+++++++++
	Two or more?	87.0	100.0	−1.0	12.0	*	++++++++++
	One extra?	87.5	96.6	−0.5	8.6	*	+++++++++
	2+ extra?	87.5	100.0	−0.5	12.0	*	++++++++++
	Overlapping and extra?	87.5	100.0	−0.5	12.0	*	++++++++++
Incarcerated?	All cases	84.0	84.0				
	Exactly one?	82.2	90.7	−1.8	6.7	−	++++++
	Two or more?	82.9	96.4	−1.1	12.4	−	++++++++++
	One extra?	83.4	93.0	−0.6	9.0	*	+++++++++
	2+ extra?	83.6	93.0	−0.4	9.0	*	+++++++++
	Overlapping and extra?	83.4	95.7	−0.6	11.7	*	++++++++++
Time?	All cases	50.0	50.0				
	Exactly one?	45.3	69.5	−4.6	19.5	− − − −	++++++++++
	Two or more?	47.3	82.4	−2.7	32.4	− −	++++++++++
	One extra?	49.6	55.9	−0.3	6.0	*	+++++
	2+ extra?	49.1	71.4	−0.8	21.5	*	++++++++++
	Overlapping and extra?	48.9	75.0	−1.0	25.0	−	++++++++++
Sentence?	All cases	49.8	49.8				
	Exactly one?	46.3	61.4	−3.5	11.7	− − −	++++++++++
	Two or more?	45.7	87.2	−4.0	37.4	− − − −	++++++++++
	One extra?	48.9	62.7	−0.9	13.0	*	++++++++++
	2+ extra?	48.9	66.7	−0.9	16.9	*	++++++++++
	Overlapping and extra?	48.4	73.8	−1.3	24.1	−	++++++++++

NOTE: Each plus and minus sign indicates one standard error, and an asterisk indicates less than one standard error.

Table E.8

RELATIONSHIP BETWEEN OUTCOME AND CASE CHARACTERISTICS
OVERLAPPING OFFENSE: ROBBERY

Outcome	Factor	Factor Present (%)?		Difference (%)		Strength	
		No	Yes	No	Yes	No	Yes
Pleaded guilty?	All cases	68.2	68.2				
	Exactly one?	65.8	80.2	−2.4	12.0	− −	++++++++++
	Two or more?	65.8	86.5	−2.4	18.3	− −	++++++++++
	One extra?	66.9	87.8	−1.4	19.6	−	++++++++++
	2+ extra?	67.5	83.0	−0.7	14.8	*	++++++++++
	Overlapping and extra?	67.2	88.9	−1.0	20.7	−	++++++++++
Found guilty?	All cases	49.9	49.9				
	Exactly one?	48.6	60.5	−1.2	10.7	−	++++++++++
	Two or more?	47.6	94.4	−2.3	44.6	− −	++++++++++
	One extra?	49.2	77.8	−0.7	27.9	*	++++++++++
	2+ extra?	48.6	100.0	−1.3	50.1	−	++++++++++
	Overlapping and extra?	49.0	100.0	−0.8	50.1	*	++++++++++
Convicted?	All cases	84.1	84.1				
	Exactly one?	82.4	92.2	−1.6	8.1	−	++++++++
	Two or more?	82.1	99.2	−2.0	15.2	−	++++++++++
	One extra?	83.1	97.3	−0.9	13.2	*	++++++++++
	2+ extra?	83.3	100.0	−0.8	15.9	*	++++++++++
	Overlapping and extra?	83.3	100.0	−0.8	15.9	*	++++++++++
Incarcerated?	All cases	92.5	92.5				
	Exactly one?	91.4	97.7	−1.2	5.2	−	+++++
	Two or more?	91.6	98.5	−0.9	5.9	*	+++++
	One extra?	92.4	94.4	−0.2	1.9	*	+
	2+ extra?	92.1	100.0	−0.4	7.5	*	+++++++
	Overlapping and extra?	92.1	100.0	−0.4	7.5	*	+++++++
Long time?	All cases	50.0	50.0				
	Exactly one?	46.5	67.4	−3.4	17.4	− − −	++++++++++
	Two or more?	47.2	71.4	−2.8	21.5	− −	++++++++++
	One extra?	49.8	52.8	−0.2	2.8	*	++
	2+ extra?	49.0	70.4	−1.0	20.4	−	++++++++++
	Overlapping and extra?	48.5	79.6	−1.5	29.7	−	++++++++++
Sentence?	All cases	49.8	49.8				
	Exactly one?	46.2	64.7	−3.6	14.9	− − −	++++++++++
	Two or more?	43.7	86.4	−6.1	36.6	− − − − −	++++++++++
	One extra?	49.4	55.4	−0.4	5.6	*	+++++
	2+ extra?	47.5	86.5	−2.3	36.7	− −	++++++++++
	Overlapping and extra?	47.8	81.1	−2.0	31.3	− −	++++++++++

NOTE: Each plus and minus sign indicates one standard error, and an asterisk indicates less than one standard error.

Table E.9

RELATIONSHIP BETWEEN OUTCOME AND CASE CHARACTERISTICS
PRIOR RECORD OFFENSE: BURGLARY

		Factor Present (%)?		Difference (%)		Strength	
Outcome	Factor	No	Yes	No	Yes	No	Yes
Pleaded guilty?	All cases	77.9	77.9				
	Arrest?	77.0	82.7	−0.9	4.7	*	++++
	Convicted?	78.2	76.4	0.3	−1.5	*	−
	Prison?	78.1	77.7	0.2	−0.3	*	*
	Juv arrest?	77.1	92.1	−0.8	14.1	*	++++++++++
	Probation?	77.8	78.4	−0.1	0.5	*	*
Found guilty?	All cases	45.5	45.5				
	Arrest?	45.6	45.2	0.1	−0.4	*	*
	Convicted?	48.6	28.9	3.0	−16.6	+++	−−−−−−−−−−
	Prison?	36.7	57.0	−8.8	11.5	−−−−−−−−	++++++++++
	Juv arrest?	45.6	40.0	0.1	−5.5	*	−−−−
	Probation?	41.7	57.6	−3.8	12.1	−−−	++++++++++
Convicted?	All cases	88.0	88.0				
	Arrest?	87.5	90.5	−0.5	2.5	*	++
	Convicted?	88.8	83.2	0.8	−4.8	*	−−−−
	Prison?	86.2	90.4	−1.8	2.4	−	++
	Juv arrest?	87.5	95.2	−0.4	7.3	*	+++++++
	Probation?	87.1	90.8	−0.9	2.9	*	++
Incarcerated?	All cases	84.0	84.0				
	Arrest?	85.3	77.2	1.4	−6.8	+	−−−−−−
	Convicted?	83.5	87.3	−0.5	3.3	*	+++
	Prison?	76.8	93.1	−7.2	9.1	−−−−−−−	+++++++++
	Juv arrest?	83.3	95.0	−0.7	11.0	*	++++++++++
	Probation?	80.1	95.6	−3.9	11.6	−−−	++++++++++
Long time?	All cases	50.0	50.0				
	Arrest?	48.9	55.3	−1.1	5.3	−	+++++
	Convicted?	49.8	51.0	−0.2	1.0	*	+
	Prison?	46.5	54.5	−3.4	4.6	−−−	++++
	Juv arrest?	50.0	48.3	0.1	−1.7	*	−
	Probation?	49.5	51.5	−0.5	1.6	*	+
Sentence?	All cases	49.8	49.8				
	Arrest?	51.4	40.7	1.6	−9.1	+	−−−−−−−−−
	Convicted?	51.4	39.8	1.6	−9.9	+	−−−−−−−−−
	Prison?	37.9	62.0	−11.9	12.3	−−−−−−−−−−	++++++++++
	Juv arrest?	49.4	54.4	−0.4	4.6	*	++++
	Probation?	45.9	59.4	−3.8	9.6	−−−	+++++++++

NOTE: Each plus and minus sign indicates one standard error, and an asterisk indicates less than one standard error.

Table E.10

RELATIONSHIP BETWEEN OUTCOME AND CASE CHARACTERISTICS
PRIOR RECORD OFFENSE: ROBBERY

Outcome	Factor	Factor Present (%)? No	Factor Present (%)? Yes	Difference (%) No	Difference (%) Yes	Strength No	Strength Yes
Pleaded guilty?	All cases	68.2	68.2				
	Arrest?	68.9	64.9	0.7	−3.3	*	− − −
	Convicted?	67.5	72.7	−0.7	4.5	*	++++
	Prison?	67.1	69.9	−1.2	1.7	−	+
	Juv arrest?	67.3	81.6	−0.9	13.4	*	++++++++++
	Probation?	68.5	67.1	0.3	−1.1	*	−
Found guilty?	All cases	49.9	49.9				
	Arrest?	51.5	42.6	1.7	−7.2	+	− − − − − − −
	Convicted?	49.1	56.1	−0.8	6.2	*	++++++
	Prison?	43.8	59.7	−6.1	9.8	− − − − −	+++++++++
	Juv arrest?	49.9	50.0	−0.0	0.1	*	*
	Probation?	46.8	60.2	−3.1	10.4	− − −	++++++++++
Convicted?	All cases	84.1	84.1				
	Arrest?	84.9	79.9	0.8	−4.2	*	− − − −
	Convicted?	83.5	88.0	−0.6	3.9	*	+++
	Prison?	81.5	87.9	−2.6	3.8	− −	+++
	Juv arrest?	83.6	90.8	−0.5	6.7	*	++++++
	Probation?	83.3	86.9	−0.8	2.8	*	++
Incarcerated?	All cases	92.5	92.5				
	Arrest?	93.1	89.7	0.5	−2.9	*	− −
	Convicted?	92.3	93.9	−0.2	1.4	*	+
	Prison?	89.3	97.0	−3.3	4.5	− − −	++++
	Juv Arrest?	92.3	95.7	−0.2	3.1	*	+++
	Probation?	90.3	100.0	−2.2	7.5	− −	+++++++
Long time?	All cases	50.0	50.0				
	Arrest?	48.9	54.6	−1.0	4.7	−	++++
	Convicted?	48.2	61.9	−1.8	11.9	−	++++++++++
	Prison?	50.1	49.7	0.2	−0.3	*	*
	Juv arrest?	50.2	45.9	0.3	−4.0	*	− − − −
	Probation?	47.8	57.5	−2.1	7.6	− −	+++++++
Sentence?	All cases	49.8	49.8				
	Arrest?	50.6	45.5	0.8	−4.3	*	− − − −
	Convicted?	51.1	42.3	1.2	−7.6	+	− − − − − − −
	Prison?	43.7	57.8	−6.2	8.0	− − − − −	+++++++
	Juv arrest?	48.6	65.2	−1.3	15.3	−	++++++++++
	Probation?	46.4	60.7	−3.5	10.8	− − −	++++++++++

NOTE: Each plus and minus sign indicates one standard error, and an asterisk indicates less than one standard error.

Table E.11

RELATIONSHIP BETWEEN OUTCOME AND CASE CHARACTERISTICS
OFFENDER OFFENSE: BURGLARY

Outcome	Factor	Factor Present (%)? No	Factor Present (%)? Yes	Difference (%) No	Difference (%) Yes	Strength No	Strength Yes
Pleaded guilty?	All cases	77.9	77.9				
	Black?	78.0	77.8	0.1	−0.1	*	*
	Hispanic?	77.5	80.5	−0.5	2.5	*	++
	White?	78.3	76.9	0.4	−1.1	*	−
	Unemployed?	74.9	82.4	−3.0	4.5	− − −	++++
	Out of state?	77.9	78.0	−0.0	0.0	*	*
Found guilty?	All cases	45.5	45.5				
	Black?	48.1	43.5	2.6	−2.1	++	− −
	Hispanic?	43.2	60.6	−2.3	15.1	− −	++++++++++
	White?	46.3	43.7	0.8	−1.9	*	−
	Unemployed?	41.3	54.4	−4.2	8.9	− − − −	++++++++
	Out of state?	44.6	61.5	−0.9	16.0	*	++++++++++
Convicted?	All cases	88.0	88.0				
	Black?	88.6	87.5	0.6	−0.5	*	*
	Hispanic?	87.2	92.3	−0.8	4.3	*	++++
	White?	88.4	87.0	0.4	−1.0	*	−
	Unemployed?	85.3	92.0	−2.7	4.0	− −	+++
	Out of state?	87.8	91.5	−0.2	3.5	*	+++
Incarcerated?	All cases	84.0	84.0				
	Black?	85.8	82.6	1.8	−1.4	+	−
	Hispanic?	81.9	94.9	−2.1	10.9	− −	++++++++++
	White?	85.3	80.5	1.3	−3.5	+	− − −
	Unemployed?	80.1	89.3	−3.9	5.3	− − −	+++++
	Out of state?	84.1	81.5	0.1	−2.5	*	− −
Long time?	All cases	50.0	50.0				
	Black?	49.1	50.6	−0.9	0.7	*	*
	Hispanic?	49.9	50.3	−0.1	0.3	*	*
	White?	50.8	47.7	0.9	−2.2	*	− −
	Unemployed?	47.8	53.1	−2.2	3.2	− −	+++
	Out of state?	51.1	31.3	1.1	−18.7	+	− − − − − − − − −
Sentence?	All cases	49.8	49.8				
	Black?	46.0	52.8	−3.7	3.1	− − −	+++
	Hispanic?	50.1	48.3	0.3	−1.5	*	−
	White?	50.9	46.4	1.2	−3.3	+	− − −
	Unemployed?	48.3	51.5	−1.4	1.8	−	+
	Out of state?	50.9	29.3	1.1	−20.5	+	− − − − − − − − −

NOTE: Each plus and minus sign indicates one standard error, and an asterisk indicates less than one standard error.

Table E.12

RELATIONSHIP BETWEEN OUTCOME AND CASE CHARACTERISTICS
OFFENDER OFFENSE: ROBBERY

		Factor Present (%)?		Difference (%)		Strength	
Outcome	Factor	No	Yes	No	Yes	No	Yes
Pleaded guilty?	All cases	68.2	68.2				
	Black?	69.0	67.9	0.8	−0.3	*	*
	Hispanic?	68.3	67.5	0.1	−0.7	*	*
	White?	67.6	71.1	−0.6	2.8	*	++
	Unemployed?	64.5	73.3	−3.7	5.1	− − −	+++++
	Out of state?	68.4	64.8	0.2	−3.4	*	− − −
Found guilty?	All cases	49.9	49.9				
	Black?	46.6	51.1	−3.3	1.3	− − −	+
	Hispanic?	51.2	39.0	1.4	−10.8	+	− − − − − − − − −
	White?	49.4	52.7	−0.5	2.9	*	++
	Unemployed?	47.5	54.3	−2.4	4.4	− −	++++
	Out of state?	49.4	57.9	−0.4	8.0	*	++++++++
Convicted?	All cases	84.1	84.1				
	Black?	83.4	84.3	−0.6	0.3	*	*
	Hispanic?	84.5	80.2	0.5	−3.9	*	− − −
	White?	83.6	86.3	−0.4	2.3	*	++
	Unemployed?	81.3	87.8	−2.7	3.8	− −	+++
	Out of state?	84.0	85.2	−0.1	1.1	*	+
Incarcerated?	All cases	92.5	92.5				
	Black?	92.8	92.4	0.2	−0.1	*	*
	Hispanic?	92.1	96.0	−0.4	3.5	*	+++
	White?	93.0	90.2	0.5	−2.3	*	− −
	Unemployed?	90.7	94.8	−1.8	2.3	−	++
	Out of state?	92.6	91.3	0.1	−1.2	*	−
Long time?	All cases	50.0	50.0				
	Black?	43.2	52.8	−6.8	2.8	− − − − − −	++
	Hispanic?	51.0	41.5	1.1	−8.4	+	− − − − − − − −
	White?	51.5	41.9	1.5	−8.0	+	− − − − − − −
	Unemployed?	48.9	51.5	−1.1	1.5	−	+
	Out of state?	50.4	43.5	0.4	−6.5	*	− − − − − −
Sentence?	All cases	49.8	49.8				
	Black?	46.6	51.1	−3.2	1.3	− − −	+
	Hispanic?	50.8	42.1	0.9	−7.7	*	− − − − − −
	White?	49.9	49.7	0.0	−0.2	*	*
	Unemployed?	47.3	52.9	−2.6	3.1	− −	+++
	Out of state?	49.7	52.4	−0.1	2.6	*	++

NOTE: Each plus and minus sign indicates one standard error, and an asterisk indicates less than one standard error.

Appendix F

CALCULATION OF RELATIVE IMPROVEMENT OVER CHANCE VALUES

This appendix describes how we made the calculations of actual and relative improvements over chance values. The first step in this process for a given outcome variable involved constructing a regression equation of that outcome on the incident characteristics. The next step consisted of regressing the outcome on the incident plus evidence characteristics. Step three involved regressing the outcome on the incident, evidence, and arrest characteristics. This process was repeated until all the variables were allowed to enter the equation. Thus, a set of equations was constructed in which each equation included all the variables that were allowed to enter the preceding equation in the set. This process was repeated for each of the outcome variables listed in Tables 7.1 and 7.2.

ACTUAL CLASSIFICATION ACCURACY

When a defendant's characteristics are inserted into an equation, the resulting value can be interpreted as an estimated probability of the defendant having the outcome. We made an outcome prediction (e.g., whether or not a defendant pleaded guilty) by ranking the defendants from highest to lowest in terms of their predicted likelihood of having the outcome and then came down this list to the point where there were as many defendants who were predicted to have the outcome as actually had it. For instance, if 60 percent of the defendants had a given outcome, then we predicted that the 60 percent with the highest estimated probabilities of having this outcome would have it (and the rest would not).

The presence of the FUZZ variable (see App. C) guaranteed that no two offenders would have exactly the same estimated probability of having the outcome, even if they matched exactly on every other predictor variable.

This approach permits a classification system to achieve 100 percent accuracy and thereby provides a common and appropriate target against which to compare the accuracy of different classification systems. The number of correct predictions is the number of cases predicted to have a given outcome (such as being convicted) who actually had that outcome plus the number of cases predicted not to have that outcome who did not have it. This sum is then divided by the total number of cases to obtain an accuracy rate. For instance, 981 of the 1,115 burglary defendants were convicted. We therefore designated the 981 defendants with the highest estimated probabilities of being convicted as those who would be convicted. We then contrasted these predictions with each offender's actual status.

The results of this comparison are presented in Table F.1. These data show that of the 981 defendants who were predicted to be convicted, 893 actually were convicted—and of the 134 who were predicted to be found innocent, 46 actually were found innocent. Thus, there were 939 correct classifications (893 + 46 = 939). Since there were 1,115 burglary defendants, this produced a correct classification rate of 84 percent (939/1115 = 0.842).

Table F.1

PREDICTED VERSUS ACTUAL CONVICTION STATUS
AMONG BURGLARY DEFENDANTS

	Predicted Outcome		
Actual Outcome	Not Convicted	Convicted	Total
Not Convicted	46	88	134
Convicted	88	893	981
Total	134	981	1,115

RELATIVE IMPROVEMENT OVER CHANCE (RIOC)

Of course, if we had just predicted some offenders would be convicted and the rest not *at random*, we would have made some correct guesses. The expected number of correct guesses can be calculated from a simple probability argument. Table F.2 shows that by chance alone, we would expect to correctly classify 16 offenders who would not have been convicted and 863 who would have been, for a total of 879 correct classifications. Thus, the 939 correct predictions from Table F.1 exceeded the chance level by 60 offenders—that is, our prediction method correctly predicted 60 more outcomes than we would have expected by chance alone.

If we had made no errors at all, we would have correctly identified all 134 offenders who were not convicted and all 981 who were, and all 1,115 predictions would have been correct. Since we would have gotten 879 correct predictions by chance alone, the best possible estimation procedure would have made 236 more correct outcomes than is possible by chance. The usual definition of *relative improvement over chance* for our particular outcome measure is thus 60/236 or 25.4 percent (Loeber and Dishion, 1983).

We made two slight adjustments to this definition.

By chance, the FUZZ variable alone sometimes revealed a small but positive relative improvement over chance (never much more than 1 or 2 percent). When this happened, we subtracted this improvement from our calculations for the same outcome measure.

Table F.2

CHANCE DISTRIBUTION OF OUTCOMES GIVEN
MARGINAL TOTALS

	Predicted Outcome		
Actual Outcome	Not Convicted	Convicted	Total
Not Convicted	16	118	134
Convicted	118	863	981
Total	134	981	1,115

It also sometimes happened that the relative improvement over chance *decreased* slightly as we added predictor variables. When this happened, we used the larger of the two values in our discussions.

Table F.3 summarizes the actual number of predicted outcomes for both strata, all outcome variables, and all predictor classes.

Table F.3

NUMBER OF CORRECT CLASSIFICATIONS WITH VARIOUS MODELS
BY OUTCOME MEASURE AND CRIME TYPE

Factors in the Model	Pleaded Guilty	Found Guilty	Convicted	Incarcerated	Long Sentence	Long Time
Burglary						
Expected	732	124	879	717	402	555
Random	743	134	877	721	412	565
Incident	737	142	895	733	432	621
Evidence	783	150	921	745	488	645
Arrest	787	162	935	743	486	643
Overlapping	807	170	937	761	526	705
Priors	803	178	943	809	562	717
Offenders	823	176	939	813	560	719
State	849	188	961	825	558	763
Site	853	196	963	843	562	771
Maximum	1,115	246	1,115	981	804	1,109
Robbery						
Expected	650	183	840	832	435	577
Random	644	197	836	829	431	568
Incident	724	205	878	855	545	657
Evidence	744	235	906	857	561	663
Arrest	734	235	906	857	581	675
Overlapping	776	247	912	865	621	717
Priors	780	249	932	865	629	715
Offenders	800	247	920	869	629	735
State	834	273	952	869	631	789
Site	836	277	966	869	623	817
Maximum	1,148	365	1,148	965	869	1,154

Appendix G

Table G.1

REGRESSION COEFFICIENTS FOR FOUND GUILTY

	Found Guilty	
Variable	Burglary	Robbery
Intercept	.2343	.2190
Had an accomplice	−.0206	−.0310
Multiple sample counts	.2956	.1907
Any victim a female	.1027	.0133
Major victim injury	.3010	.0551
Two or more victims	−.0829	−.0155
Nighttime incident	−.0912	.0664
Vulnerable victim	−.1661	.0603
Weapon threatened	−.1524	.0723
Eyewitness	.1152	.0992
Fingerprints	.0023	.1016
Property recovered	−.0260	.1201
Weapon as evidence	.2153	.0018
Arrested at scene	.1444	−.0213
Arrested after 24 hours	−.0242	−.0681
Under influence of drugs	.2576	−.0591
Exactly one overlapping case	.2142	.0817
Two or more overlapping cases	.4635	.4347
Exactly one extra case	−.0875	.3774
Two or more extra cases	.5733	.4535
Overlapping and extra case	−.3980	−.2339
Prior adult arrest	.0356	−.0137
Prior adult conviction	−.1224	.1101
Prior adult incarceration	.0922	.1405
Prior juvenile incarceration	−.3820	.0078
Probation, etc., when arrested	.0458	.0394
Offender black	.0641	−.0075
Offender Hispanic	.1011	−.1389
Offender white	.0576	−.0203
Defendant unemployed	.0465	.0151
Out-of-state defendant	.0639	.1530

Table G.2

REGRESSION COEFFICIENTS FOR DISPOSITION TIME

Variable	Disposition Time	
	Burglary	Robbery
Intercept	.2162	.2186
Had an accomplice	−.0143	−.0026
Multiple sample counts	.0232	.0225
Any victim a female	.0304	.0351
Major victim injury	.0490	.0334
Two or more victims	.0195	−.0071
Nighttime incident	−.0178	.0029
Vulnerable victim	−.0319	.0243
Weapon threatened	−.0233	−.0008
Eyewitness	−.0109	−.0013
Fingerprints	−.0008	−.0241
Property recovered	−.0317	.0143
Weapon as evidence	.0376	−.0158
Arrested at scene	−.0134	.0117
Arrested after 24 hours	−.0015	.0054
Under influence of drugs	.0108	−.0252
Exactly one overlapping case	.1001	.0943
Two or more overlapping cases	.1980	.1452
Exactly one extra case	.0101	−.0083
Two or more extra cases	.0104	.0174
Overlapping and extra case	−.0148	−.0172
Prior adult arrest	.0079	.0193
Prior adult conviction	.0318	.0503
Prior adult incarceration	.0510	.0182
Prior juvenile incarceration	−.0294	−.0179
Probation, etc., when arrested	−.0417	.0187
Offender black	−.0346	−.0767
Offender Hispanic	−.0507	−.0963
Offender white	−.0575	−.0764
Defendant unemployed	.0393	.0167
Out-of-state defendant	−.0381	.0389

Table G.3

REGRESSION COEFFICIENTS FOR CONVICTIONS

	Convictions	
Variable	Burglary	Robbery
Intercept	.6702	.6353
Had an accomplice	−.0115	−.0046
Multiple sample counts	.0556	.0716
Any victim a female	.0085	.0154
Major victim injury	.1324	−.0180
Two or more victims	.0113	−.0053
Nighttime incident	−.0248	.0423
Vulnerable victim	−.0779	−.0279
Weapon threatened	−.0778	.0592
Eyewitness	.0264	.0416
Fingerprints	−.0069	.0532
Property recovered	.0650	.0716
Weapon as evidence	.0157	.0103
Arrested at scene	.0857	.0317
Arrested after 24 hours	.0610	−.0503
Under influence of drugs	.0657	.0038
Exactly one overlapping case	.1000	.1167
Two or more overlapping cases	.1138	.1905
Exactly one extra case	.0698	.1674
Two or more extra cases	.0937	.1632
Overlapping and extra case	−.1031	−.1553
Prior adult arrest	.0088	−.0338
Prior adult conviction	−.0438	.0488
Prior adult incarceration	.0085	.0581
Prior juvenile incarceration	.0556	.0500
Probation, etc., when arrested	.0083	−.0143
Offender black	.0533	−.0126
Offender Hispanic	.0675	−.0650
Offender white	.0334	.0142
Defendant unemployed	.0457	.0456
Out-of-state defendant	.0267	.0335

REFERENCES

Abrahamse, A., P. Ebener, and S. Klein, *Criminal Justice Policies and Outcomes Database User's Manual*, RAND, N-3165-BJS, 1991.

Boland, B., C. Conly, L. Warner, R. Sones, and W. Martin, *The Prosecution of Felony Arrests, 1986*, Bureau of Justice Statistics, U.S. Department of Justice, Washington, D.C., 1989.

Bureau of Justice Statistics (BJS), "Tracking Offenders, 1984," *Bureau of Justice Statistics Bulletin*, 1988.

Clarke, S., and S. Turner-Kurtz, "The Importance of Interim Decisions to Felony Trail Court Dispositions," *Journal of Criminal Law and Criminology*, Vol. 74, 1983, pp. 476–518.

Justice Statistics, U.S. Department of Justice.

Klein, S., J. Petersilia, and S. Turner, "Race and Imprisonment Decisions in California," *Science*, Vol. 247, February 1990, pp. 769–892.

Loeber, R., and T. Dishion, "Early Predictors of Male Delinquency: A Review," *Psychological Bulletin*, Vol. 94, No. 1, 1983, pp. 68–99.

Petersilia, J. R., A. F. Abrahamse, and J. Q. Wilson, *Police Performance and Case Attrition*, RAND, R-3515-NIJ, October 1987.